MONGOLIAN MEMORIES

Modern Mongolia and its Twentieth Century History

MAAIKE VAN HOEFLAKEN

TABLE OF CONTENTS

MAAIKE VAN HOEFLAKEN

PREFACE

Mongolia was my home from 1999 to 2006 while I was working as a project manager in the financial sector for donors such as European Union, Asian Development Bank and the International Finance Corporation (World Bank Group). The job I had from 2002-2004 took me away from my easy expat life in the capital Ulaanbaatar with its hikes, western restaurants, poker games and parties and brought me into exclusive and close contact with Mongolians, particularly those living in the rural areas. My job involved spending a lot of time visiting families and businesses, sometimes sitting in the middle of the steppe, sometimes at home in the ger (more commonly called a yurt in the West) of the client and sometimes in our car. I spent even more time with my Mongolian colleagues accompanying me, listening in fascination to the stories they told about how they grew up. I became intrigued by their life, their upbringing during the socialist era in which communist ideals mixed with traditional pastoralist traditions, and the struggles they faced trying to cope with the changes forced upon them by Mongolia's transition to a market economy. I thought again and again: I need to write this up!

So that is what I did. In this book I use anecdotes from the years I lived, worked and traveled in Mongolia and interviews with elderly Mongolians as an entry point to bring their 20th century to life. During that century, the abjectly poor, unhealthy, illiterate and oppressed population of the Manchu province of Outer Mongolia managed to successfully fight for independence, initially forming a Buddhist state but soon thereafter aligning itself with the Soviet Union. During its communist years Mongolia's authoritarian regime ruthlessly purged the opposition — notably the Buddhist establishment — but also hugely improved the living standards of the whole population. When the Eastern Bloc imploded, an educated, independent and rowdy bunch of Mongolians entered the 21st century. Not all Mongolians fared well, however.

*May 2007. **Lun soum.** We drive up to a small encampment in the barren tan landscape with patches of snow. I am not feeling too well, maybe a small flu or a stomach bug that made me vomit several times last night, forcing me to go to the flimsy outhouse in a blizzard, where I have to hang myself precariously over the drop, struggling to get my pants off while not being able to bend my injured leg and hoping not to get frostbite in the process. But I brace myself: my discomfort does not begin to compare to what I encountered in the gers I visited that morning. Most families we found in the morning were sleeping, exhausted from being up all night saving as many animals as they could in the blizzard. I felt horrible to bother them with my survey questions and might not have gone through with it if it hadn't been work.*

The afternoon has become sunny and we stop at the two gers and animal enclosures. There are clumps of iron — Soviet-era machinery parts — hanging from the side of the gers (gers need to be weighted down so they don't take to the air in a storm) and a dead fox has been tied to the roof. Two horses are tied up to a line between two posts, a motorcycle is parked beside the larger ger, and young animals frolic in a sunny enclosure. A dog runs to our car and sits looking up expectantly. It looks friendly enough, but we know better than to go out and wait for someone to call it off. It is cashmere season and this family is up and about and combing the goats, but the lady of the house is happy to take a break and answer my questions. After the formal interview (I am doing a survey among herders about their livelihoods, a tiny part of a large World Bank project) she talks more informally about their life. She is happy enough with her herding life but tells me that her daughter, who graduated from college in Ulaanbaatar, has come back to live with them because she couldn't find work. That is her big worry: she had wanted her daughter to get out of herding and make a better living for herself.

My story is biased. I am drawn to rural areas and remote places and it was by traveling through the Mongolian countryside, meaning everything outside Ulaanbaatar, that I became interested in

Mongolian history. It was also in the rural areas that I saw most poverty and stagnation. The 20th century trend towards an ever more sedentary lifestyle and ever-deeper penetration of services into the remote backcountry, where children went to school in soum (something like a county in the US) and aimag (something like a province) centers, and where professionals worked in the tiniest settlements as veterinarians, teachers, doctors, nurses, all paid by the state, was reversed in the last decade of the century. At the same time, the number of herder households (who depended upon those services) increased by more than 250 percent because people lost their jobs when the centrally planned economy collapsed. These people have center stage in this book.

Housekeeping

I didn't intend to go back as far as 1900, I just wanted to tell the stories of the elderly people I interviewed. However, the logical starting point for this book receded further back as people started talking about their parents and as I attempted to understand the world they were living in. Their stories needed at least some historical background in order to be comprehended and I needed a beginning and an end. A simple sense of symmetry and wholeness made me decide to try to present the 20th century in its entirety, including Mongolia's independence from the Manchu dynasty, alliance with the Eastern Block and transition to a market economy. I am not a historian, but I have nevertheless tried to tease a bare minimum of historical facts from — occasionally conflicting — English-language sources (see Bibliography). Many subjects have been left out but I hope I have made 20th-century Mongolia more accessible to people who, like me, are interested but don't know anything about what happened there.

      I have not been consistent in my transcriptions of Mongolian words and names, trying to use the spelling that is the most recognizable to people who are not familiar with Mongolia. But not always: the best-known Mongol is still the guy we foreigners are familiar with under the name Genghis Khan. The Mongols call him Chinggis Khaan and have named so many places and items after him that it would be madness for me to hang on to our western Genghis Khan; he is Chinggis Khaan. Similarly, the character we call Diluv Khutagt is referred to as Dilowa Khutugtu by the Mongols. I shall use that name.

Nowadays, the capital of Mongolia is spelled as Ulaanbaatar — UB among expatriates — but in the past the name was usually spelled, Russian-style, as Ulan Bator. The city was named Ulaanbaatar (Red Hero) in 1924, before that (1911-1923) it was called Niislel Khüree (Capital Settlement) and before 1911 it was referred to as Urga by foreigners and by Mongols as Ikh Khüree (Big Settlement).

Mongols do not use surnames. They have a first name, preceded by a patronymic (first name of the father — or mother, if the father is not known), as was customary among the Russians. The patronymic is usually just written as an initial, which confuses many foreigners who mistakenly use a person's father's name instead of his or her own name.

English-language honorifics such as Mr. and Mrs. do not have an adequate translation: they do not exist. I shall use them in cases where I would use them in English but leave them off for friends, colleagues and generally for people in more informal settings.

I use the word Mongol when focusing on the ethnicity and cultural identity and the word Mongolian when focusing on nationality. The Kazakhs living in Mongolia are Mongolians but not Mongols.

Maps

Map1: Mongolia and its Neighbors

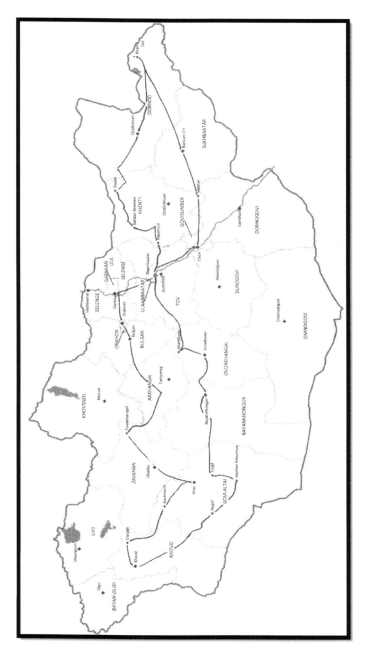

Map 2: Aimags, Aimag Capitals, Travels of 2012

INTRODUCTION

An inauspicious beginning

Early in 1999 I received a call enquiring whether I was interested in a possible assignment in Mongolia to replace the manager of an economic development project who had unexpectedly decided not to take the job. I didn't know anything about that part of the world because Mongolia had been part of the Eastern Bloc or Second World and as such hadn't been included when I studied Third World development. For that reason I was about to turn down the opportunity when my husband Terry sighed and said: "I've always wanted to go to Mongolia; I represented that country in a model UN when I was in high school!" Planning one's life is overrated and in any case not feasible when trying to make a living as an independent consultant for large international donors. We went.

August 3, 1999. Ulaanbaatar, Mongolia. I wake up hot, half awake, sweating, drooling, squinting at the sun shining in my face as we have just moved in and don't have any curtains. Something in my mouth, I spit and it moves, disgusting: a big cockroach! I start retching. I get up disoriented, drenched in sweat, in the empty flat where I have been lying on a mattress on the ground, no furniture yet. Then the awful truth strikes me — Terry had a heart attack last night, he is in the hospital! A memory pops up of the change in the expression of the doctor when she saw the ECG — I was watching her intently — from neutral to alarmed. I panic: what hospital, where is it? I don't know! I kind of remember the Russians sedating me and taking me home in an ambulance. I don't know the town and have no phone number. The

Russians. . . yes, the Russian hospital, it was. I call Javhlan, my project assistant, who had stayed in the hospital because they wouldn't take Terry unless I provided 24-hour interpreter services. Thank God for mobile phones, I resolve to get one as soon as possible! I manage to find the huge cavernous, half-empty building that is the Russian hospital and Terry's room in intensive care. This is actually a storage room and broom cabinet, but it is also the intensive-care unit because it is next to the nurse station.

Terry is lying on his back with both his arms pinned down with needles in them. We are both shocked and scared — Terry more than I. Dr. Mike, the German doctor who had been contacted by Javhlan and arrived in time to administer the nitroglycerin that saved his life, surreptitiously (he is not registered as a doctor in Mongolia) takes some of Terry's blood to an outside lab to confirm the diagnosis of a heart attack. The treating physician is Dr. Tatiana, a smartly dressed platinum-blonde middle-aged Russian lady with a warm heart. She is doing her best in that broom cabinet and that is not easy with the lack of modern medicine and equipment. The Russian doctors and nurses make up for it with 24-hour personal care of this American who has fallen in their lap.

The American is not an easy patient, however, he expects different treatment than what he gets (quite apart from the greasy eggs with bacon the heart patient is served for breakfast). After the first few days it is time to change the needles in his arms. He asks the nurse to put a needle in one arm only. The quick answer is: Njet! Terry is not a man to take no for an answer. He glares at the nurse and tells her they are going to get only one arm. Njet! Njet! More nurses appear. Njet! Njet! Njet! The interpreter is working overtime and I am summoned away from my new job. By that time I have hired a car and driver to shuttle me back and forth from my office to the hospital. Terry raises his voice, balls his fist and states that he wants to be able to scratch his balls (I tell my interpreter not to translate this) and that anyone who tries to put a needle in the second arm will be punched in the nose. Njet! Dr. Tatiana is summoned. Dr. Mike is summoned. The director of the hospital is summoned. All of us cram into the storage room. Tatiana appeals to me: "Please tell your husband that we are doing the best we can to keep him alive." I know it is true; they simply have nothing to work with, no money, no modern equipment, no modern medicines. They just have their truly big Russian hearts to give. In the end Dr. Mike *defuses the situation by producing a needle that branches into three parts so that the drips can all go into one arm. Only the nurses are unhappy; they are not used to inserting the modern delicate and flexible needles into veins.*

This is the beginning of a series of emergencies to which I am called. Tatiana and I become friends. She implores, "Could you please tell your husband not to talk so much? It is not good for him. And he gets too many visitors." He does get a lot of visitors and I hope that Terry, who has one hand free, sticks to talking and doesn't heed the advice of one of my colleagues that Russian ladies — i.e. the nurses — like to be patted on the rear. I commiserate with Tatiana, but decide not to discourage Terry from talking. He will probably die if he isn't allowed to talk.

While in the process of interviewing candidates for my project, I get another call: "Please come quickly to the hospital." I go and find the by now familiar scene: nurses, doctors and the Hospital Director around Terry's bed. The Director stands center at the foot-end of the bed bellowing that the hospital is like a symphony orchestra and that he, the Director, is the conductor and that all would be well if only staff and patients did exactly as he directs. At issue is exercise, which Terry interprets as being allowed to walk around the corridors and the Russians interpret as Terry being allowed to sit up in bed and put his feet on the floor while seated — once a day. Terry yells at me that I should explain PATIENT'S RIGHTS to them. I tell Terry to shush, that there is probably not an equivalent term in Russian for the concept of patient's rights. Njet patient's rights! There are many subsequent issues: Terry wants to use a bedpan in privacy with the door closed when the nurses threaten to administer an enema (he wins that one). After two weeks he wants to go to the toilet and to take a bath. He wants to know how long they will keep him. He wants to know if he has a chance to survive.

Tatiana asks me again if I don't think they are taking good care of my husband, why he seems unhappy. They are really trying very hard and I feel for them. I conspiringly (disloyally and not doing my own country's hospitals justice either) whisper to her that he is an American and that the habits and customs of Americans are quite different from those of us Europeans and that one of the issues is transparency, as in Terry not being given any information at all about what is wrong with him, how long he might have to lie in the hospital bed, if he might die soon. No diagnosis, no prognosis, nothing. That this makes Terry very unhappy because, in America, patients get such information from their doctors. She exclaims in a shocked voice that knowing might not be good for his heart. Now I am not reassured either. Then she mulls over what I have said and decides that a small measure of glasnost will not be fatal. We agree that she will talk about Terry's condition every day at 11 a.m., provided I and a good interpreter (by now the 24-hour interpreter requirement has been watered down) be present at the briefing.

After a few weeks of this Dr. Mike and the insurance company decide that Terry can be safely med-evacuated to Amsterdam. Again Tatiana calls me to her and asks if I don't think they are taking good care of my husband. She says the traveling might not be good for his heart, that heart patients normally stay in hospital for many months. I explain that they are taking very good care of him (true, they are doing what they can), but that I think he would be more comfortable in my country and that the hospitals in my country are richer and have more up-to-date equipment and facilities. They very reluctantly let him go.

My first job in Mongolia

My project, funded by the European Union, was to establish a credit fund in support of the small businesses that had sprung up all over Mongolia after the country had, in the early 1990s, precipitously transitioned from a Russian-style socialist state to a democracy depending on a market economy. The centrally planned political, economic, and social system was dismantled before there was anything to replace it and the country descended into a deep Depression. I was one of many financial and economic consultants plucked from around the globe to work in internationally funded donor projects aiming to fix the economic crisis.

That job gave me a fascinating insight into the many ways in which people were trying to survive in a capitalist world that was new to them after their familiar planned economy had been abolished. Everywhere behind the facades of the aging, decrepit concrete buildings there were well-trained individuals, many of them college graduates, who had lost their livelihood when their jobs disappeared, setting up their little businesses. People were running medical clinics, pharmacies, veterinarian services, producing honey from wildflowers, preparing intestines for export as sausage casings, operating bars, restaurants, hotels, laundry services, flour mills, making sausages, providing borehole logging services for the mining industry, processing wood, running a minivan business for transport of mail and passengers between towns. These businesses were more often than not invisible because the concept of advertising one's services wasn't well understood — that hadn't been a part of the centrally planned socialist economy. The really fun part of my job was the field-days when we went out to meet our loan applicants for a first assessment — when I got to meet all these experimenting entrepreneurs.

I found out early on how people struggled to get their small businesses going. One of the things that confounded me within the framework of lending money to small businesses was the disconnect between what was put down on paper (financial statements and forecasts, business plans and any other required forms) and reality. Maybe it was still a leftover of the socialist time when bureaucrats worried more about filling in all the blanks on a form than whether the content matched reality. Bank lending programs to companies presuppose that a business plan including the stated purpose of the loan reflects the real intentions of the entrepreneur, but sometimes this was not at all the case.

✳ ✳ ✳

2000. Our European Union project has created a financial institution called Credit Mongol to lend to deserving small businesses. The preparatory period has been long and tortuous but now we are ready to go. After careful fact-finding and investigation of our first lenders the first three loans have been approved. One is to a poultry farm in Darkhan, two hundred kilometers north of Ulaanbaatar. The owner of the company requested a loan to buy a back-up generator for the incubator that he had managed to procure from a former State poultry farm because he sustained considerable losses caused by frequent power outages.

The Chicken Man, as he has been dubbed by our staff, has defaulted on his second repayment installment. I immediately send the loan officer up to Darkhan. He returns without having been able to find the client (the first indication that a loan is going bad is generally that the client turns off his mobile phone and cannot be found). The Director of Credit Mongol and I look at each other: this is our first loan! A default? Impossible! How can we request more loan funds from the EU if our very first loan goes bad? We decide to investigate then and there

(Mongols do not lack initiative and immediate action), jump in the car, drive to Darkhan where we arrive after dark, check into a hotel and start looking for our man. Had I ever imagined when I decided to become a development worker that I would end up hunting down non-performing clients in the dark Mongolian night?

Of course we find him, Darkhan is a small enough town that people know each other. We sit on his couch, drink salty tea and listen to his embarrassed story. Mr. Bolorsaikhan is a graduate of the Mongolian Agricultural University and his thesis was titled "Quality of the Domestic Chicken Egg and Recovery of Eggs/Incubations"; he had received an excellent mark for it. He has been raising poultry for several years and is generally successful (and reliable, we had thought). What we hadn't known was that he has a dream. It is to raise Beijing ducks. China wants to keep its monopoly on Beijing ducks and he has never had the opportunity to get his hands on any Beijing ducks even though he usually buys his fertilized chicken eggs in China. After he cashed his check for the full amount of the loan, he did not buy the generator as agreed but traveled to China and bought a large number of fertilized eggs, including Beijing duck eggs. He got caught at the border, his duck eggs were confiscated and all his legal chicken embryos died in the ensuing delays as well. That is the whole sorry story. We lecture him on responsible financial management and ask him to come up with a repayment plan. I am faced with the task of having to explain the debacle to the EU bureaucrats in Brussels.

We ended up restructuring the loan and he earned the money to repay the loan by setting up a container selling coffee and home-made preserves (his sister pitched in) at the entrance of the local market. Several years later I visited a poultry farm near the western city of Khovd. When I asked where they bought their one-day old chicks, they said they had a good, reliable dealer in Darkhan, 1700 kilometers away. It was our Chicken Man!

This is a typical post-transition story. Our dreaming poultry expert had graduated in 1991, the year everything changed and, in contrast to previous generations, graduates weren't guaranteed jobs in the new market economy. He found work in a pig farm until he had enough money to start his own poultry farm raising chicken and geese. In 1995, he managed to get a loan and bought an incubator from the socialist-era national poultry farm, with a capacity of 15,000 eggs, at the time the only incubator available in the country. Despite the sleep I lost over Mr. Bolorsaikhan's dream, I remember my first Mongolian entrepreneur fondly, sap that I am.

Strangers in a foreign land

Mongolia now feels like home: familiar, welcoming, easy, close, even ordinary to me. That wasn't so when Terry and I first arrived in Mongolia in June 1999 — sans our personal effects, which were still en route from Paraguay (the location of my previous assignment) to my home in Amsterdam. I was unburdened not only by material belongings but also by any background knowledge whatsoever about the country, as there had been no time to prepare. My first impressions were vivid and naive.

Landing in Ulaanbaatar I noticed the smells first of all: the pervasive odor of boiled mutton and humid wool in the buildings and, as we stepped outside, the fresh smell of aromatic herbs and mountain meadows, which I later identified as sage, chamomile, thyme, and an assortment of wildflowers. On the short drive into town, in the state of heightened awareness that accompanies arriving jet-lagged in a new country, I took in exotically garbed Mongols with funny hats racing their horses beside the road; huge water-pipes with crumbling grey insulation (was that asbestos?) connecting the power plants to the city; dreary run-down Soviet-style housing developments; Eastern Bloc embassies in decline; huge polluted industrial parks in disarray; and livestock wandering in the center of town, grazing in the small parks lined with larches that surrounded the forbidding-looking Parliament House.

Green wooded hills surrounded the city and charming Soviet-era buildings dominated the quiet center: the opera house, the post office and other official buildings, housing blocks with children's playgrounds in the courtyards. In Sükhbaatar Square (recently renamed Chinggis Khaan Square) old-fashioned photographers arranged their clients, serious-looking groups and families from the countryside, in stiffly postured groups around props. Fortune-tellers sat in the park next to the square, their grubby old anklebones displayed in front of them. Looking south, I could see the roofs of the tranquil Choijin Lama temple (now a museum) and next to it the more modern, square, white Wedding Palace. Behind the large

Children's Park stretched to the south towards the Naadam stadium, the river and the sacred Bogd mountain behind, covered with dark green forest. The Mongolians boast that it the oldest national park in the world.

Walking in the city involved stepping through broken-down fences and wading through weedy, empty lots and Mongolian office workers used to carefully clean and polish their fashionable shoes after arriving at the office. I started doing the same with my more sensible shoes. The streets were dark at night and I took to carrying a flashlight. Shops were not immediately apparent, and where were the taxis? How to communicate? Answer: there were no taxis, but most cars would stop for you and take you wherever you wanted to go, if you knew where that was and were able to communicate by pointing or saying "left", "right", "straight ahead" and "stop" in Mongolian.

We had been booked into the small, modern Edelweiss Hotel — edelweiss is a common flower in Mongolia — close to the Children's Park with the same open view to the south. Nowadays you see only apartment buildings from the hotel. My first tiny office was in the old tower of the Bulgarian embassy on Karl Marx Street (now Olympic Street) just a few minutes' walk away on Embassy Road. It was a suite of two tiny rooms where people had to enter sideways between the desks, one in each room, and the wall; the project assistant sat in the front office and I in the back.

The most shocking thing I remember about that period, coming straight from a tropical country, was the slowly deepening cold of that first winter, seeing the Mongols still blithely sauntering down the streets with their coats hanging open even though the temperature hadn't been higher than -10°C in weeks. In fact, the minus sign is not mentioned in winter, "thirty degrees" means -30°C. Ice-cream vendors appeared on the streets when it was cold enough that no refrigeration was needed to keep the ice cream frozen. The ingenious freezer in our apartment — a formerly upper-class place in the center of town — consisted of a space hollowed out in the two-meter-thick walls with openings to the outside and a wooden door to the inside. The apartment itself was boiling hot, well insulated with heaps of dusty, greying cotton-wool stuffed between the double windows — most of which did not open, and, because it was located in the city center closer to the power plants than the outlying suburbs, the water was still very hot when it reached our building. No adjustments to the temperature were possible other than opening two tiny, unaligned windows that were difficult to reach. It became a daily winter-morning struggle to dress quickly for moving from the cozy 25° in our apartment to the unimaginable -35° (or lower) outside without becoming soaked in sweat before stepping outside.

Mongolia would become my home for years but those first six months I was a foreigner, very much lost in a strange land. I didn't know who the Mongols were, how this country had become what it was, how long I would stay, how quickly everything was changing.

Just two weeks after our arrival we had to leave our comfortable hotel because they were booked full for the Naadam festival. There were no other hotel rooms available in town so my assistant found us a ger camp to the north where we could stay for a week or so. A ger camp is a resort or hotel where tourists sleep in gers, the traditional Mongolian felt-lined tents. There were facilities such as showers, even toilets — they understood that tourists want that kind of thing — but the women's facilities had floor-to-ceiling windows facing the center of the camp and no curtains. There was nowhere to hide! This prepared me for the facilities in the offices we rented a few months later in the Zorig Foundation building in the center of town: the women's toilet-stall had a window without shades or curtains and faced the offices of the Ministry of Foreign Affairs.

The owners were just establishing the ger camp — we might have been the first Western visitors — and smothered us with hospitality. We were stuffed with food all day long. We had a large Thermos with salty milk tea and a Chinese ceramic pot of at least eight liters of airag (fermented mare's milk) in our ger. Terry refused it; I like a small bowl of airag — but eight liters?

If there is one subject that sets expats off into fits of helpless giggling it is Mongolian food. A few days after our arrival Terry and I went to lunch in a Mongolian place close to my office and we had soup. I glanced at it thinking not bad, nice cauliflower, but the cauliflower buds turned out to be nice, round globs of mutton-fat. The smell of boiled mutton in Mongolia essentially denotes being Mongolian, and if the Western mind associates Buddhism with vegetarianism, it would be sadly mistaken in Mongolia. A Buddhist expat running an orphanage was seen by many Mongols as torturing her charges by feeding them a vegetarian diet. Mongols traveling abroad for the first time are appalled by the diet in Western countries. Russian influence is still visible in modern-day Mongolia where mutton dishes often include potatoes, cabbage and winter carrots, either fresh or pickled, the main ingredients of old-fashioned European no-frills peasant food. Shops in Ulaanbaatar also used to sell caviar and wine from former Eastern Bloc countries; now, with the mining wealth coming in, you can buy anything from anywhere. When Mongols get together, particularly in the more traditional countryside, there are snacks of cheap bonbons, sweets, Korean cookies called Choco Pies, all washed down with vodka and producing a particularly nasty hangover. There was a US-brand three-in-one instant coffee with milk and sugar. When I first tasted it, I said: "This is where I draw the line," but I later made exceptions in remote areas when served three-in-one by officials, not wanting to be impolite.

I had to learn how to deal with alcohol, particularly alcohol in the workplace. At first we drank a glass of wine on birthdays, we opened a bottle of wine for happy hour on Fridays, we drank to celebrate the approval of an important loan. Pretty soon we were polishing off two bottles of vodka instead of the one bottle of wine among the six of us until I regretfully put a stop to it. At parties hard liquor was free while it was difficult and expensive to procure a bottle of soft drink for my non-drinking husband.

What intrigued me most were the apparent contradictions: people in exotic-looking clothes, living in gers and adhering to traditional customs within the ger, turned out to be literate, well-educated and knowledgeable about the world. They had open-minded discussions on religion and whether God existed; they also reverted to soothsayers on the pavements and consultations with lamas on subjects such as identifying favorable dates to start a journey, to move house, or even whether the person you want to marry is compatible with you. Highly educated professionals circumambulate piles of rocks laced with prayer-flags, broken vodka bottles, crutches and other discarded items — and when and why did I start doing the same? I learnt the small things, such as shaking the hand of the person you accidentally bump into, to re-establish harmony. This was only after having embarrassed myself the first month I was there by stepping on the robes of a young monk and trying to disentangle myself while he tied us into knots by whirling around desperately trying to shake my hand. Only later did I understand what had been going on.

The Mongols have assimilated many foreign ideas and habits into their culture during the past century. The similarities in thought and ways of looking at life between the Mongols and myself, I believe, are the result of the Russian influence and include an enlightened secular outlook (communist ideology had effectively eradicated and taken the place of the Tibetan-style Buddhist culture of the early 1900s), a belief in and knowledge of western scientific concepts, widespread high-school education, understanding of world history, a high degree of equality between men and women, to name but a few. In many ways I experienced the Mongols to be as Western — nay, as Dutch — as I am.

Continuing to work in Mongolia

Mongolia was unlike any of the previous countries I had worked in because of the similarities in outlook between me and the Mongolians, and because of the rapid development that the country was going through while I was there. My project staff worked extremely hard and were well schooled. Lack of English-language skills was a problem, but I asked for a reallocation of some project funds to pay for English lessons for the staff, which they greatly appreciated.

The Non-Bank Financial Institution we created immediately had as a problem that we didn't have sufficient funds to lend out and grow as fast as the market allowed. This was in contrast to previous credit funds I had been involved in where the staff weren't able to lend monies out fast enough (or not as fast as had been foreseen in the project documents) and had difficulties getting it back. Repayment rates were high in Mongolia because there was so much demand for the loans that it was easy to cherry-pick reliable borrowers.

The problems we faced were unique. The most difficult one was that there was no regulatory environment for financial institutions and the inexperienced staff and governors of Mongolia's Central Bank (most of whom were in their 20s and 30s) had to figure things out as they went. Serious about coming up with solid policies, rules and regulations, they were reluctant to license new financial institutions, which clashed with my mandate to get the allocated funds circulating fast. Another one was that the somewhat vaguely formulated loan agreement between the EU and Mongolian government stipulated that the Financial Institution lending the money would be a non-governmental organization (NGO) while the ministry that had requested the project wanted the funds to be amalgamated with their own small-business fund (which had mostly non-performing loans and was beginning to show a deficit) and the Mongolian National Bank stipulated that the financial institution be a private company. In most countries where I had worked and that had much experience with foreign aid, the politicians would say one thing to the donor and pressure the project manager to do something else, but in Mongolia the issues were fought out in the open which made them easier to deal with. I knew where I stood.

After initial delays during which these issues were sorted, the project went well and in the years that followed I got caught up in my work, made friends, both Mongolian and expatriate, and settled down. My original 15-month job in Ulaanbaatar became 25 months, after which I left the country in 2001 for good. Or so I believed.

Several months later, while I was back in Mongolia for a few weeks doing a short-term assignment, I was asked to urgently replace someone who had left a project after just one month. Could I please decide within a day? Terry was doing a short-term job in Ethiopia and I wanted to discuss it with him. I had just one night before I left to do fieldwork and only a few minutes left on the phone card by the time I was connected. The low-quality, long-distance conversation went more or less as follows:

"Terry, this is Maaike."

"What a surprise! How are you doing?"

"I got a job offer I'd like to talk to you about."

"How is it to be back, did you play poker last night?"

"Yes, I played. I want to talk about this job—"

"Who all were there?"

"There were Ron and Mike and Nasankhuu and Zol. I got offered this job—"

"Did you win?"

"Yes, I won. I am wondering if I should take the job—"

"Go ahead, dear. How much did you win?"

"It would mean I won't come home next week, I'll only be able to come home in six months."

At that point the phone card expired. I had heard "Go ahead, dear" and took the job.

A week later, in May 2002, I met my new Mongolian counterpart Shombodon, with whom I was to be responsible for the implementation of an agriculture-sector lending program. Shombodon was 55 (seven years older than me), thin, of average height and dressed in a dark suit that reminded me of the socialist past; his manner was polite, quiet and unassuming. He spoke English carefully and precisely, having learned it in the 1980s, a few years before the fall of the socialist system, already aware that English would supplant Russian in Mongolia's future. Our job within the Agriculture Sector Development Project (which had other components such as rehabilitating water wells, improving veterinary services, vegetable growing, etc.) was to lead the credit component. The Asian Development Bank loaned the credit funds to the Mongolian government at concessional interest rates to support the agriculture sector in certain aimags (provinces). The funds were to be lent out through commercial banks with the objective that the banks would learn how to deal with the herders and farmers (at the time the banks weren't lending any money to the agriculture sector) and find that providing credit to the sector was profitable. Our project provided training and monitoring to bank staff and clients through five credit specialists, one for each aimag. The credit specialists were trained and supervised by Shombodon and me.

The project was located in four of the western aimags and the northern aimag of Selenge, requiring us to be on the road at least 50 percent of our time on a one-month on, one-month off schedule. National flights on Mongolian Airlines (MIAT) had been banned by the Asian Development Bank because a MIAT helicopter had crashed two years earlier, killing nine people. We were therefore obliged to go by car and hired Shombodon's son, Enkhbayar, a quiet and shy young man who didn't speak English, to drive us.

Shombodon asked me to inspect the Russian jeep that Enkhbayar had identified for our travel. What did I know about Russian jeeps? But I perceived that they want me to be involved so I accompanied them to the car dealer and looked at the engine, peered under the chassis, touched the interior and pronounced it a good buy.

I happened to know the budget didn't allow anything more fancy. The color, grey, was also fine with me. We knew that new Russian jeeps normally came with fake parts that needed to be switched out during the first months of driving. Besides, Russian jeeps had the advantage that they could be fixed anywhere in the country, right? I conveniently overlooked the fact that the reason they could be fixed anywhere in the remotest corners was that they needed a lot of fixing. We brought a retired mechanic, Shombodon's cousin, along with us on our maiden voyage.

I asked Shombodon whether Enkhbayar knew the way in the western Aimags and the answer was a resounding "No" — however, delivered with a hint of a smile. Apprehensively I purchased a GPS and detailed military maps. We didn't need those as it turned out: Shombodon hadn't considered it necessary to tell me that he knew his way around western Mongolia. He needed only to look at the shape of the mountains around us anywhere in our half-a-million square kilometer work-area to know where we were. We bought camping equipment, food, bottles of vodka and sweets for presents. Traveling by Russian jeep, I knew, would not be the most comfortable way to get to the west; safety policies and regulations required overland traveling to be done with at least two vehicles and a satellite phone in one — but our project didn't have the budget for that. We were going it alone.

What trips they were, lodged so vividly in my mind! Our first stop, Altai, the capital of Gobi Altai aimag, was about a 24-hour drive from Ulaanbaatar — two long bumpy days measured under good road conditions. Only the first 150 kilometers were asphalt — actually 50 percent asphalt, the other 50 percent potholes. A large number of the snapshots I made while traveling in Mongolia show somewhere in the background our jeep with the hood up and Enkhbayar bent over the engine or lying under the car. Enkhbayar turned out to be a steady and careful driver, but many Mongolians are prone to reckless driving. On one occasion I, reluctantly and feeling prissy, admonished the driver of the car guiding ours to drive at a slower, more reasonable, speed. An hour later the front of his car dove into the sand while its front wheel rolled on ahead of us through the desert steppe. The driver was gracious enough to thank me for having told him to slow down: he didn't think they would have come out of it alive at his original speed.

MONGOLIAN MEMORIES

We experienced rain and snow, smelling of mutton, car breakdowns, and not being able to recharge the laptop. Sometimes we looked for our herder-borrowers and couldn't follow them across the river or had to sit and interview them in the middle of the desert or in the car. I found that I preferred camping to staying in soum center hotels or family gers, because I like camping and because I can "check the horses" (the polite Mongolian way to say you are going to the toilet) in private without waking everyone up or stepping on kids sleeping on the floor. However, we normally stayed in the soum centers where, in some cases, I couldn't check any horses during the night because "the unfriendly dogs" were loose at night.

One last trip

I did a third assignment in Mongolia from 2004 to 2006, based in Ulaanbaatar but it was the second job (2002-2004) that brought me into contact with the Mongolian countryside, gave me a flavor of what the country must have been like during the socialist era and hooked me on the country. Shombodon was ever my guide: not only was he able to find specific families in gers out in that empty nowhere, but he was also the only person who spoke English so all my communication went through him. Together we worked, sat in the car for days on end, walked in the hills to stretch our legs and talked. We became friends. Slowly the stories of the past that I heard through Shombodon grabbed me and I started understanding a little bit more about the people. At the same time I realized that I needed the background of history to truly understand the Mongolians. I carried the idea of writing this book with me until, in 2012, Terry gave me the opportunity to turn the idea into reality. He took a job in Salt Lake City, Utah, and I started reading about Mongolia's 20th century.

I had never made notes on anything apart from work-related issues before (of course, I had sent emails to friends and family) and I had never seen the eastern part of the country. These were good reasons to go back and fill in the gaps of my knowledge. I asked Shombodon to accompany me again as guide and interpreter and he said yes. Enkhbayar, his son, would again be our driver and at the last moment we were joined by Terry's cousin David, who is a professional photographer and captured many gorgeous photos of our trip. This time round we had a comfortable Isuzu Bighorn instead of a Russian jeep.

Mongolia is a large country — roughly the size of Alaska — and has only a few paved roads, but with a 4x4 you can get to most places during the summer months, although you might get stuck crossing a river when it rains. Driving in winter is a different matter: I had traveled in fall and spring before and those seasons translate into winter as far as I'm concerned. I remembered seriously worrying about survival one night in March when a blizzard came up and we couldn't see the road any more in the dark and it was -20°C with an insane wind-chill factor. This time round it was going to be summer or not at all.

It was good to be back in the summer of 2012 and Shombodon, Enkhbayar and I fell into an old and comfortable routine. We bought a road-map of the country, left getting the car ready to Enkhbayar, sat in their tiny office, unfolded the map and companionably started plotting. Our first destination was to be Khalkh Gol, in the far eastern tip of Mongolia on the Chinese border (the autonomous region of Inner Mongolia, to be more precise), where an important battle was fought in 1939 between the Japanese on one side and the Russians and Mongolians on the other. Neither Shombodon nor I had been there before.

It was luxury: this time we could go where we wanted to without our work constraining us. What did we want to see? I knew that there were, in reality, few places of great historical significance and even fewer places where there was tangible evidence of the past, so any place where there were people to interview would be significant.

This narrative, a reflection on a place and time that was already past when I first arrived in Mongolia, is the result of me trying to understand and satisfy my curiosity about what happened in Mongolia while I was growing up in a separate world. It is my personal story, based on my experiences during the seven years I worked and traveled there (1999-2006), a series of interviews with elderly Mongols in 2012, visits to sites where important historical events took place, and reading books on Mongolian history. It is a travel book in that it communicates what I have seen, heard and read, but I have made an effort to summarize what happened to the region that became modern-day Mongolia because the stories don't make sense without at least a summary of recent history.

My story is biased not only by my affinity with rural areas but also by the fact that I have mainly interviewed elderly people. Many of those people and places benefited little from the transition from socialism to capitalism. Also, the elderly all over the world tend to idealize the world in which they were young and many elderly Mongols are bothered by the negative way people nowadays talk about their socialist past. Just like the people who were resentful of the way their history, culture and religion were repressed during socialist times, others — and sometimes the same people — are put out by the fact that everything they have ever known and worked for during their lifetime is now being maligned. It would have been a different story had I interviewed young, urban professionals. But the latter would have less memory of the period I found so fascinating and Ulaanbaatar has changed faster and more profoundly than the rest of the country.

I have worked with, listened to and talked with (not to speak of getting drunk with) many ordinary Mongols, which has given me an understanding of how they perceived their history. That unique perspective is what I offer the reader. My focus is the lives of ordinary people; the history of political events is backdrop. I have also attempted to present the stories in a way that is easily digestible and entertaining to read. While I was gainfully employed, I didn't have the time and energy to plow through academic books on Mongolia. I would have chosen something easier to digest. Something like this book.

Tourist brochures depict the Mongols as nomadic herders who live much the same way as they did in Chinggis Khaan's time, but modern Mongols do not live as their ancestors did in the 12th and 13th centuries, not even the herders, however picturesque and authentic they look. Neither do they live the same way as their forebears did in 1900. Their livelihoods, culture and beliefs have radically changed in the course of the 20th century and continue to change under the influence of events on the global stage; they have modernized.

At the turn of the 21st century, roughly half Mongolia's population still lived in traditional gers, mainly because of poverty. Most would prefer to live in apartments, however small, inadequate and depressing in our eyes — and who wouldn't, really, the average temperature in January in Ulaanbaatar being -25°C. The traditional dress, "deel", is cheap, warm and comfortable in the rural areas, but young people and those who move to urban areas or become government officials wear western-style clothing. A colleague of mine was none too happy playing the role of traditional hostess during the celebration of Tsaagan Saar (lunar new year); she hissed under her breath to me that once a year she would respect the past by borrowing her mother's deel and waiting on the men before the women were served. I understand her: Do I want to go back to the traditional — maybe even Dutch Reformed — society where women promise to obey their husbands at marriage, are not allowed to vote, are barred from attending university? Do I wear clogs?

Yet despite their similarities to the Dutch that struck me initially, the Mongols, who were propelled into the modern world in the 1990s and started interacting eagerly with it, carry with them cultural heritage that harks back to their nomadic roots, to the empire that Chinggis Khaan founded, to their Buddhist religion, and to their subordination within the Qing empire by the end of the 19th century. One cannot understand Mongolian society without some knowledge of its history. This book is my attempt to provide readers who are unfamiliar with the country with a summary of that history.

1. A BRIEF INTRODUCTION TO THE LAND AND PEOPLE

A day in my life of Mongolia

A popular theme in paintings is "A day in the life of Mongolia", generally a large canvas with delightful scenes of Mongolian daily life depicted in great detail against an expanse of bucolic background. The longer you gaze at it, the more detail you find: gers; blue-and-white traveling tents; horses tethered to a line; people riding horses; camels, goats and sheep; dogs and children playing; people making felt by dragging large rolls of wet wool behind horses, cooking, making music. My years in Mongolia feel like that painting: a huge canvas with patches of exquisite detail against a grand backdrop — days of my life in Mongolia. For example:

October 2002, on the road. Shombodon, Enkhbayar and I have left Khovd this morning accompanied by a few friends and colleagues who are keeping us company for two days while we make our way to Uliastai, the next aimag (provincial) capital where we have an office. This is the first year on this job and, despite the cold, my new friends want to make sure I appreciate the country they live in: we contemplate the Khovd river at the bridge, and further downriver our friend Togtogbaatar spends some time fishing while we walk around. On the other side of the river bare eroded hills show bands of chocolate brown and reddish brown with in front a few gers and a mud shed on tan dried grass with a few camels in front. Later, when the sun goes down, we stop at several large lakes in the process of freezing over. The soft pastels of

the lakes and shimmering mountain ranges, deeply frozen. The world around me so quietly and intensely cold, the full moon on the horizon and the stars already so bright and close that I feel I am standing alone in the universe. A fleeting moment too cold to savor at leisure.

May 2003, on the road. In Gobi-Altai our colleagues talk us into making a detour to visit a site of natural beauty, 300-kilometer-long sand dunes. We pitch camp and climb a dune behind us. When we move the whole dune starts vibrating and produces an eerily weird low-pitched hum like a deep airplane-engine a short distance away. I have never heard of "singing sands" before and am much impressed. Then we collect dung for our barbecue. Shombodon instructs me as to the suitable age and dryness of the droppings but then feels embarrassed that he has a foreign expert collecting dung and suggests that I shouldn't tell Terry about it. But I am happy to collect dung, feeling pretty useless otherwise. Besides, Shombodon and I both know that collecting dung is traditionally women's work in Mongolia. The mutton tastes very good but I try hard not to think what it has been lying on top of. I am happy sitting in the pungent dung-smoke (against mosquitoes) with these four unsavory-looking Mongols, drinking vodka and gnawing bones. Such a scene would have been unimaginable in many other countries and I conclude that civilization is internal; it does not reside in silverware, crystal, tablecloths, not even in spic and span toilets; it is what makes you feel safe and at ease with your fellow human beings.

May 2003, on the road. A mixture of windy sleet and wet snow is falling when we arrive late at night at the Chandmani soum hotel, Khovd aimag. The hotel is, in actual fact, a kindergarten, which is not at all unusual in rural Mongolia. Immediately we receive a stream of visitors: the chairman of the local people's Khural (assembly); the soum governor; Togie, who works for us as the rural credit specialist from Khovd with the aimag director of Post Bank, a tough lady and a favorite of mine because she runs a good lending program. Also, four plump ladies with rosy cheeks who are in charge of the hotel enter and make a fuss over us, ask us what we want to eat and make sure we are comfortable. I am extremely tired and cold — way beyond being hungry — and want everyone to go away so that I can go to sleep but, of course,

I sit up and am professional and polite. After they leave the roof starts leaking on Shombodon's bed. Now it is a little before midnight and the four ladies want us to move to another part of the building but the door is nailed shut and they have to fetch a carpenter from somewhere to help them pry it open so that they can move our beds. I grump that I do not want to move, but they move us anyway. Shombodon laughs and says that the four ladies don't often have such important visitors and that they are going to make us as comfortable as possible and aren't I having fun? I ungraciously say I'll have fun by the time I am allowed sleep. It's after midnight when we are finally fed and left alone but I still have to find the outhouses. I wander the freezing dark corridors of the cavernous building with my small flashlight, aware there might be obstacles such as pipes crossing the corridors three inches from the ground, emerging in the dark stormy night with horizontal snow whipping around the corners and then trying to fold myself into one of the tiny outhouses constructed for infants.

Back to Outer Mongolia

The enduring metaphor of Outer Mongolia denoting a romantically exotic and remote place was coined by the American explorer Roy Chapman Andrews in the 1920s, after his travels there. At the time the country was already changing, but around 1900, Outer Mongolia, situated on the northern frontier of the Manchu (Qing) Empire, was just that: a remote and inaccessible land where exotic nomadic peoples roamed, their world-view a mixture of animism and a form of Buddhism that featured demons wrapped in strings of skulls with large bulging eyes and evil grins crushing their enemies beneath their feet, and where lamas used objects made from virgins' thighbones in their ceremonies. Today Outer Mongolia is an ancient memory, its skeletons locked up in the closets of decaying museums. A visit to Ulaanbaatar, the capital, shows only a fast-growing, chaotic and polluted Third World city with traffic jams, high rises, fast food and office workers in suits scurrying around. My own staff, professionally dressed and taking every opportunity to wipe the dust off their well-polished shoes, were highly educated, hard and enthusiastic workers, and spoke multiple languages. How can I begin to resurrect the past, not that long ago, really, and yet so far?

The country was visibly and rapidly evolving when I was there, but it had been evolving for quite a while. In fact, the changes that had taken place in the 20th century were much more profound and took place in a shorter space of time than the changes that had taken place in the roughly seven centuries since Chinggis Khaan's era. By the beginning of last century the Mongol territories had shrunk to unimportant outposts of the Manchu empire called Inner Mongolia and Outer Mongolia. Over the course of that century, however, the situation was to radically change: Inner Mongolia would be irretrievably incorporated into modern-day China, its Mongol population becoming a 17 percent minority among ethnic Han Chinese immigrants; the Outer Mongolian region became the independent country of Mongolia.

Before 1900, the Mongols were there already there. Who were they? And what was their territory like? Permeating all my memories of my trips through Mongolia is my awe of the grand empty landscape around us and usually of the cold as well.

Mongolia's southern border snakes through craggy mountain ranges in vivid colors, red, black, greenish, tan, many with white snowy tops floating over them, interspersed with bright yellow sands, seasonal rivers and lakes rimmed with golden grasses and the dry flat steppes called gobis that give the Gobi desert its name. In autumn the gobis turn an unworldly pink, yellow, green, purple, and ghostly tumbleweeds are blown around by Siberian winds while the snow creeps down to lower altitudes. In winter the days are cold and still under icy blue skies, the colors turning pastel between day and night. Two-humped Bactrian camels thrive in these cold deserts; with their thick woolen coats they plod through snow that never seems to melt until the temperature shoots up for a short, hot, dry, and miserable summer. These rugged, ill-tempered animals survive the staggering range of temperatures and are powerful beasts of burden — but their time is past. Herders prefer motorcycles and generally use trucks for their seasonal moves. In spring vicious sandstorms sweep the southern part of the country, causing weakened animals to die, disorienting the people who stumble around trying to find and collect their herds, and sandblasting the paint off vehicles.

To the north and west, mountain ranges tower above wide valleys, fresh- and salt-water lakes, bordered by rocky badlands and sweeping steppes. The highest mountains are in the majestic Altai range in the west, close to where Russia and China meet. Their snowy peaks rise above 4000 meters and feed several large lakes. I visited the Altai mountains once in May and will never forget the sound of the nearly-melted water streaming out of the lake: it was the sound of tens of thousands champagne glasses tinkling in the stream. At higher altitudes shaggy yaks are the beast of burden; in my mind I see them startle and scamper off with their bushy tails ridiculously pointing up.

In the middle of the country the Siberian taiga encroaches southward with its hills and mountains covered with pines, larches and birches, and its cold and deep rivers and lakes, the largest and most beautiful of which is Lake Khovsgol, a miniature of its more famous sister, Lake Baikal. It is cold, clear, more than 250 meters deep and holds 0.4 percent of the world's fresh water. I have drunk the water straight from the lake without any treatment. The Khangai mountain ranges, a little west of the center of Mongolia, stretch out south of Lake Khovsgol, most of their peaks around 3000 meters, with one exceptional — and holy — mountain called Otgontenger of a little over 4000 meters. Most of the rivers that originate in this region flow north towards Siberia or into salt lakes.

Further east, the lovely Khentiis, eroded to soft rounded hills covered with forests, gently give way to seemingly endless rolling steppes that spread east towards the border with China, the part that is commonly referred to as Manchuria, where herds of thousands of gazelles still wander. It is the least populated part of this thinly populated country. The landscape is less spectacular and more monotonous than in the West. Nowadays there are large oilfields and the steppes are much degraded; only a few places are as pristine as when the Manchu emperor's herds of horses were grazed in the area.

In 1900, these isolated lands of 1.5 million square kilometers were inhabited by impoverished peoples, most of them ethnic Mongol tribes, who were subjugated to the Qing dynasty that ruled the whole of China. China and Mongolia had first been united in one empire in the 13th and 14th century under the Yuan dynasty established by Chinggis Khaan's grandson, Kublai Khaan. The ethnic Han-Chinese Ming dynasty took control of China after collapse of the Mongolian Yuan dynasty, but the territories beyond the Great Wall were not conquered by the Ming and stayed under Mongol rule.

In 1644 the Manchu, an ethnic group from north-eastern China overthrew the Ming dynasty and established the Qing dynasty in Beijing, the political center of China. They conquered and formed alliances first with the southern and eastern Mongol tribes living in what is now Inner Mongolia, and in the 1690s they also formed an alliance with the northern Khalkh Mongols against the invading (western) Oirad Mongols. The Oirad nation was eventually vanquished by the Qing dynasty in 1755 but what started out as a more or less equal partnership between Manchus and Mongols over time became Mongol subordination to the Qing dynasty. The final years of the Manchu domination were, perhaps, the most precarious period in the history of the Mongols because the survival of a place where Mongols would be able to maintain their identity and control their own destiny hung in the balance.

That uncertain period is where this narrative starts but it seems long ago, blurred by time, and predated the memories of people I talked to. Moreover, the history books don't dwell on individual experiences or the lives of ordinary people. I was therefore happy to encounter a most enlightening and enlightened source of information concerning the period. A high-ranking Buddhist leader, the Dilowa Khutukhtu (often spelled Diluv Khutagt in English: Appendix 4 for a summary of his life), dictated his autobiography to the Mongolia scholar Owen Lattimore. The Dilowa Khutukhtu, who turned 17 in 1900, gives us a rare first-hand account of monastic life and politics in Outer Mongolia at the beginning of the 20th century. I shall use some of his stories as a first-hand witness account.

Nomadic herding roots

The Mongols, like many other Central Asian ethnic groups, were nomadic pastoralists moving seasonally between different pastures to ensure optimal feed for their livestock year-round. This enabled them to subsist in the extremely harsh Mongolian environment, characterized by long severe winters, low and irregular precipitation, and generally unpredictable variations in temperatures and growing seasons. Cropping under these conditions was insufficiently reliable to depend on for livelihood. Spring blizzards come up out of nowhere and cause temperatures to drop by 20°C within the hour — as Terry and I experienced our first year in Mongolia when we went for a walk in our T-shirts one fine spring morning and nearly froze to death in the hour that followed while we were trying to make it home. The traditional Mongol livelihood, therefore, is herding and even that is a hard and risky livelihood.

The Dilowa Khutukhtu mentions that the year he was born, 1884, his family lost most of its livestock during a dzud. Dzuds, the greatest danger to the livelihood of Mongolian herders, are extremely severe winter weather conditions that happen every few years and result in catastrophic losses of livestock. There are different kinds of dzud, such as white dzud (deep and long-lasting snow cover that prevents grazing), black dzud (lack of snow leading to the freezing of surface-water sources, so the animals cannot drink), and dzuds having to do with blizzard conditions and extreme wind-chill factors.

A devastating dzud occurred the first winter of my stay in Mongolia. Living in Ulaanbaatar and working with mainly urban enterprises at the time, I heard about the livestock losses the same way I hear about other catastrophes that happen around the world — it didn't sink in. I donated some money and that was that. However, few years later a dzud occurred in the Gobi region where we were experimenting with loans to herder families and I was confronted the phenomenon first-hand.

May 2002. Bogd soum, Bayankhongor aimag. On a freezing spring morning, a colleague and I travel to Bogd soum to assess the damage to our lending program in the dzud-affected area. In the sandy desert with tan polls of dried grass and small bare shrubs, there are desiccating and slowly decomposing carcasses lying around. We visit ger after ger of our borrowers — a painful task for us, who are representing their creditors. We encounter bone-weary and shell-shocked families, many of whom had lost their livelihoods. They give accounts of how many animals they had lost — usually all their cows and a percentage of their other animals as well. We are received as usual with salty tea, but without milk or butter. Most say they will pay back their loans because nearly all the loans would come due at cashmere-combing season and I learn that you can comb the cashmere from dead animals, no problem. We keep our visits short — no use increasing the burdens of the families by reminding them of the hardships to come.

It is heartbreaking. My young colleague — unusual for a Mongol — cries when she asks me what we could do. Which is nothing. If you let people get away with not repaying loans, word will get around and no one else will repay either. Your fund will collapse and you can close shop for good. Better hope some of the emergency relief services will step in and be able to finance activities next year. I very much doubt we will get any money back and start thinking about how to limit damages to the dzud-affected areas.

As it turned out, most of the loans got repaid and the herder loan program continued. The visits to those gers gave me a visceral understanding of the precarious nomadic pastoralist livelihood of the Mongols and their dependence on a harsh environment and fickle climate.

Mongolian identity is rooted in the nomadic pastoralist lifestyle and culture of their ancestors. This entails living in mobile dwellings (gers), having a strong preference for meat and dairy products, a love of livestock in general and horses in particular, and a love of wide-open spaces. I also associate nomadism with rugged independence, hospitality, practicality, unapologetic frankness and an aversion to meekly conforming to rules.

Mongolian shelter, food and drink

A ger is a round felt tent that is draped over a wooden frame consisting of latticework walls and a door, connected to a top-wheel with spokes. It can be taken apart and loaded onto camels, ox-carts or trucks and set up to form a new seasonal encampment. Gers are related to the dwellings of Turkic nomads roaming the Steppes of Central Asia from Anatolia to Mongolia and are found, in different forms, in Afghanistan, Turkmenistan, and Kazakhstan. The oldest evidence of a ger, an image in a tomb in southern Iran, goes back to 600 BC.

Gers have become a national symbol for Mongolia the same way clogs, windmills and tulips are symbols for my country. They have been used and adapted for glamping all over the world — and in Mongolia itself. Favorite weekends out for expats and Mongols alike are to rent one or more gers in a ger-camp and go hiking, running, or fishing. I love staying in gers, their cozy round shape with the colorful orange spokes against the white canvas, the beds around the side where you can recline and still be part of the group, the little stoves in the middle that heat up the interior quickly. But when it goes out the temperature quickly plummets to outside levels — which was minus 30°C one of the first nights I spent in one (and realized the outhouse was fifty meters away and the same temperature).

Present-day gers are larger than they were at the beginning of the 20th century. The heavy contemporary wheels are normally supported by two posts, but that was not necessary for the smaller gers with lighter-weight wheels that were used in earlier centuries; those wheels were often made of woven willow branches and were simply held up by the spokes.

The internal organization of gers in the Mongolian countryside is still similar to that of traditional yurts. The door faces south or southeast, the fire (or stove) is in the center below the smoke-hole in the wheel, the place of honor is at the back against the north wall, where Mongols usually display an altar, family photographs, medals and precious belongings. Traditionally the women and their belongings stay in the eastern side of the ger and the men and their belongings in the western side. Guests, particularly male guests, are generally seated in the northwest — close to the altar and warmly away from the door; weak or newborn animals were often kept in the southwest. It is customary to move clockwise around the stove, as it is when one circumambulates a sacred place such as an ovoo (usually a cairn of rocks or wood piled in the form of a tipi that marks a Shamanist or Buddhist meaningful place or boundary: they are generally covered with prayer flags and offerings of money, rice, tea, incense, or discarded crutches). With the door facing south, the interior of the ger also functions as a sundial, as the sun shines through the wheel and describes a path onto the walls of the ger. Mongols are accurate when giving directions, referring to the points of the compass. This is more accurate than the "left" and "right" we use when giving directions, because it is not necessary to know what direction a person is facing before starting to follow directions.

We expats often laughed about traditional Mongolian food because it doesn't conform to our tastes and ideas of what a healthy meal should look like. For instance, we Dutch traditionally mention the vegetable that is mixed into the potatoes to identify our main meal. We don't say we eat steak, we say we eat carrots, meaning carrots mashed with potatoes, or sauerkraut (mashed with potatoes) or kale (mashed with potatoes) — we do not mention the 80 grams of sausage that go with the mash. Laugh if you will. A Mongolian friend who visited the Netherlands for military training confided that he had been miserable there for the first several weeks because he couldn't face the food (apart from mash, we eat a lot of sandwiches). That is, until he found a place that sold lamb-burgers; after that he enjoyed his stay.

Survival in Mongolia's harsh climate precludes any kind of waste: all parts of a slaughtered animal are eaten (intestine soup provides much-needed vitamins). In summer it is not necessary to slaughter animals, so only "white food" (dairy products) is eaten. Going by descriptions of Mongolian food from Chinggis's time that didn't change much until the middle of the 20th century when state and collective farms were introduced and, with those, Russian staples such as potatoes, vegetables and bread. However, throughout the socialist era most factories and other businesses owned herds in order to provide meat and dairy products, healthful airag (fermented mares' milk) in particular, to their employees. When I started working with the credit fund, I found that all official formats in which business accounts had to be presented contained lines for animals: adult animals were categorized as fixed assets, young animals as current assets.

Nevertheless, it would be a simplification to think that Mongols exclusively ate meat and dairy products before the 20th century: People picked berries, mushrooms and herbs such as wild onions, of which there is abundance in the steppes, and harvested wild grasses and made flour from those. In some corners of the country they still do: in Gobi Altai a lady we interviewed presented us with sacks of different types of flour hand-milled from several grass species and included information on the healthful properties of each. Shombodon was familiar with those types of flour and was happy to take them home.

Some herders planted crops such as millet and barley and traded with their neighbors for items they did not produce themselves; there were even families around Lake Khovsgol who dedicated themselves to farming as their main livelihood at the beginning of the 20th century. One man I talked to about his childhood in the 1940s and 50s said his family used to plant barley and rye on one hectare in the southwestern aimag of Gobi Altai using manual irrigation. The grain was roasted and then ground with a hand-operated mill-stones (quern-stones) in a technique that dates back to the Neolithic era. Shombodon said that he and his sisters loved flour but didn't get it often because the whole process of roasting, milling and preparing it was very labor-intensive and time-consuming for their parents. The flour was mixed with cream, butter or sheep-tail fat and eaten with tea for breakfast and lunch. Mongolian salty milk-tea is more like soup than like tea. It is made by boiling milk in the huge wok-like cooking pot, which generally makes it taste like mutton and feel a little greasy, mixing in green tea and salt while beating it vigorously and finally pouring it through a strainer, usually into a large thermos. Sometimes butter or cream is added or meat or dumplings. I like it as broth but prefer to have my early-morning tea without milk, salt or mutton-fat.

Alcohol has been part of the culture since time immemorial. Getting drunk on vodka, as became common during the Russian-influenced period, was easily adopted by a people that has been guzzling gallons of airag since Chinggis Khaan's time and before. Airag is believed to have significant health benefits: in particular, it is supposed to improve digestion and treat respiratory diseases such as tuberculosis. For that reason it was an important benefit extended to socialist workers during the time of the planned economy — on the same plane with free education and medical care.

The religious establishment wasn't known for abstention either: in Dilowa Khutugtu's autobiography he says, "Mongols do not like to drink alone, like Chinese and Tibetans they like to drink competitively, urging on their companions and proud if they can drink them under the table."

Religion

The Mongols were originally shamanists and worshipped the heavens, mountains, streams, caves and their own ancestors, and to this day many geographical features are considered holy. They loosely adopted Buddhism during the Yuan dynasty; after the fall of the dynasty and in the absence of centrally organized religion, they reverted to shamanism.

The Tibetan Gelugpa (or "Yellow Hat") strain of Buddhism was re-introduced to Mongolia at the end of the 16th century as a result of an alignment of interest between the Gelugpa order that was seeking military and moral support against rival sects and Mongol Khans. The Khans, even while competing with each other, were seeking a unifying religion to bring together the Mongols and to expose them to the high levels of learning transmitted through Tibetan scriptures rather than exclusively through Chinese texts, thereby counteracting Mongol subordination to Chinese culture. Altan Khan (Golden Khan) of the Tümed Mongols, trying to obtain legitimacy to go with his military might, took the initiative to invite Sodnomjamts, head of the Gelugpa order, to Mongolia. The latter accepted in 1577 and the Golden Khan bestowed the title "Dalai Lama" upon him. The Mongolian word dalai means "oceanic" or "vast"; in fact, the Tibetan name Sodnomjamts already incorporated the concept of oceanic, "jamts" meaning large surface of water. In any case, the title Dalai Lama originates in Mongolia (more precisely Inner Mongolia where the Tümed Mongols had settled).

The Dalai Lama remained in Mongolia to proselytize among the Mongols while the Golden Khan enacted laws imposing fines for practicing shamanist rites, particularly the rites that involved killing slaves and servants to accompany their deceased masters to the other world. Tibetan monks were imported to convert the Mongols to Buddhism; Buddhist temples and monasteries were built. The Erdene Zuu monastery, the oldest in the country, was built in 1585 on the ruins of Kharkhorin, the ancient capital of the Mongol empire, and was always an important religious center. It is the largest temple complex that partially survived the purges of the 1930s and is again functioning as a place of worship (and tourism). Lamaist temples were often constructed on ancient sacred sites, and shamanist spirits and ancient demons, soothsaying and belief in magic permeate Mongolian Buddhism to this day.

The conversion of Mongols to Buddhism between the 16th and 18th centuries resulted in the rise of a strong ecclesiastical Yellow Hat establishment, Tibetan-Mongolian in nature (Tibetan was spoken and written in the monasteries alongside Mongolian), next to the secular feudal establishment. Tibetan Buddhism influenced Mongolian culture and in time became a unifying force. To counteract it, the Manchu administration exerted control over the lamaist establishment by requiring the registration of all lamas, restricting the movements of Mongolia's religious leader, the Bogd Javzandamba Khutukhtu, and directly appointing the head of the civil administration as well as the Da Lama ("Lama Superior") of the monasteries.

In Tibetan, and therefore Mongolian, Buddhism, the concept of reincarnation and in particular the reincarnation of historical holy personages has led to the practice of identifying and grooming infants to succeed high-ranking religious officials. The Dilowa Khutukhtu, himself the reincarnation of an ancient saint, starts his autobiography by explaining how there is the Soul and its vehicle, the material body. The (reincarnated) Soul may appear and act very differently when in a different body. When a Khutukhtu, or "living Buddha" as the Dilowa refers to that high rank, dies, the Soul finds another body as its vehicle and this new reincarnation needs to be found. He sheds light on how reincarnations were discovered: "Messengers were sent to all the other living Buddhas to ask help in finding the new Dilowa. Some recommended the best direction in which to search by the casting of dice, some by the system of divination based on the rosary of 108 prayer beads and some by contemplation and inspiration. Sorcerers called Choijin were also consulted, who speak when inspired, and after recovery do not remember what they have said."

The search for reincarnations is one of the areas where politics and religion sometimes clash. The head of the Buddhist religion in Mongolia, the Bogd Javzandamba Khutukhtu (the reincarnation of the Indian God Javsun Darnat), was always an influential figure. After the second Javzandamba Khutukhtu, who was a direct descendant of Chinggis Khaan, supported a rebellion against the Manchu in 1755-1756, the Manchu administration prohibited further Mongol reincarnations. From the third Javzandamba Khutukhtu onward the reincarnations were imported from Tibet.

The Yellow Hat faith is strongly monastic and there were some 600 to 750 (sources vary in their estimates) monasteries and temple complexes in the Outer Mongolian region, holding about 20 percent of the province's wealth. Monasteries were also trade centers and the Manchus had established branches or agents of Chinese trading companies at them that traded Mongolian goods for Chinese wares such as tea, silks, and tobacco. The original name for Ulaanbaatar, Ikh Khüree, is usually translated as "big monastery", demonstrating how the town was perceived. In actual fact, the word Khüree stems from a group of herding camps that were positioned in a circle with their wealth (the herds) in the middle, so as better to defend themselves. It might be better translated as "settlement".

Monasteries acquired wealth and dependent herder households, just as the nobility did, alongside the esteem and power that religions usually hold over the faithful. At the beginning of the 20th century it was the principal Mongolian socio-economic power; it was also decentralized and a web of monasteries crisscrossed the country. Despite the strong support of the faithful, the lamas were seen as corrupt, venal and parasitic by the laypeople and popular folklore depicted them in an unfavorable light as being stupid and dishonest.

By the 1920s perhaps a third of the Mongolian population either lived in their territories or as their hereditary bondsmen. The Buddhist faith and its monasteries were the only Mongolian (as opposed to Manchu or Chinese) sources of organization, education and power in the country. Shombodon told me that it used to be common for families to send at least one of their boys to become a lama, which must have bound the monasteries and the general population tightly together.

Agvaanluvsanchoijinnyamdanzanvanchigbalsambuu (that was really his name!) was the eighth Bogd Javzandamba Khutukhtu and the highest authority in the Mongolian Buddhist establishment at the turn of the century. In 1874 the five-year-old from Tibet had been identified as the reincarnation of the Bogd Javzandamba Khutukhtu and sent to Mongolia the same year, where he was joyously welcomed and elevated to the Bogd Throne, receiving the corresponding title and rank from the Manchu Emperor in Beijing, along with the golden diploma of entitlement and a golden seal. He was accompanied on his trip to Mongolia by his parents and five other family members and never returned to Tibet. He was to become the symbol for Mongolian independence movement against the Manchu and in 1911 became the first sovereign of the independent state of Mongolia.

Even before then he met foreign dignitaries. The most amusing of these encounters with the Bogd Javzandamba Khutukhtu was written up in the memoirs of Count Alfred Kaizerling, on a mission to strengthen friendship between Russia and Mongolia that took place around 1887. During the first meeting, Kaizeling presented the youthful Bogd Javzandamba Khutukhtu with gifts, among them a prototype telephone and a music box. The Bogd was, according to Kaizerling, heartily amused by the music box, particularly by a tune that sounded to him like horses galloping (how very Mongolian!). The next day, during a reception, the Bogd invited him to a game of chess. Kaizeling recorded: "When we were playing chess, devout Buddhists came crawling one after another and got his blessing. On occasion, the Khutukhtu blessed them with a chess piece he was holding. When doing so, he was humming and what surprised me was the tune. It was the one he had heard the day before. He checked and then checkmated me while blessing his subjects to the tune of Strauss' waltz."

Despite the humorous description of their encounter, it draws a picture of two men from different cultures who got along well and it was definitely not a dumb move by the Bogd to cozy up to the Russians at that time, as we shall see.

Horses, sports and arts

It would be difficult to write about traditional Mongolian culture without mentioning horses. The first use of horses is, just like the first gers, often linked to the Scythians who roamed the Eurasian continent between the third and eighth century BC; in fact, the Scythian horse-based culture seems to have been very similar to Mongol culture and some of their art uses the same motifs as the ancient deer-stones found in many parts of Mongolia. Chinggis Khaan was able to conquer the world because of the speed and hardiness of the Mongolian horses and the superb use the Mongols made of them. The use of stirrups is usually attributed to the Mongols, enabling them to shoot their arrows accurately from horseback. Today herders still make extensive use of horses. One of the advantages of Mongolian horses is that they fend for themselves even in Mongolia's harsh climate and require very little care. They live in a half-wild state and have to be broken in again after each winter.

Mongols love their horses and Mongolian art and culture is suffused with horse-imagery. Mongolia's most famous instrument is the morin khuur or horse-head fiddle, a two-stringed instrument played with a bow. The morin khuur has a carved horse head at the peg head. The legend of the origin of the instrument is that a herder, grieving over the death of his favorite horse, lovingly crafted a horsehead fiddle in memory of the deceased.

Important religious ceremonies used to be accompanied by festivals and competitions featuring horse racing and other competitive sports. The core of these annual Naadam festivals are formed by the three so-called manly sports: horse racing, archery and wrestling. Another manly sport that is making a comeback is anklebone-shooting, one of many games that are played with the ankle bones of sheep or goats. I have seen it played only once and I didn't understand the rules but remember the very authentic-sounding ancient chanting that accompanied it, as well as the concentration and enthusiasm of the men flicking bits of bone from a polished wooden tray at anklebones sitting on a wooden stand a few feet away. The anklebones are the size of dice and represent different animals (horses, camels, goats, sheep), depending on what side is up.

The rules of Mongolian horse races are simple: the fastest horse that still has a rider on it at the finish line wins. Only male horses race and in order to give one's horse an edge, its jockey has to weigh as little as possible, which is why children, boys (and in modern times girls as well) ride the horses, often bareback. The race goes from point to point, a distance of about 15 kilometers, but the horses start at the finish line and first have to ride out to the starting line. That is where some of the excited children lose the race: they tire their horses out by starting out too fast on the 15 kilometers before the actual race. When I attended races in 2012, children from seven onward were allowed to race, up from age five or six several years earlier. There are discussions about letting children race; in 1999 an eight-year-old girl racing in the national Naadam festival fell from a horse and was dragged to death, sparking outrage and opposition from children's rights advocates.

July 2012. It's a grey and wet morning in Baruun-Urt, the capital of Sükhbaatar aimag, and I'm still tired of the driving we did the previous days. Last night we were able to rent a ger in the huge ger-camp that the city has erected to house all the visitors this Naadam festival. The gers are crammed together, the camp is noisy, and filled with small beetles that are attracted to the lights inside. David has decided to sleep in as he is feeling a bit under the weather but Shombodon was up bright and early, exclaiming: "Now we are going to have some fun!" While I could have done with a bit more sleep, I don't want to miss anything so here I am standing in the mud among throngs of Mongolians dressed in their best deels under plastic ponchos or umbrellas. The first race is about

to begin and a large group of horses with their tiny jockeys in their colorful clothes is milling about, waiting for the sign to leave for the starting point of the race, out of sight beyond the horizon. We stay in the car so we can keep dry while waiting for the racers to come in.

When the excited crowd starts quickening we get out of the car and maneuver to find a good place to watch the finish. We see the first horses coming towards us and soon the winning horse flashes by in the pouring rain with the tiniest slip of a girl in a bright pink plastic raincoat hanging on. She and the other kids of the small head group of three are riding bareback. They disappear from sight as the crowd surged towards them to wipe off some of the winning horse's very lucky sweat. Behind I see a horse that has fallen in the soggy mud — I was later told it died. I muse that it is still a fairly unsophisticated sport! In any case, winning horses are superheroes and their fame rubs off on their owners. Poems and songs are written about them and statues are erected for them. The jockeys are just kids and nothing special.

Wrestling is certainly the most manly of the three manly sports and the only one that is reserved for men only. Legend has it that Khutulun, the great-great-granddaughter of Chinggis Khaan, wrestled so well that men couldn't win against her (making it difficult for her to find a suitable husband). Apparently women were relatively free to take part in war and excel in sports during the heydays of the Mongol Khans but somewhere in the subsequent centuries culture and morals changed against that freedom. In order to prevent women from wrestling, modern costumes are designed in a way that women can't hide their gender in them, the dainty tops cover just a part of the arms and a tiny bit at the back; furthermore, during the winner's "eagle dance" the victor flaps his arms like an eagle and thrusts out his naked chest for all to see.

Mongolian wrestling, traditional-style, is as straightforward as horse-racing. There are no weight-classes and if the stadium is large enough all participants are paired off and fight at the same time in the first round. The winners fight each other and then again until there is one final winner left. You lose if any other part than your foot or hand touches the ground. Bouts of severely mismatched pairs take just a few seconds, while evenly matched contests seem to go on forever. In the national Naadam competition, the full contingent of wrestlers that participate is 512 or even double that number in very special commemorative years.

Archery is a sport for both men and women: the only difference is that the men stand a bit farther from the targets. The competitors wear traditional deels and shoot from a standing position. The judges stand close to the targets, and sing out the result of each shot in a traditional melodic way (fall short, overshoot, wide or bounce). Shooting from horseback must have gone out of fashion somewhere between Chinggis's time and the present.

Mongols love to sing and many of the traditional long-songs (each syllable of the song is drawn out) are about the beauty of the landscape, a beloved horse and one's mother — in that order. Beautiful girls are usually allotted short-songs, I gather. Herders might sing while riding their horses or at get-togethers. The most well-known ancient singing style from Mongolia (and Tuva) is throat singing (Khoomii) or overtone singing, in which the singer manages to amplify the overtones of the fundamental frequency of a tone so that these are heard at the same time. The fundamental frequency usually sounds like one long low growling tone deep in the throat and the overtones sound like Irish tin whistles. The first time I heard it, I didn't realize the singer was actually making the whistling tunes in his throat instead of using an instrument. I find it interesting but not attractive to listen to for prolonged periods of time. Some people who are not used to listening to throat singing, don't even know what to listen for and only hear the low growling sound.

Another traditional Mongolian art that has survived to this day and has become world famous is contortion: the world's top contortionists, working for such as Cirque Du Soleil, are Mongolian girls. It is a strange and wonderful art where the performers' heads seem disconnected from their bodies and pop up in unexpected places. A popular stance is a contortionist bending backwards until her feet are comically placed on both sides of her head. Mongolia is rightly proud of its art of contortion and is trying to get Unesco to recognize contortion as a Mongolian intangible cultural heritage.

There are many other traditional art forms and games that are disappearing in these modern times, such as bielgie dancing (a dance form that was designed to be performed inside the ger), a variety of board games and games involving stones, ankle-bones or dried goat droppings.

2. THE FINAL YEARS OF THE MANCHU DYNASTY

Uliastai

August 2012. Uliastai. *We are sitting in a sumptuous setting: The wallpaper features bold gold-and-silver floral patterns against a royal-blue background; shimmery silvery-grey curtains, neatly draped, set off matching net curtains; a gold-colored polyester damask tablecloth adorns the table; and we are eating from pretty gold-rimmed plates. This is a typical VIP room, still common in many restaurants, particularly in the aimags. During the classless socialist era some people were a little bit more equal than others and they dined privately in such VIP rooms. We are hosting Mr. Lhasuren, a friend and former colleague of Shombodon, who can hopefully tell me something about the Manchus here in Uliastai, the capital of Zavkhan aimag. We have ordered food and weathered a lively discussion and consternation about David's order (fried onions, peppers, mushrooms and rice — but no meat). After worried glances in his direction and assurances that he really doesn't want meat, the waitress leaves, the meal comes and he eats it with relish — a fact I note with relief, as he has not been very open-minded about Mongolian food and has resorted to eating cookies instead.*

In 1900 the Manchus exercised direct control of the vast territory of Outer Mongolia through their main administrative and military center Uliastai, and through offices in Khüree (now Ulaanbaatar), Khovd and a resident representative in the border town of Khiagt which was an important trading post giving access to Siberia and beyond. Uliastai sits in a valley where two rivers meet amid high and rugged mountains — the most sacred mountain of Mongolia, Otgontenger, is less than 60 kilometers away. In this lovely setting

Shombodon and I are happy to reconnect with our former credit specialist, Badamkhatan, whom we first met 10 years ago. He was our youngest credit specialist and was always laughing and clowning around, making faces while eating the peppery and supposedly healthy spring prairie crocus. One day, after having spent a week together with our credit specialists for training and meetings in a resort close to Uliastai, the older generation (Shombodon, the trainers and I) were so tired from the nightly parties that we crept away and fled into the countryside where we set up our tents in order to rest up and get a good night's sleep, but Badamkhatan, an avid wolf-hunter, knew the area better than we did and our pupils hunted us down with leftover snacks and vodka. Today we are here to try and learn something about the Manchus; Badamkhatan, all mature, is with us, helping us set up some of our meetings.

Against the formal setting of the dining room, Mr. Lhasuren, in his 60s with slightly receding hair, glasses and laughing crinkles around his eyes, looks relaxed in a shirt without a tie and an informal dark jacket. He is happy to see his old friend Shombodon and delighted to tell me whatever I want to know about the Manchu period. He is used to someone taking down his words and he and Shombodon give me time to make my notes. Even though he didn't live in that period himself, his parents and other older people told him about that precarious time when the Mongols were at their weakest.

He tells me that the town of Uliastai was first established as a fort in 1733 at a place called Sanguin Khot between two rivers and that the Amban (equivalent to a governor or viceroy) of Uliastai represented the Manchus in North Mongolia had and had broad powers. The selection of the location for Sanguin Khot was excellent, centrally located in Western Mongolia, and also favorable for planting vegetables with which the Chinese supported themselves. The current vegetable fields around Uliastai, where some of the clients of our former loan-scheme farmed, are inherited from the Chinese.

Uliastai is about 1800 kilometers from Beijing and Mr. Lkhasuren starts talking about communication and transportation within the enormous empire of China. The "pony express" system of mounted couriers that was allegedly established in the early 13th century (it was probably earlier) by Ogodei Khaan, a son of Chinggis Khaan, to govern his empire, was still vital to the administration of the Chinese empire 700 years later. It is called the örtö system in Mongolian and provided fast and reliable services to transport messages and officials between Beijing and the Mongolian centers and forts of Ikh Khüree, Uliastai and Khovd. The örtö system transported important passengers, mostly Manchu officials, between the main garrisons. Örtö points were established every 30 kilometers where the passengers were fed, accommodated and provided with fresh horses. Local herders were forced to support the örtö points by providing their best horses, guides, food and accommodation. The guide would take back the horses.

Herder households were appointed by the Manchu administration to service the örtö system but labor shortages meant that local herders were pressed into service; people from the four Khalkh aimags (tribes) who had rebelled against their nobles or otherwise made a nuisance of themselves were also sent to perform örtö service. The "black and white khoshuu" in the area that is now Aldarkhaan soum surrounding Uliastai was so called because its population came from many different ethnic groups that had been sent there to provide örtö services. The pony-express system enabled the Manchus to transport people from Khovd to Uliastai, a distance of over 500 kilometers, in one day. I am impressed: that is the maximum distance we manage in a day in our car. The system was so efficient that it was replaced by motor vehicles only in 1949. The Manchu officials transported that way, each rank with its own banner according to protocol, were preceded by criers who called "We are coming!" and had to be fed and accommodated immediately.

The Department of Protocol was important in the Manchu empire, as described in the Dilowa Khutugtu's autobiography: "According to protocol, a Living Buddha of the rank of Khutugtu was entitled to a ceremonial two-wheeled cart with a blue covering over it. After three state visits to the (Manchu) Emperor of China, he was entitled to be presented by the Emperor with the green canopy instead of the blue one." After the fall of the Manchu Empire, the Bogd Khaan, who had been enthroned as head of the new and independent country Mongolia, appropriated the right of the Manchu emperor to bestow privileges of protocol to the deserving: "On this occasion, the Bogd bestowed the honor of a green canopy to me. He also bestowed on me the orange bridle. The Imperial yellow was a bright golden color. The color bestowed on lower ranks was a deep orange-yellow." And a few pages later, he mentions that in 1918 the Bogd bestowed upon him the yellow bridle and yellow canopy for his Cart of State. The huge and elaborate Manchu administration had generated a profusion of ranks and titles, not only among the lamas: there were six different ranks of Mongolian princes ("princes" were direct descendants of Chinggis Khaan) and even more for nobles. The lower classes were divided into commoners (ard) who paid taxes and labor to the Manchu, and feudal serfs who were subject to princes and nobles. Some of the latter would run away and live as commoners.

Mr. Lhasuren tells us that Chinatown, the Chinese commercial center, was established where the center of modern Uliastai is located, across the river from the fort against rocky outcrops below the mountains in the west, and that there used to be a red bridge over the river connecting the garrison with Chinatown for Manchu officials and other travelers to cross without getting their feet wet. Chinatown was a market place — traders collected wool from this area in exchange for goods from China. The town had a one-meter-thick wall around it with a gate and a strong wooden gate of 10 centimeters with large nails in it. Chinese were still living in Uliastai until the 1960s, but the last of them have since died. About 30 Chinese had been married to Mongolian women. Although I have heard differing opinions about the period of Mongolian independence and the socialist era, the Mongols are united in being convinced of their destitution under Manchu rule. Modern-day Mongols are graphically reminded of Manchu brutality in oppressing them through depictions of the nine Manchu punishments: grisly pictures displayed in museums throughout the country illustrate how the Manchu tortured Mongols though beating, burning, hanging, flaying and shackling them in various contorted positions or in small crates with just a hole for their heads to stick out.

East of town, the rectangular outline of the Manchu mud-brick walled fort and surrounding moat is still there (Google Earth shows the outline very clearly) but it is fading. The fort was about 400 by 500 meters and looks tiny in the huge landscape; the site is surrounded by snow-capped mountains and long-forested slopes but the valley floor is bare of vegetation. Shombodon told me that the acacia shrubbery that originally grew there was cut by the Manchus to prevent the Mongols creeping up on them unnoticed. It didn't look to me as if they would have been able to control the immense region militarily from their few flimsy fortifications — acacia shrubs or not — but of course they didn't have to as they governed through a system of Mongolian nobles and Buddhist officials who were loyal to the Manchu emperor.

In 1910 the town had a population of 3000, two thirds of them Chinese and one third Mongol. There is nothing left of the original buildings: by the 1970s Chinatown had completely disappeared with the exception of one last building that was used as a wholesale center — but it too is now gone. We walk about town and point out some of the places where Manchu buildings had stood. Then we say goodbye to Mr. Lhasuren after having spent a pleasant afternoon with him and go to our next appointment.

Decline of the Manchu empire

In the second half of the 19th century, the Manchu dynasty was severely weakened by events such as the Taiping Rebellion (1850-1864), the Boxer Rebellion (1898-1901), the first Sino-Japanese war (1894-1895) and Russian occupation of the Manchurian territories in 1898 and 1900. Indeed, the Dilowa Khutukhtu mentions in passing that during the period of the Boxer Rebellion, when the troops of Zasagt Khan aimag mutinied but not those of the neighboring aimag of Sain Noyon Khan, "If those two had united, they could have taken Uliastai."

The Manchus were also aware of the danger of being assimilated by the overwhelmingly numerous mainstream Han Chinese — rightfully so, after the fall of their dynasty they ended up losing much of their original culture and language. While in power, therefore, their policies aimed at keeping the Manchu ethnicity "pure" and these policies covered the Mongols as well. Mongolian ethnicity, language and culture was, during the Manchu dynasty, protected by laws prohibiting travel, speaking each other's language and intermarriage between the ethnic Chinese and Mongols, and by prohibiting Han Chinese to settle in Outer Mongolia.

Russia increased its influence in Outer Mongolia during the second half of the 19th century by opening its first trading company in the 1850s and by making efforts to establish good relationships with the Mongolian nobles. The main product that was transported from China to Europe was tea, compressed into hard bricks. By the end of the 19th century, Russia had negotiated duty-free trade rights across Mongolia and permission to open additional consulates in Khovd and Uliastai. The Russians were strategically more interested in Manchuria and the Pacific coast to the northwest, but Mongolia itself was also seen as a potential prize. The Russians did not want to confront the Chinese powers directly but opened their first consulate in 1860 in Khüree (which they called Urga) and a lot of strategic positioning went on behind the scenes between 1880 and 1910. By the end of the century the Russians had several hundred Cossack troops stationed in Mongolia to protect trading posts against incursions of Chinese Muslim rebels, and in 1900 an additional 200 Cossacks were stationed in Khüree, ostensibly for similar purposes, but in reality Mongolia was already seen as a potential buffer between the increasingly important Trans-Siberian Railway, which opened in 1891, and China.

Japan's power was also on the increase and it developed imperialist tendencies that worried Korea, China and Russia. When it became clear that the Manchu empire was failing, hostilities between Japan with its commercial and industrial interests in the Korean peninsula, and Russia with its interests in protecting its Chinese eastern railway project, broke out over Manchuria in 1904. Russian-held Port Arthur fell to the Japanese in 1905, and Russia lost a large part of its Baltic fleet that had sailed halfway around the globe around the Cape because Britain had denied it passage through the Suez canal. Korea became a Japanese protectorate. In the peace negotiations brokered by Theodore Roosevelt, for which he received the Nobel Peace prize, Manchuria fell under the Japanese sphere of influence and Outer Mongolia under the Russian sphere. Nevertheless, Japan did not fully relinquish its hope of gaining control of a larger part of the continent.

By the end of the 19th century the Manchu administration tried to compensate for the loss of income from the south of China by increasing tax revenues from their other regions, including Inner and Outer Mongolia. The Mongols were compelled to pay their taxes in silver instead of livestock as had been the custom, forcing them to borrow the silver from Chinese merchants and moneylenders at usurious interest rates. The loans were repaid in livestock and the number of livestock exported to China increased exponentially, decimating the Mongolian herds, the only source of survival for the Mongols. The Manchu administration devised other ways to increase taxes by modifying the old system in which the khoshuus paid tax and in turn taxed their households. For instance, in Khovd they introduced a new tithe system based on combining 10 households, called aravts, and imposed taxes on the 10 together; if a household couldn't pay, the others had to compensate. The aravts paid to the soums which in turn paid to the khoshuus, increasing the tax burden on the population[1].

The tax burden is mentioned by the Dilowa Khutukhtu who traveled to Tsteserleg in 1902 to the "great assembly of Aimags" to petition for relief of taxes in his region, which was "very impoverished". He goes on: "In my twenty-first year (1904), I made two more trips to Uliastai to see officials there because of the very heavy debts owed by the people of my monastery territory to Chinese merchants, so heavy that every payment of interest was becoming very difficult." Many years later, in spring of 1926, he was still working on resolving the debt issues of his people.

In addition to increasing their tax revenues, the beleaguered and debilitated Qing dynasty tried to counter Russian and to a lesser degree Japanese designs on Mongolian territories by introducing a large reform program. This so-called New Administration included the creation of a Frontier Defense Bureau to train Tibetan and Mongolian soldiers — paid for by the Mongolians, naturally — and the introduction of a policy of cultural assimilation in Mongolia. Laws that had formerly segregated Mongolia and Chinese were abolished and plans were made for Han Chinese to colonize Inner and Outer Mongolia and turn them into regular Chinese provinces. Despite resistance, Inner Mongolia was opened up for immigration and in 1910 a more aggressive Qing administrator, Sando, was appointed as Amban of Urga to force through the New Administration reforms in Outer Mongolia as well.

These changes, together with the increased tax burden, threatened the very existence of the already impoverished Mongols and rebellions started breaking out. Inner Mongolian nationalist leaders, having fled to Outer Mongolia after unsuccessful revolts, bolstered Mongolian nationalism — they had seen the end of the nomadic Mongolian livelihood caused by Han Chinese settlements at

---

1. Interview with Mr. Ganbold, history and ethnography professor at the University of Khovd (22 August 2012).

home. The Manchu had truly gone from allies to oppressors during the two-and-a-half-century Qing dynasty.

As early as 1895 the Bogd Javzandamba Khutukhtu started seeking support from Russia by sending a secret mission of two high-ranking lamas to the Tsar to deliver a letter soliciting assistance for Mongolia to become independent from Manchu rule. The Russian response was cautiously favorable, advising the Mongols to bide their time, secretly unite, and prepare for rebellion. Apart from these secret inquiries and circumspect contacts, incidences of rioting, rebellions by troops and Buddhist monks started taking place with increased frequency around the turn of the century.

The Mongolian rebellion

Mongolian insubordination, at first involving scattered mutinous incidents many of which involved Buddhist lamas, crystallized into a more coherent independence movement around 1910-1911. In July 1911 a group of Khalkh nobles and the Bogd Javzandamba Khutukhtu (the one with the long name) organized several secret meetings in which Mongolian independence was discussed, and a clandestine delegation was dispatched to St Petersburg bearing a letter, signed by the Bogd and the Khans of the four Khalkh clans, requesting assistance in establishing the independent nation of Mongolia.

The Russian government wanted Outer Mongolia to function as a buffer state against China and Japan but was equivocal in its response because it didn't want its powerful neighbors to interpret its role in Mongolia as an act of aggression — it opposed inclusion of the regions of Inner Mongolia, Barga and Uriankhai (now Tanno Tuva) into an independent Mongolia as the Mongols had envisaged. It therefore ambiguously strengthened its consular guard in Urga and informed the Manchu government of the Mongolian mission to St Petersburg expressing concern regarding the complaints of the Mongol delegation. Sando saw the writing on the wall, tried to intercept the returning delegation, forbade further Russian-Mongolian negotiations, and threatened to bring in Chinese troops and provide arms to the Chinese population. He failed and was left without support when in October 1911 the Manchu administration itself completely collapsed.

After that, things moved quickly. In November the Khalkh-Mongol insurgents and the Bogd Javzandamba Khutukhtu took advantage of the situation and formed a Provisional Government of Khalkh. On November 28 the Provisional Government ordered the mobilization of 1000 soldiers from each of the four Khalkh aimags. On December 1 it proclaimed an end to Manchu rule and the founding of a Mongolian state with the Javzandamba Khutukhtu at its head. On December 5 Sando, who had only 150 troops at his disposal, was expelled from Mongolia with support from the Russian consulate. On December 29 the Javzandamba Khutukhtu was formally enthroned as Bogd Khaan (Great Khan) of the independent Mongolian state. The town of Ikh Khüree was re-named Niislel Khüree (Capital Settlement).

After the enthronement of the Bogd as Khaan, the remnants of the Manchu rule were mopped up. In January 1912, the Manchu Amban in Uliastai (formerly the main center of Manchu rulers in Mongolia) did not resist deportation. According to the Dilowa Khutukhtu: "At the beginning of the winter of 1911-1912 I had gone to Uliastai. At the time nothing violent had yet happened there but there were many rumors and everyone inquired for news. The Manchu Amban of Uliastai was a man named Ma. Ma had been appointed three years before, but had managed to delay taking up his post. He finally arrived in that summer and fled the winter of the same year, the year that the Urga Living Buddha became Khaan." I feel a twinge of pity for Ma, who happened to be a civil servant at the time of the collapse of his civil service and was left hanging in Outer Mongolia. Of course he fled! The Northern garrison-town of Ulaangom was taken in May. In August Mongolian troops with support of militant lamas and the local population liberated Khovd.

It is difficult to assess what the Bogd Khaan's role in the struggle for independence was, or indeed what kind of man he was. Sources give wildly differing views of him, depicting him either as a wise leader playing an important role in starting off the national liberation movement, or as an alcoholic fop who was instrumental in oppressing and exploiting the Mongols. That he drank to excess is mentioned in many sources and attested to by the Dilowa Khutukhtu, who at the same time affirms he was a very able politician: "The Bogd was very hard to do business with because he was such a fearful drinker. He would sometimes sit cross-legged for a week drinking steadily night and day. The officials attending him would be changed frequently, but he would go on drinking, never lying down to sleep and never moving except to go out to the toilet. At times he would seem to be completely unconscious, with his head lying on his chest; he would seem not to understand anything that was said to him; then he would raise his head and demand another drink, and the new drink would sober him up so that he could conduct business." I ask myself, however did the Mongols manage to become independent?

Historians during the socialist era were, in line with communist ideology, against religion and accordingly belittled the role of Bogd Khaan in the independence movement, suppressed evidence that he was an astute politician, and portrayed him as an inept, doddering drunk. In fact, he was aware that the window of opportunity for independence that opened at the collapse of the Manchu empire should be seized at once before it closed. He understood and shrewdly dealt with Mongolia's superpower-neighbors as well as with the Buddhist and secular Mongolian leaders representing different clans, each pursuing their own interests. Shombodon told me that the Mongols always respected the Bogd Khaan, even during the socialist period, and had continued to pray for him "within their sleeves", meaning secretly. Anyone familiar with Mongolian dress will smile at this saying because traditional deels have sleeves that hang down to a person's knees and flare out like bells. The Mongols could have had quite a lot up their sleeves, if they wanted to!

Mongols at the beginning of the 20th century

From 1912 onward, several years of relative tranquility descended on the country, enabling the newly independent country to start navigating its own course. The Mongols started building their state-institutions while the foreign powers were looking the other way: in 1914, significant for most of us as the start of World War One, the Mongols were quietly forming a government that resembled modern Western governments with a two-house parliament, consisting of the Ikh Khural and the Little Khural, a cabinet and prime minister. They were also working on their legal code, which they adopted a year later.

Shombodon wanted to make sure I included information on the Bogd Khaan's reign in my book so in Khovd he found me an informant.

August 2012. Khovd. School is out at the University of Khovd and the building is large and empty, but the professor of history and ethnography, Mr. Ganbold, has been talked into giving me a short lecture on the history of the Kazakhs in Western Mongolia. He sits in a bare narrow room with a high ceiling with a long desk along one wall. The only item on the large white expanse of wall is a portrait of his beloved teacher, the famous ethnographer S. Badamkhatan. Mr. Ganbold was a youngish man who gives me the impression he might have had better things to do than talk to an ignorant foreigner, but he nevertheless give me an impromptu lecture in answer to my question about ethnic minorities.

Kazakh groups had settled in Outer Mongolia during the Manchu period, he says. The Kazakh families that were living in Mongolian territories paid taxes for the use of pastureland to the nobles reigning over the Khoshuus. Those nobles had to pay a fixed amount in taxes to the Manchu administration and were happy that these taxes could be shared among a larger number of households (as were the Mongolian households living in those Khoshuu, no doubt). After Mongolia proclaimed its independence, in 1917, the Kazakhs officially petitioned the Bogd Khaan to be allowed to continue to live in the territory of newly independent Mongolia. The Bogd Khaan agreed, on three conditions: 1) that the Kazakhs wouldn't move in and out of the country, across the border; 2) that the Kazakhs follow Mongolian laws and decrees; and 3) that they continue to pay pasture tax for use of the pastures. The Shiruz and Kiru tribes of the Kazakhs agreed to the conditions and officially settled in Mongolia.

Mr. Ganbold makes the point that the Mongols lost some of their territory to the Kazakhs through this agreement. But that is hindsight; the loss of territory for Mongol use was not seen as a problem at a time when the population of this country of 1.5-million square kilometers was around 600,000.

I try to picture the Mongols as they lived around that time. Few in number and barely surviving, they lived in small, dispersed herding camps, paying tribute to their overlords or monasteries who were themselves indebted to Chinese traders and bankers. Some sources suggest their numbers might even have been declining due to high mortality rates related to disease, bad nutrition, absence of health care and the high proportion of boys joining Buddhist monasteries. The Chinese held the more profitable occupations of trader, banker, stonemason and carpenter. That period is now more than a century ago and the people I interviewed do not go as far back, but the father of one of the people I interviewed was born in 1905.

* * *

August 2012. Tsogt Soum. At the end of our trip through the Western Aimags, I look for a man in Tsogt soum, possibly a lama, who, I had heard, was resurrecting Buddhism and had some interesting stories to tell. We are driving back from a visit to the sacred mother mountain when we come to Tsogt soum late afternoon. We first drive to the tiny new temple situated just outside the soum center. It is locked. A passerby tells us that the lama is staying in his summer camp, herding; he'll be back in a few weeks. We go to buy petrol and ask if there is anyone else who knows the history of the soum. That would be Mr. Luvsanjamts, we are told. We find his compound and introduce ourselves. He turns out to be an energetic man in his 50 who looks younger than his age. In T-shirt and jeans with a shaved head and expressive features, he is a striking and charismatic figure. He invites us into his cozy and well-kept ger where he lives with his wife.

Not unusually, he does not need much prompting to start his story. I explain that I am trying to get a sense of the Mongolia of the 20th century. "Ask", he commands, so I ask him the first thing that came to mind: "Are you a lama?" That was all he needs to start talking. After briefly mentioning that before the transition he worked as a driver for a high-level Party official (in fact, the Ideological Secretary of the Party) in Ulaanbaatar and then as the head of the soum Party organization, he races through history, mentioning people and events from the 17th century, early last century and the recent past. We receive a lecture in Mongolian Buddhist beliefs. We hear legends about the Ja

Lama. We hear about his father who entered the monastery in 1911 at age six.

That was the year the Bogd Khaan was to be enthroned as head of state! Herders and monks in the more remote areas of the country at the time might not yet have been directly affected by independence but they would have known about it. The Dilowa Khutukhtu's autobiography is a testimony to the amount of contact between the monasteries and the extensive travels of high-level lamas. The enthronement of the highest religious leader, the Bogd Khaan, on December 29 1911 as head of state must have been seen as an auspicious omen for the future of Buddhism in Mongolia. Little could anyone foresee that the ensuing chain of events would instead annihilate the religion with little hope for it to ever return.

The night darkens and the temperature drops below freezing, so we send Enkhbayar and David to find a hotel or any place to stay. They find none so Mr. Luvsanjamts invites us to pitch our tents next to his ger, after which he continues his fascinating stories into the night while his wife prepares food for us.

The fact that Mr. Luvsanjamts's father became a lama was not surprising as, according to some estimates, there were nearly 100,000 lamas at the time, one third of the male population. I puzzled aloud over how girls could find husbands, given that Mongolian society was essentially monogamous. Shombodon answered that they didn't: it was no wonder that both his grandmothers had been single mothers. Lamas were supposed to be celibate, but it was not exceptional for lamas, especially high-level lamas, to marry or at least live with a woman. Dilowa mentions that the third Narvanchin Gegeen (a Gegeen is a high-level lama, sometimes translated as saint) lived like a layman and had a wife and three children. The Bogd Khaan himself married a woman from Khentii aimag in 1902 and they had a son and adopted children from families that couldn't care for them. The marriage earned him a reprimand from the Dalai Lama, who had taken refuge in Urga in 1904 for nearly two years after the British invasion of Tibet under Younghusband.

Labor shortages, exacerbated by the high percentage of sons entering the monasteries, have long been bottlenecks for herding households. This was partly solved by sending lamas home to assist their families at times when extra labor was needed (harvest, cashmere combing, lambing seasons). I assume they occasionally fathered children. The labor of women and children was also important to survival of the herder families and valued accordingly. While women played a subordinate role in the traditional patrilineal and feudal society with a high regard for warrior-type macho attributes, scholars nevertheless agree that, traditionally, Mongolian women had higher social positions and more autonomy than in surrounding countries. Their role bearing children was appreciated as well, as delicately expressed by authors Worden and Savada who wrote an important report on Mongolia for the US Federal Research Division in 1989: "Mongols valued fertility over virginity and did not share the obsessive concern with female purity found in much of Southwest, South and East Asia." Couples established their own household when they married (as opposed to the girl joining her husband's parents' household in a subordinate position) and women performed traditionally male tasks when the menfolk weren't around, which was often as many of them joined monasteries, went to war or spent time in remote herding camps.

In any case, life was harsh at the beginning of the 20th century: traditional pastoral nomadism did not produce a lot of surplus to begin with, and the tax increases imposed by the dying Manchu regime had led to abject poverty. Learning was limited to the monasteries and included religious subjects as well as practical branches of learning such as medicine. There was also local knowledge of medicinal plants among the population; herders who were accustomed to looking after animals performed simple medical procedures such as setting bones at home. Family members such as husbands or mothers would assist women giving birth, and there are stories of women managing by themselves while herding. Dealing with contagious diseases, however, was a problem without modern knowledge of bacteria and viruses and how these spread.

Mongols were and are mobile and used to traveling great distances. The country is geographically large but socially small and close-knit. Particularly in summer, people visit and meet at festivals and sporting events. What did they think about contemporary events, these Mongols roaming Outer Mongolia around the turn of the century, their unique culture for many centuries shielded from the outside world because they inhabited a marginalized outpost of the Manchu empire? They had taken control of their country while being swept into the 20th century like a raft on a fast-flowing river: steering doesn't influence where you're going but it can prevent you getting shipwrecked and perishing before you get there.

Daily life in herding camps

At the lowest level of social organization Mongols live in herding camps, named Khot Ail, consisting of just a few households, usually related to each other — for instance, a young couple forming a Khot Ail with one set of parents. Each household lives in its own ger and sometimes there are separate kitchen gers and storage gers. Herders still live in Khot Ail today and collaborate during the milking season to form a Saakhalt, a neighborhood of sorts. The name stems from the word for milk, the reason for forming the community. Each Khot Ail has its own flocks of goats and sheep. In spring and summer, the mothers have to be kept separated from their lambs and kids so the herders can milk them; every morning after feeding, the kids and lambs are taken from their mothers and exchanged with the lambs and kids of a neighboring Khot Ail because the mothers let only their own young suckle. At night the lambs and kids go back to their mothers. Exchanging kids and lambs is labor-intensive and usually performed by young people. This used to be an important way for young people to mingle and meet potential marriage partners, which was not easy for the geographically dispersed youngsters at a time when children did not go to school.

Trade connected those living in the Khot Ails to sedentary agriculturalist peoples and the world beyond. From ancient times, nomadic herding peoples from the Northern Steppes traded livestock, skins and hides, meat, dairy products, and wool with the Chinese for items they didn't produce themselves such as tea, barley, millet, wheat, silk fabrics, ceramics, and metal items such as pots and pans — or they raided the Chinese for these items. The Great Wall of China's main function was defense against invasions and raids. By the early 1900s traders traveled around and sold items such as Russian leather boots, copper utensils (milk cans, kettles, pots and pans, bowls), ornamental snuff bottles, religious pictures and a large variety of silk, wool and cotton fabrics and clothes. The Mongols did not accumulate large quantities of belongings or bulky or heavy items, as these were not suitable for their nomadic lifestyle.

Hospitality has always been an important part of nomadic life, particularly in times gone by when traveling involved riding horses or camels and being exposed to the weather. Staying out in the Mongolian cold is life-threatening so travelers are made welcome in the ger, fed and warmed by the fire or stove. That hospitality is still in force today and Shombodon, Enkhbayar and I had to ask for shelter a few times when we found ourselves faced with extreme cold, snow banks too deep to cross and darkness falling. We were always generously and warmly received as guests.

The Mongols had their own traditions and ceremonies surrounding life's important events such as birth, surviving infancy, marriage and the like, in which the lamas played a major role. While Buddhism was exterminated during socialist times, some of these traditions continued through the 20th century, more in the countryside than among the urbanized population. I received an unexpected lecture from Shombodon's cousin, Tsengelmaa, who gave me some insight into remnants of ancient Mongolian customs that weren't Russianized and persisted throughout most of the 20th century.

August 2012. Altai. We meet Tsengelmaa, a chubby and bubbling youthful woman who talks rapidly, giggling at her own memories, in our hotel in Altai, the capital of Gobi-Altai aimag. She was born in 1969 as the ninth child of 11 children and describes her own birth in 1969 from stories and her knowledge of Mongolian traditions. At the time, the health system had penetrated deep into the countryside and each soum had a health center, an ambulance and often also maternity accommodation where women could check in a few days before giving birth and stay a few days. Despite these advances in the provision of services for pregnant women, many women from herding households could not easily reach the soum center and gave birth at home in their gers.

This is what Tsengelmaa tells me about her birth: In the 1960s it was common in the rural areas for fathers to handle births of their children. The person who handles a birth is referred to as "white mother" or "foster mother" whether they are male or female. A person should visit her white mother during her lifetime. In her own case her white mother was her father. After giving birth, a woman has to sit next to the arag (a rectangular wicker basket that is used for collecting dung for the fire, as well as packing and transporting goods, children and baby animals on camels during moves) for three days and nights for the afterbirth and blood to come out properly. She tells me that she handled the birth of the daughter of her elder brother in 1996. Shombodon adds that it was often the grandmother who helped with giving birth and clarifies that when a woman gave birth traditionally in a ger, the woman would sit next to the arag and hold it while giving the birth. His uncle helped when his sister was born. Only his two younger sisters were born in the hospital, plus a brother who died an infant, so three out of 10 kids were born in hospital, the others at home in the ger.

Tsengelmaa continues: After three days the newborn has to be washed and they celebrate the washing ceremony. They invite relatives and prepare food; a sheep is slaughtered and meat offered. The baby is named at the washing ceremony: a boy's name is whispered three times in his right ear and girl's name is whispered three times in her left ear. Relatives and parents present animals (horses, sheep) or fabrics or whatever they can. Her own name, Tsengelmaa, is Tibetan for "to be full of happiness". She so clearly is!

She doesn't remember her haircutting ceremony but knows how these ceremonies are done. Parents, with advice from the lamas, determine the day for it. The household prepares for that day — they prepare a long cake called "ul boow" and decorate it. The dough has to be refined with milk, butter and sugar. All the children help with kneading the dough, passing it around. Father puts it in the form in the correct way. Mother cooks it. Then they have airag and milk and cream and cook a whole back of a sheep, sometimes even one or two whole sheep! They do not eat ordinary food such as noodle soup. Meat is divided among guests according to traditional hierarchy, based on closeness of kinship; for instance, the shoulder blades (scapulae) go to the uncles. They invite neighbors and relatives, who bring presents for the infant.

The ceremony is held at five years of age for a boy and three for a girl. (Shombodon adds that this was usual in their region, not everywhere in Mongolia.) Guests come the afternoon of the previous day or on the haircutting day itself and then they start the celebration. The children look after the horses of the guests.

The exact date and time of the ceremony is specific to each individual child. The animal sign of the birth year has to be aligned with an auspicious hour of the day; the hours of a day are also associated with the animals after which years are named. In any case, the birth year of the infant is combined with a lucky hour, giving the time when the haircutting ceremony should begin. At the start a lama gives a religious reading. The person to start the ceremony should also be identified according to his birth year in the lunar calendar. A man with a compatible year should start the haircutting.

Scissors and knives could be considered weapons, so they start with a knife-shaped piece of wood, slightly oiled. If it is a boy, they start at the right temple and if it's a girl at the left. They don't really cut, at first, but mainly anoint it with butter while cutting only a few hairs. After that they use real scissors that have been kept inside a khadag (prayer scarf). Absolutely new scissors must be used and the hair put inside the khadag. The scissors must then be tied inside the khadag as well and kept until the child is grown and gets married. Then the parents give it to the grown-up child. Similarly, at the washing ceremony, the shinbone is kept after the mother has eaten the meat off. Between the lama's reading and the haircutting ceremony, someone should say a "yorool", a long, ritual invocation to secure a prosperous future for the child. The haircutting must be done clockwise for both girls and boys.

Even during socialist times local people sought advice from (married) ex-lamas who still had religious tools and knowledge. Other ceremonies, for instance weddings, have a master of ceremony who opens and closes the ceremony, but the haircutting ceremony is not closed: they say it goes on for 70 days and during that time people come and visit. It is said that attending a haircutting ceremony gives good energy and extends life, so anyone who hears about it wants to come. After the ceremony, they clean the stubs with a very clean knife and put butter and a hat on the infant's head. The hat must be kept on for a day. Tsengelmaa still has her hair with her. She doesn't have any of her gifts left: they were sheep, horses, sweets, sugar, fabrics. First they used a one-meter long cloth hanging from ger-spokes as a bag to hold presents, then the presents were put in her suitcase and it was full of gifts. Her parents would use the cloth for sewing.

She goes on to describe day-to-day life when she grew up. For toys they used anything: broken cups, stones with a pretty shape and color. Last year she and two of her sisters went back to visit Bugat soum, the place where they were born and grew up. That was so nice, she says: they found shard of broken cups of long time ago and it was pleasant to remember those times. When she was a child their household had two gers, the big ger for living and a storage ger for saddles and tools used for herding. Mother cooked and served father first. Then she served the children by age, the oldest first. She ate last. They all slept lying in that same order. It was crowded. The children were very obedient. If a visitor came the kids were sent outside and told not to listen to the conversation. They did their chores such as looking after young animals and collecting dung for the fire.

Tsengelmaa gave me this small window into intimate ger-life that has carried on throughout the 20th century but has been changing, slowly fading even in the rural areas. Shombodon said he didn't know these customs as well as his cousin because they weren't practiced in the cities any more. I assume that under socialism, the modern Mongols who had been educated abroad viewed the old traditions as superstitious and unscientific.

3. MONGOLIA'S FOREIGN DEVILS

Steppe Inne

1999. Ulaanbaatar. During and after any revolution, when the old order of things breaks down and creates a power vacuum, this isn't a really a vacuum at all: it is everyone's fate and fortune thrown into the bag, shaken and up for grabs. Foreigners are part of the mix, and so am I. I find myself standing next to a shipping container nursing a beer that is in the process of congealing in the -20°C temperature and dropping, thinking I need to get away before my bladder becomes uncomfortably full. There are no restrooms and I do not want to emulate the men who pee outside against the Embassy wall — the need would have to become a little more urgent before I would sink to such levels of impropriety. (A few months later this awkward state of affairs will be rectified by the female UK ambassador who has proper restrooms built.) It is 1999 at the Steppe Inne, a weekly drinking hole run by the British Embassy where I socialize with other expats, a mix of adventurers looking for uncharted territories; Buddhists interested in the country's Buddhist past and wishing to assist its resurrection; missionaries seeing an expanse of atheists to convert; miners and mining corporations looking for riches; entrepreneurs sniffing out new business opportunities; and the usual misfits who are attracted to less-organized places. These mingle with the more boring diplomats, schoolteachers and development workers such as myself and the place is buzzing with excitement.

I am a member of this container-club. My colleague who coordinates the projects of the European Union, a retired Scottish military man, saw to it that I joined the first week I arrived in Ulaanbaatar, telling me that it is one of my duties as project team leader (one that is not written up in my job-description) to drink beer at the

Steppe Inne on Friday nights after work. He will be there so I can repay him in beer for favors regarding the interface between my project and the government. That is his job and his beer is well earned. On one occasion he raises his military voice at the governors of the Central Bank on behalf of my project, a feat I am unable to perform myself. At issue is whether the legal entity we have created is entitled to receive a license to become a "non-bank financial institution" and start operating (issuing loans). The Central Bank is taking its sweet time to make a decision while my project is paralyzed and spending EU money without being able to do business. It is the perennial problem: development projects have deadlines while government administrations on which the projects depend do not, putting project managers in a difficult position. But we get the license and my man gets his beer.

The container-converted-to-bar at the back entrance of the British Embassy compound is too small for all of us to fit, which is why we are standing outside, whatever the temperature. The mix of people who frequent the place provides ample occasions for social faux pas: an ex-mercenary adventurer pinching a genteel bottom; someone's dog barfing on an ambassador's shoes (after which dogs are banned from the premises); a retired Japanese officer enquiring from newly arrived males, regardless of status (be it student, volunteer or diplomat) whether they are getting enough sex and if he can be of assistance finding a partner. I have recruited my hiking friends at the Steppe Inne and we spend a lot of time sitting on the mountain giggling and gossiping about the absurd social interactions we have observed the night before.

It is time to go — there is a Chinese restaurant next door with a blessed toilet and warmth and food and a group of us will end up there for dinner.

* * *

In 1999 I had caught the tail end of the transition period that followed the switch from a centrally planned system to a market economy. I hadn't had much time for reflection, was trying to come to grips with a challenging job while contending with the fact that we didn't know yet what Terry's recovery after his heart attack would look like. The Steppe Inne was a weekly safe-haven where I could talk informally about my project, or talk rubbish, drink and giggle in wonder and amazement at the assorted crowd. Only now that I have become more involved with the place than I ever thought I would, do I realize that such an eclectic mix of foreigners, in which adventurers, misfits, gold-diggers and fugitives are prominent, is typical of the aftermath of revolutions when there is a power vacuum to be filled and order to be made out of chaos. So it was after Mongolia's first revolution as well.

I have been lectured repeatedly by people I interviewed on the three Mongolian revolutions of the 20th century: the revolution of 1911, the revolution of 1921, and the revolution of 1991. In the chaotic years that followed their first revolution and the collapse of the Manchu empire the Mongols were not yet able to control their destiny. Consequently, during their first 10 years of statehood, they contended with an influx of uprooted foreign fugitives generated by global revolutions and wars, who saw opportunities in the politically weak and militarily unprotected wild backwaters of Mongolia where the old (Manchu) order had broken down and had not yet been fully replaced by a new order. They played roles that under normal circumstances would not have been possible. Apart from the Chinese warlord Xu Shuzheng, who tried to recapture the country for the Chinese, there were Japanese spies, European diplomats, a checkerboard of Red (for the communists) and White (for the Tsar) Russians and Buriats from Siberia on the run. I wish I could have been there to see it! Two characters are especially noteworthy: The Ja Lama and the German-Russian Baron von Ungern-Sternberg.

The Ja Lama

In 2012 while back in Mongolia to learn about its history, I started hearing about the Ja Lama. At first I didn't understand that people were talking about the same historical personage when they talked about the militant lama Dambijantsan, the Ja Lama who had supernatural powers, and about a Kalmyk (these were ethnic Torgut Mongols who lived in Russian territory) called Dambijá. After having heard many stories about the legendary Ja Lama, the main facts that I distilled about him are that he entered Mongolia in the late 1800s, passed himself off as a lama, was a warrior in the struggle against the Manchus and later against invading Kazakhs from southwest China, and carved out a power base in what is now Inner Mongolia. In the few photographs of him, Dambijantsan is depicted as a large, defiant-looking character, clutching a flintlock rifle. He was a very strong man who could lift a heavy saddlebag that other men couldn't onto a camel, and spoke the predominant Khalkh Mongol language fluently. The strange thing is that very little is known about him while he is so dominantly present in popular Mongolian imagination. For instance, the Dilowa Khutukhtu, who knew Dambijantsan in person, dedicated a whole chapter of his autobiography to him — yet in the first paragraph he attests to the mysterious nature of the man: "He called himself a lama, but nobody knew if he really was one. Nobody knew his real age. Nobody knew the real truth about him."

He played a small role in Mongolian history at the beginning of the century and would not be worth much mention if he hadn't become a mythical figure about whom people in the eastern aimags tell stories to this day. I started paying attention when I heard about him from Mr. Luvsanjamts who wanted me to know about the importance of his region to Mongolian history, making the point that here was where Dambijá (the Ja Lama) operated. According to Mr. Luvsanjamts, Dambijá was a Kalmyk who came to Mongolia with two white camels and was respected in the area because he fought against Kazakhs from China who were raiding these places and stealing animals. He collected soldiers from the neighborhood, fought the Kazakhs and expelled them. Dambijá first came to Tsogt soum in March 1918 while recruiting people from Tsogt, Erdene, Shinejist and neighboring soums with whom he then established his own fortress named Gonpojén as the base from where he operated. There he had workers, animals, herders and a military unit.

After the 1921 revolution he was put to death by the new government who disliked him because he was religious and was against Red Russians. Many were also critical of him because, according to Shombodon, "he took away nice young ladies and also took strong young men for his military". The nobles in the Tsogt area were against his execution because he had liberated them from the Kazakhs but, while they were meeting about it, revolutionary government forces simply went and shot him. In fact, according to Mr. Luvsanjamts, some subterfuge took place: the letter supposedly from the Aimag governor ordering three specific people to ascertain whether the dead man was indeed the Ja Lama and to cut off his head as evidence, was actually signed by the governor's younger brother, who was a radical and who had illegally kept and used the real governor's seal. The local population had requested to be shown his head if they had killed him so it was hung from a religious flagpole for a day and a night. A relative of Mr. Luvsanjamts's father, the ex-lama Baanchig who had converted out of his monastery and had become the watchman for the soum governor's office, sat and watched his head for a day and a night. It ended up as exhibit "No. 3394, head of a Mongolian" in the Kunstkammer of the Hermitage in St Petersburg. Go figure.

After this introduction to the Ja Lama by Mr. Luvsanjamts, I heard many stories about this intriguing figure, many of them demonstrating that he has become a legend and that mystical powers were ascribed to him. Shombodon, who came from Bugat soum in the southwest of Gobi Altai Aimag, grew up hearing stories about him. His mother used to talk about the Kazakh raids and how Kazakh kids simply took lambs from the Mongolian children looking after them and killed them for lunch. He told a story about his grandfather who was on border protection duty when his unit came across a group of Kazakhs intending to steal camels from nearby monasteries. They sent him to Tonkhil monastery to inform Dambijá, who immediately rode forth with a number of soldiers and ambushed the Kazakhs on their way back south towards China. He shot the first man and then caught the first bullet coming their way in his hand, showing his men that they wouldn't die. Thus encouraged, the Mongols then overcame the Kazakhs and captured some alive. They skinned one and grabbed the heart of another which lay, still beating, in the palm of his hand. Those two died there and then, but a third was put bareback on a horse and sent back to the Kazakhs as a warning. A fourth captive was taken to Tonkhil monastery, tied from neck to feet with hide ropes on the flagpole, and had his head chopped off with a sabre. I wonder how much of this story is fact and can only say that the Dilowa Khutukhtu also mentions the Ja Lama skinning someone alive: "This skinning alive is done by shooting the victim in such a way that he loses consciousness. Then the skin is taken off whole." The beating heart doesn't seem such a tall tale either, considering that Mongols today still kill their animals by inserting a hand in the live animal through a small incision and squeezing off the blood supply to the heart. The business with Dambijá's head fits right in.

Many of the supernatural powers ascribed to the Ja Lama had to do with mind-reading, fortune-telling and magical feats involving guns and bullets. The Ja Lama was alleged to be able to cure sickness with gun magic, meaning that the treating magician fires a gun in the direction of a sick man, who is instantly cured even if hundreds of miles away. The Dilowa Khutukhtu mentions matter-of-factly that another lama he knew, the Narvanchin Gegeen, was also a magician of that kind. Many other mythical stories of the Ja Lama have him reading minds, catching bullets, and hitting a wolf by shooting from the doorway of his ger in the darkness of the night.

These myths easily took root in an illiterate society where news traveled by word of mouth, where the Mongolian version of Buddhism was influenced by Shamanist spirits and, I suspect, the stories told were enhanced by the spirits of airag and vodka. Soon after his arrival, the Ja Lama tried to gain acceptance from existing powers such as the Dilowa Khutukhtu, who mentions that as early as 1913 the Ja Lama approached him to establish relations, calling himself his disciple and asking him to pray for him. When he was disinclined to establish close relations, the Ja Lama sent troops for him and tried to order him to join and command those troops: "It took about three months of negotiation to rectify this situation." Further unpleasantness was averted when in 1914 the Russians arrested Dambijantsen and carried him off (he was still a Russian citizen). When the Russian revolution broke out in 1917, the Ja Lama immediately traveled back to Mongolia and he slowly made his way southward to an area called Maajin Shan, just south of the current border with China, attracting followers as he went (including fair maidens).

The Dilowa Khutukhtu recounts how he first acquired his riches by ambushing a group of about 50 rich Tibetan traders who had decided to return to Tibet (presumably because of the chaotic situation in Russia, Mongolia and China): "They turned their wealth into gold, silver, silks and valuable furs, and started off with many camel loads and a strong armed escort. The route they took passed near the Maajin Shan, and they were ambushed by Ja Lama. Some he ransomed and let go, others he kept as hostages, and he kept all the camel loads and arms so he became a wealthy and powerful man. He also had Chinese growing opium near his stronghold and made quite a revenue from that." He adds another strong reason for the government to get rid of the Ja Lama: "At this time one of the princes of Zasagt Khaan Aimag, one of the original aimags under the Manchus, Taij Eregzen, raised a cry that, rather than submit to Red rule, all good Mongols should go south and be ruled by Ja Lama. It was this threat to their authority that caused the new Government at Khüree to send a detachment south and execute Ja Lama." This they did in 1922, demonstrating that he was not immune to bullets after all.

Continued threats to Mongolia's independence

The turmoil on which the Ja Lama thrived was global, with World War One in Europe its center stage. In Central and East Asia, complex power struggles took place between colonialist tendencies of Russia, Japan, France and Great Britain — with some business interests of other nations such as the US thrown in for good measure. Russia and China, superpowers in turmoil, each regarded Mongolia as a buffer against the other and determined the course of events there. Chinese, Russians and, to a lesser degree Japanese, contributed to maintaining a chaotic situation within the country. The historian C.R. Bawden talks about Mongolia being tossed about like a shuttlecock at the mercy of foreign interests. Not since Chinggis Khaan's time had Mongolia been so connected to global politics — but this time round the Mongols were fighting for the survival of their own nation instead of conquering the world.

Tsarist Russia supported the Mongolian independence movement with military training and affirmations of Mongolian autonomy from China but, not wanting to directly confront China, continued to demonstrate cautiousness, even reluctance, to get involved. In earlier agreements, a Tsarist protectorate over Outer Mongolia was envisaged. In the friendship agreement of 1912 between Mongolia and Russia, the latter acknowledged Mongolian autonomy and sent military advisors to assist with the training of a Mongolian army and in return secured commercial privileges.

An account of the signing that took place in November 1912 was written up in the diary of the then Russian ambassador, Ivan Korostovets, who led the diplomatic mission to Mongolia. It mentions that the Mongol noblemen did not appear at the specified time because they had consulted astrologer-lamas to establish the favorable time to sign such an agreement. I smiled when reading this: during my first job, we had the misfortune of having to move our office five times, which did not faze my professional staff but did cause them to consult lamas each time while setting the date on which to move. By the fifth move I had had it with the lamas: they indicated an auspicious day that was inconvenient to me. No problem, I was told, I needn't worry about a thing, a chair would be ritually moved on the auspicious day, after which I could move our office at my convenience.

Korostovets's diary fell into the hands of the White Russian general Andrei Bakich, who later had to flee the Reds and managed to escape to Harbin and from there to Australia. His granddaughter, Dr. Olga Bakich, ended up living in Canada and in possession of the diary, which she eventually got published at the University of Toronto's Department of Slavic Languages and Literature. The friendship treaty of 1912 was followed three years later by the tripartite Khiagt treaty between China, Russia and Mongolia, which ambiguously described Mongolia's status as "autonomous under Chinese Suzerainty". Russia's attention was subsequently drawn away from Mongolia when it became involved in World War One and had its internal revolutionary struggles that would end in victory for the Reds (Marxist-Leninist Bolsheviks) in 1917.

Japan's imperialist ambitions also played a role. Japanese-Chinese relations remained hostile after the first Sino-Japanese war of 1884-1885 in which Japan gained control of the Korean peninsula. Relations between Russia and Japan were also hostile as both empires tried to take advantage of a weakened China in the late days of the Manchu dynasty. Around the time of independence, nationalism in Inner and Outer Mongolia as well as among the Uriankhai and Buriat Mongols included the idea that a Mongol nation that united all the territories where Mongols lived might be possible. In Urga, Inner Mongolian refugees (after unsuccessful revolts back home) and Buriats played political roles alongside the dominant Khalkh Mongols and supported a pan-Mongol concept.

Japan tried, unsuccessfully, to influence the course of events in 1911-1912 by contributing arms and money to the Mongolians and later, in 1917, encouraging and supporting an anti-Bolshevik pan-Mongol movement led by Buriat Mongols. Participants in a pan-Mongolia conference held in early 1919 in Chita, Siberia, decided to establish a Mongol state comprising Outer Mongolia, Inner Mongolia, and Buryatia. However, Khalkh-dominated newly independent Outer Mongolia refused to participate and the movement failed.

China, which had now become the Republic of China, had let possession of Mongolia slip through its fingers when the Manchu dynasty fell, but maintained that both Inner and Outer Mongolia should remain part of China. In 1917, the year of the Russian revolution, China took advantage of Mongolia's lack of Russian support by invading the country again, imprisoning freedom fighters and putting the Bogd Khaan under house arrest. Resentful Mongols, who had fought for their independence less than a decade earlier and who had treaties with the Manchus, not the Chinese, resorted to violence against the remaining Chinese population living in Mongolia, particularly the merchants and bankers to whom they were indebted. Tensions rose and in 1918 the Dilowa Khutukhtu was invited to Uliastai to have prayers read in his honor by the city's combined Mongol and Chinese communities. In 1919 the Chinese residents of Uliastai requested the Bogd Khaan that the Dilowa Khutukhtu be stationed there as a kind of resident protector of them (the Bogd Khaan considered this unnecessary). The Dilowa Khutukhtu mentions disturbances that broke out in the western Uriankhai area in 1919 that reflected the powers that played in Mongolia at the time: "The trouble was being caused because the most powerful men in the region were two high lamas, one of whom was the leader of the White Russian faction while the other was pro-Chinese, although most of the people were pro-Mongol."

From 1914 Chinese traders had been moving back to Urga/Khüree and diplomatic relations between the Bogd Khaan and the Chinese Commissioner, Chen Lu, were cordial. Ceremonies started resembling former Manchu times where Mongols gifted horses and camels to the Chinese and Chinese bestowed honors on the Mongols. When the Russian revolution started, Chinese control tightened and Chinese troops trickled into the region that was already under Chinese financial control and more so after the post-revolutionary collapse of the Russian ruble.

In 1919 the Chinese tried to cajole and bribe the Mongolian government into canceling Mongolian autonomy. As a last resort, they sent the warlord Xu Shuzheng to settle the matter. In November 1919 Xu, accompanied by three infantry divisions, arrived in the capital where he immediately intimidated the government and the

Bogd Khaan into relinquishing autonomy. He followed up by organizing an official abolition of autonomy ceremony where he demeaned and insulted the Mongols by forcing the Bogd Khaan and other leaders to kowtow before the portrait of the Chinese Prime Minister (standing in for the traditional portrait of the emperor) and the Chinese flag. He then demobilized the Mongolian army and the larger part of the honor guard, seized their arsenal, and proceeded to harass and rob monks and foreigners (among them White Russian refugees).

These brutal humiliations only strengthened the resolve of the independence movement of the Mongols — revolutionaries founded the Mongolian People's Party and initiated contacts with the Bolshevik movement in Russia. This would eventually determine the outcome of the independence struggle, but not before another interlude of chaos and turmoil. In 1920 the Bogd Khaan asked the Dilowa Khutukhtu to join a delegation to Peking, headed by the high-ranking lama Jalkanz Gegeen, ostensibly to convey greetings to the President of China but in reality to win support of foreign countries such as the US and of Chinese officials for restoring the autonomy of Outer Mongolia. After several delays, "The mission was finally able to start in the first month of summer, and we left for Kalgan [now called Zhangjiakou: it is located where the Chinese provinces of Hebei, Inner Mongolia and Shanxi meet] by motor car. There we were delayed for a few days by a Chinese civil war, but we were eventually able to go by train to Peking." It was a high-level mission indeed, traveling by a new-fangled motorcar! Even so, the delegation did not accomplish anything in the month it stayed in Peking: the Mongols saw the President of China, had interviews with the US minister and military attaché, and paid a ceremonial visit to the deposed Manchu boy-emperor Pu-yi. And their mission soon became irrelevant with the arrival of a new conquering power in Khüree: Baron von Ungern-Sternberg.

The mad baron

The Ja Lama was not the only outlandish character to whom the turmoil and power vacuum afforded an opportunity to play a noteworthy role in Mongolian history. The "Mad Baron", Roman Nicolai von Ungern-Sternberg made a thankfully brief but remarkable appearance as well. More is known about the larger-than-life figure of von Ungern-Sternberg than about the legendary Ja Lama, but he hardly ever came up in talking with Mongols. A fascinating biography by James Palmer enlightens us about the man who invaded Mongolia leading White Russian troops at the end of 1920, defeated the Chinese at Urga in 1921, and ruled the country for about five months before being ousted in turn. Palmer writes in his introduction: "He was an appalling human being in almost every way; virtually his only admirable characteristic was his fierce physical bravery, and perhaps parts of his fascination with the East."

Von Ungern-Sternberg, born in 1886 (two years after Dilowa Khutukhtu) to ethnic German nobility, grew up in Estonia, then a part of the Russian Empire. He was expelled from the schools his parents sent him to, first the Nicholas Gymnasium in what is now Tallinn and later the Marine Academy at St. Petersburg, for being obstinate, savage, and continually at odds with authority. At 19 he joined the military as an ordinary soldier and was sent to the front of the Russo-Japanese war in Manchuria for his first short-lived stint in the far East. The Russians were defeated in September of 1905 and Corporal von Ungern, having had his first taste of war and been awarded a service medal, found himself back in Russia where the imperial order he knew and had fought for was unraveling. Workers demonstrated and were violently subdued; peasants rose up against noble houses, burning and destroying handsome manor houses and all kinds of property — including that of his family. The young von Ungern-Sternberg, who "had a fundamental sense of arrogant privilege", convinced of his superior race and of the rightness of the old tsarist order, was outraged. He enrolled in the military academy and trained to become a cavalry officer.

During this period he seems to have developed an interest and belief in Buddhism, occultism and other esoteric and fringe beliefs that were in vogue in certain elite and reactionary circles in Europe. Romantic and mystic ideas extolling the virtues of simple, pure cultures such as the nomadic peoples in the East and of good old-fashioned monarchy struck a chord with him. After graduation he chose to serve in a Cossack regiment in Transbaikal along the Mongolian and Manchurian borders. Buddhist Buriat Mongols made up about 12 percent of the Transbaikal Cossack army and von Ungern's fondness of the Far East and its peoples deepened as he studied their customs, religion and language. His fondness for drinking also deepened; his move from the Transbaikal Cossacks to the Amur Cossacks was the result of a drunken duel with a fellow officer.

In 1913 he rode into the near-empty wilds of northeastern Mongolia, receiving the customary hospitality from the Buddhist monasteries and scattered herders while making his way to the capital Ikh Khüree (Urga to foreigners) and Khovd. In those towns he sought out the men of the Russian garrisons, which included members of his former regiments. In Khovd he served briefly as an out-of-staff officer in the Cossack guard detachment at the Russian consulate where he was said to go his own way in relative isolation from his countrymen, learning Mongolian, talking to lamas and riding out. In 1914 he returned shortly to Reval from where he was again mobilized at the start of World War One. He was not only among the seven percent who survived the East Prussian front, but actually thrived on the thrills and gory violence of the battlefield, excelling as a soldier. His brutality deepened, drunken incidents continued and he was imprisoned, only escaping more severe punishment due to his excellence on the battlefield.

In 1917 he fought in the Caucasus where he befriended Grigory Mikhaylovich Semyonov (Semonov), who was of partial Buriat-Mongol descent from Eastern Siberia. Semonov was involved in the Buriat-led (and Japan-backed) Pan-Mongolian movement. That same year the old Tsarist order fell, much to von Ungern-Sternberg's dismay: he hated the Bolsheviks. In the far East (Transbaikal and Manchuria), he and Semonov started raising Tsarist White Russian troops that included Buriats, Cossacks, Mongolians, Chinese mercenaries and even a Czech Legion trying to get home by traveling east around the world to fight the revolutionary Bolsheviks and their Red Army. They secured support from the Japanese and other foreign powers (British, French) that had an interest in the region.

Von Ungern settled in Dauria, the area east of Lake Baikal, for nearly two years and started to establish his own domain there. Becoming more and more brutal, he robbed and plundered as source of funding. His headquarters became a regional execution camp and the bodies of executed Bolsheviks were simply dumped on hills and in rivers around the camp. In 1919 he married an aristocratic 19-year-old Chinese woman in Harbin, which seems to have been a political move to give him a Manchurian title. The marriage might never have been consummated as she went back to her parent's house after the wedding and he back to Dauria, which was clearly not a place to bring one's bride.

Von Ungern's forces grew slowly more independent from Semonov and in February 1920 they formed the Special Manchurian Division. By summer the White Russian resistance had collapsed in most part of Siberia and it became clear that von Ungern couldn't hold his position much longer. In August 1920 he divorced his wife and moved into Mongolia with his forces of about 1500 men. He had lost everything — his home in Estonia and the Russian imperial cause to which he had pledged his loyalty. The imperial army to which he was closest had lost the war and he judged that his best friend Semonov had become a corrupted tool of a foreign power, Japan. The one thing left was his belief in the uncorrupted and pure Mongolian people who must be led to reinstate the empire of Chinggis Khaan, according to esoteric Mongolian prophecies.

So he marched on Urga where the warlord Xu Shuzheng held power, and offered the Bogd Khaan that he would liberate the capital. His ranks had swollen with refugees, renegade soldiers and bandits of different nationalities. His offer was speedily accepted and on October 26 1920, a date deemed propitious by the oracles, von Ungern started attacking the Chinese in their garrisoned town of Maimaichen a little to the west of Urga.

His first attacks were poorly planned and failed but his emaciated rag-tag cavalry — his men had nothing to lose — frazzled the Chinese and increased their xenophobia and harsh treatment of all non-Chinese: foreigners and Mongols alike were robbed, raped and killed. Von Ungern seemed invulnerable in battle, highly visible, wild, and adorned with amulets. People started believing he was immune to bullets — just as they believed that the Ja Lama was immune to them — and started ascribing divine characteristics to him, linking him to the God of War. Insanely cruel, he maintained sadistic discipline. While everything about the man is repulsive and insane when we read about it now, he lived in a time and places where his extreme character served him well. His superstitious dealing with charms and amulets, and his dependence on the oracles regarding the date when to go to battle, were normal in the Mongolian context.

Apart from the looting and killing sprees, the Baron was lighting nightly fires in the hills overlooking Urga leading the Chinese to believe his forces were larger than they were, a tactic once employed by Chinggis Khaan's army. By the end of January 1921 von Ungern, having fueled the fears of the nervous Chinese over time, planned his attack more carefully. An important element was to liberate the Bogd Khaan from house arrest in his winter palace. The Baron's Tibetan troops whisked the Bogd Khaan and his wife over the Bogd Mountain to the monastery of Manzshir on the south side, which was no mean feat considering the huge bulk of the Bogd who had to be balanced on both sides after having been heaved onto a horse. The day after, the Chinese officers fled the city, heading north towards Kyagta in their motorcars and the abandoned Chinese garrison was overrun and most of the troops slaughtered. A three-day orgy of "rape, torture and murder" ensued, after which von Ungern reinstated order. He made an exception, however, for the Jews: they were systematically and viciously purged as had been his practice for years.

After von Ungern's victory over the Chinese, the Bogd Khaan was restored to his position of head of state. The state oracle (the Bogd's brother) was consulted on the most auspicious day for the Bogd to triumphantly return to Khüree as Khaan of Mongolia: he chose the lunar New Year. Von Ungern ordered his soldiers to rid the city of the mutilated corpses that were lying strewn about, fought over by dogs. Fortunately the average temperature that time of the year is around -25°C so at least the corpses were frozen solid. He also had the textile factory produce new uniforms for his men and surprisingly — he was notoriously scruffy — for himself. He was weirdly declared the reincarnation of the fifth Bogd Gegeen, just like the Bogd Khaan himself, and had a hereditary princedom and the title of "Outstanding Prosperous-State Hero" bestowed on him.

The second coronation of the Bogd Khaan was effected with pomp and pageantry, preceded by a marvelous procession, the highlight of which was the Bogd Khaan and his wife on a Chinese carriage, directly followed by the Baron on his white horse. This must have been von Ungern's finest moment, given his fervent belief in divinely sanctioned monarchy as the natural order of things. The Bogd Khaan, much maligned by later communist-inspired historians and certainly having qualities that could be ridiculed and criticized, demonstrated he was also a politically astute operator. He hedged his bets vis-à-vis both powerful neighbors by claiming he had been abducted by force by the Baron, that he had nothing against either regime and was willing to collaborate with them.

Initially the Baron was welcomed as a popular liberator and divine Buddhist hero who restored order to the ravaged town and reinstated a government that included the second-highest-ranking Buddhist, the Khutukhtu of Manzshir, Tserendorj, who became the Prime Minister. He released prisoners, restored the power-generating station — a novelty for that time — and started reopening mines and factories and constructing bridges, hospitals, and veterinary laboratories. He also took pains not to alienate the foreign community and ensured that his statements were promulgated in Russian, Mongolian, Chinese, Tibetan and Manchurian. The justice he meted out was less sadistic and draconian than what had been usual in Dauria and among his forces, but severe measured by any other standard. Not only common criminals were punished, but a crude political cleansing was carried out in an attempt to eliminate anyone sympathetic to the archenemies of divine monarchy, namely revolutionaries and Bolsheviks. The witch-hunt involved torture and butchering of anyone who might have been a Red. After von Ungern proclaimed that a third of an executed person's property should go to the informer who turned him in and the rest to government, the last bit of restraint was thrown to the wind and murder became the norm: around 10 percent of the expatriate community was executed and those who could fled Urga. Though the Baron had Russians executed in other parts of Mongolia as well, he did not have the power to persecute all revolutionaries in Mongolia, particularly not the Mongolian Reds.

This could not and did not last, as the prevailing political wind was blowing from a different direction. The Baron's short reign probably strengthened nationalist anti-religious feelings and as a result the socialist ideology of the People's Party. It brought Mongolia to the attention of Bolshevik Russia, which had not wanted to antagonize China by entering Mongolia but certainly didn't want Mongolia to become another refuge for the White Russian enemy. The Baron's threat to Soviet Siberia was an excellent pretext for deploying troops into the country. It also drove the Mongolian nationalists into the arms of their revolutionary comrades who had taken over Russia. The Political Bureau of the Bolshevik Party approved a plan to send troops to Ikh Khüree with the objective of supporting revolutionary movements in China and Mongolia, cleansing the Mongolian stronghold of White Russians, and supporting autonomy for Mongolia under the Chinese federation. The Baron fled Khüree before the Red Army arrived, but was captured, tried and condemned to death by firing squad in August 1921. And that was the end of that story.

Urga

Contemporary Ulaanbaatar doesn't look anything like the town it was in the early 1900s when it was called Ikh Khüree, or Urga to foreigners. An important trading center on the route from Beijing to Russia and the nominal capital of the powerful Khalkh Mongol tribes, it was where the diplomatic community was located and the seat of the Bogd Javzandamba Khutukhtu and other high-ranking reincarnated lamas. This made it very much the Mongolian capital, which it formally became after the ouster of the Manchus whose center of administration had been in Uliastai. By the beginning of the 20th century it was no longer the mobile town it had been in earlier centuries. There were temples, permanent residences for monks and laymen, warehouses, businesses, a large Chinese district, the Russian consulate and residences of foreigners. Estimates of the number of permanent residents of the capital city vary but sources agree that roughly between a third and half of the population were monks.

I stumbled upon a rare collection of photographs of Khüree from 1913. They can be seen on the website of the Albert Kahn museum in France. Kahn was a wealthy French banker who, between 1909 and 1937, financed cultural and scientific expeditions around the world to preserve for posterity images of the societies and ethnicities of the period. The photographs show a wide-open, bucolic Tuul river valley with separate neighborhoods of fenced plots for temples, houses and gers. One shows the broken palisade wall that had protected the Chinese fort until they were expelled two years before the picture was taken. Scattered through the valley are groups of felt-covered gers (without the white canvas covers used today), wooden-wheeled ox-carts, livestock, stupas, altars and separate palace-temple complexes. Besides the deels still seen today, the women wore ornate traditional costumes with unwieldy headgear and the many monks are wearing red and yellow robes. The variety of creative head coverings, pointed, rounded, with silk tassels, fur brims, shimmering Chinese silk, or simply looking like a hairy mat perched on top, stand out. An expat friend once called Mongolia the "land of silly hats", but these are fast disappearing on the streets of Ulaanbaatar: a standardized version appears in many tourist shops.

How different the valley in the pictures is from today! But the Bogd mountain that I endlessly explored in weekend hikes was right there to witness the events I read about in history books. Other reminders left of the time that Ulaanbaatar was once predominantly a temple city are the Chojjen Lama temple, the Gandan monastery and the Bogd Khaan's Winter Palace (from where he was removed by the Mad Baron).

I also read the American explorer and naturalist Roy Chapman Andrews's travel books and note differences and similarities with my own experiences. Of the Ulaanbaatar of 1920, he mentions the golden roofs of scores of temples giving back the sunlight, the moaning chant of praying lamas, Mongols in half a dozen different tribal dresses, Tibetan pilgrims, Manchu Tartars, camel drivers from far Turkestan. He also describes the custom of leaving corpses just outside town, on the banks of the Tuul river, to decompose and feed birds, wolves and dogs. That custom has disappeared, fortunately: I have made many a pleasant walk along the river banks, not a corpse in sight.

In Andrews's time cars were still exceedingly rare in Mongolia; most transportation took place by camel, horse and oxcart. I saw the occasional movements of herders by oxcarts and by camel caravan, but these had become sporadic and unusual. Nevertheless, his exclamation "Woe to the men who venture into the desert with an untried car and without a skilled mechanic!" strikes a chord. Shombodon and I did not make that mistake in 2002.

More recognizable is what Andrews writes about the dogs: "The dogs of Mongolia are savage almost beyond belief. They are huge black fellows like the Tibetan mastiff, and their diet of dead human flesh seems to have given them a contempt for living men. Every Mongol family has one or more, and it is exceedingly dangerous for a man to approach a yurt or caravan unless he is on horseback or has a pistol ready." These ger-dogs are still a source of concern for those of us who hiked the countryside nearly a century later. Terry gave me mace, a Taser and a collapsible dog-whip for when I went to the countryside. I remember going for evening runs accompanied by our jeep with Shombodon, armed to the teeth, riding alongside with the door open to protect me from dogs. Of course, the one time I had left the dog-weapons in our car when we went for a walk, we got stalked by three of the brutes. They had separated and approached from three directions; Shombodon and I barely made it to the car walking back-to-back and throwing stones all the way.

Another thing that caught my eye was Andrews's description of a monastery that he referred to as the great lamasery at Turin, located on the main route to China, about 170 miles from Urga: "Three temples lie in a bowl-shaped hollow, surrounded by hundreds upon hundreds of pillbox dwellings painted red and white. There must have been a thousand of them and probably twice as many lamas. On the outskirts of the 'city' to the south enormous piles of argul [dried dung used as fuel for make fires] have been collected by the priests and bestowed as votive offerings by devout travelers. Vast as the supply seemed, it would take all this, and more, to warm the houses of the lamas during the bitter winter months when the ground is covered with snow. On the north the hills throw protecting arms about the homes of these half-wild men, who have chosen to spend their lives in this lonely desert stronghold. The houses are built of sawn boards, the first indication we had seen that we were nearing a forest country."

Shombodon thinks Andrews is referring to the Zuun Choir monastery: it was by far the most important in the region — estimates of the number of lamas vary between one and two thousand — and the main road would have passed it. We visit the ruins, about 270 kilometers from Ulaanbaatar, late one fine summer day under a blue sky with woolly white clouds. There is little left of the place: it amazes me how totally the monasteries have been destroyed! There is an image of a goddess sculpted into the eroded rocks, freshly painted with four new prayer-wheels in front of it and fenced off with prayer-flags. We poke about and talk about Shombodon's father-in-law who served here and the Mad Baron who made camp here. I reflect that Shombodon's father-in-law was here when Andrews passed because he was born around 1900, probably entered the monastery as a child and lived there until the monastery was destroyed in the late Thirties. Andrews described lamas as half-wild men leading a lazy, worthless existence but I have difficulty squaring this with Shombodon's description of a quiet, dignified man who was a loving father and doting grandfather.

4. MONGOLIAN NATIONHOOD

The banks of the Khovd river

Summer 2003. *Shombodon and I have taken the afternoon off because one of us — or both? — are feeling a little under the weather and Shombodon lets me know that a true and tested Mongolian cure for feeling poorly is to sit next to a stream and listen to the sound of flowing water. We are in the western city of Khovd and decide that the bank of the Khovd river is the ideal place to sit and listen to the water quietly gurgling by. Fortunately it is a warm summer day without mosquitoes. When there are mosquitoes even I, not easily fazed by bugs, cannot manage to stay outside the car for more than 30 seconds — and I have tried, believe me. We are not the only ones here: in summer the whole city of Khovd moves out of their stuffy apartments and into their gers that they erect by the river. The ger-city has the feel of a festival during the short and glorious summer season. We sit a bit upstream from the gers, con template the lazy day under the blue sky, and chat. We talk about the existence of God or not (I think we agreed that He probably does not). We talk about the relationships between girls and boys in school. We talk about homosexuality (pretty much a taboo subject for his generation). We talk about our childhoods.*

The Khovd Agricultural Technical School is Shombodon's alma mater; he boarded with a family in their ger more or less at the very spot where we are sitting. I feel embarrassed when he says he used to get up at four in the dark freezing cold to do homework and read Marx's Capital, and that the students went out in the weekends to assist with voluntary labor-brigades. We weren't that dedicated as college students; we also wanted to contribute to a more socialist (anti-imperialist in the case of Third-World sociology students) society and we wanted to learn,

75

but we nevertheless had plenty of time to drink beer, smoke pot and party. Actual learning was low on my list of priorities, though fortunately some learning must have taken place despite my efforts to the contrary. In any case, Shombodon's stories put me to shame.

What is communism?

After the Mad Baron fled and was captured and executed, the Mongolian revolutionaries, together with the Red Army, mopped up the opposition. The Chinese were defeated at Khiagt (near the present-day northern city of Sükhbaatar) and the White Russians were expelled from Urga in July 1921. Mongolia was again an independent nation, this time for good. July 11 was set as the official date of independence from China and the annual Naadam festival from then on was scheduled for 11-13 July to commemorate the Revolution of 1921.

From 1921 onward the Mongols were able to exert influence over their destiny but they weren't powerful enough to maintain independence without a strong ally and that ally became the Soviet Union. Because they had become part of the Eastern Bloc, we in the West never learnt much about them or their political and economic system. So I need to shed a bit of light on the terms "socialism" and "communism" because both terms are used to describe the Mongolian socio-economic and political system from the 1920s to the 1980s and many westerners, particularly the younger generation, have no idea what they mean. And maybe neither did I, precisely. I was corrected several times by elderly Mongols who indicated that I did not know what I was talking about when using the word "communism"; they wished to describe their system as socialist.

The term communist has been used indiscriminately for the political and economic systems of countries that were governed by a one-party system and introduced an economic system based on the 19th-century ideology referred to as Historical Materialism or Marxism. The Marxist theory was developed by two German philosophers, Karl Marx and Friedrich Engels, and had its roots in criticism of the capitalist system that, according to this theory, inevitably leads to exploitation, misery and destitution of "the workers", "the masses" or "the people". (That is why the official name of the Communist Party is the Mongolian People's Revolutionary Party and the official name of the country used to be the People's Republic of Mongolia.) Those masses with nothing left to lose would then be ready to revolt. The theory embeds the idea that the only way to effect change is through a total revolution and switch of power. Permutations of these ideas became popular in the first half of the 20th century and political parties based on those ideas built strong, military-style organizations. One, the Bolsheviks, under the leadership of Vladimir Ilyich Lenin, overthrew the Russian Tsarist regime in October 1917 and subsequently became the Communist Party. After ruthlessly consolidating power, the Communist Party formed the Soviet Union (USSR) around the former Russian empire: it functioned as one authoritarian state and headed a group of satellite communist countries, including Mongolia, that became known as the Eastern Bloc.

In its early years, the USSR extended its influence and control through an organization called Comintern. Comintern, an abbreviation for the Third Communist International, was an aggressive international organization headquartered in Moscow, with the ultimate objective of instating worldwide communism by any available means, whether armed struggle, subversive cells, political pressure or ideological warfare. In satellite countries such as Mongolia, it functioned between 1919-1943 as a means to control them and keep them aligned with the Soviet Union. Marxist theory and ideology was supposed to guide the USSR and its allies towards a utopian communist society, but, although the theory analyzed and criticized capitalism and went into detail on how to fight and overthrow capitalism, little thought had gone into what ideal communist society should look like after the revolution actually succeeded, and what to do in countries where the capitalist system didn't exist in the first place. It was a militant theory geared towards revolution and overthrowing established powers and the ideologies that justified the status quo, such as the churches and religion in general.

The word "socialism" was originally defined as a stage in the economic development of a country before attaining the ideal of full-fledged communism. Lenin, the first leader of the USSR and its primary political theorist, understood that revolutionary Marxist theory implied that there was a capitalist system that should be overthrown and was therefore difficult to apply to non-capitalist countries such as Mongolia. During Comintern's Second Congress in

1920 he expediently asserted that underdeveloped countries could attain socialism directly, bypassing capitalism altogether. This assertion was immediately accepted by the Third Congress and sums of money were allocated to support revolutionary movements in the Far East, among other places. The Mongolian People's Revolutionary Party (MPRP) joined Comintern in 1924 and Comintern became the instrument through which the Communist Party of the USSR wielded power in Mongolia in the Twenties and Thirties. Despite the fact that the word "communism" was normally used for the political system of the USSR, I shall generally refer to "socialism" because it is more commonly used in Mongolia.

Mongolian resistance and heroes

The new nation's socio-economic structure after independence was much the same as before. The majority of Mongols were poor, illiterate nomadic herders while their feudal lords and the monasteries that acquired many of their sons owned most of the livestock. The economy was extremely undeveloped, with virtually no farming or industry and only rudimentary transportation and communication services. Chinese and Russians controlled key sectors such as banking and trade. The population continued to be squeezed by high taxation because the government itself was indebted to Chinese bankers. The religious establishment under the Bogd Khaan held most of the power; assassinations of the political opposition, many of them from nobility, were common. But change was coming.

The revolution of 1911 and its turbulent aftermath spawned a group of educated youngsters who had been involved in the independence movement and in designing the new government and who by the early 1920s constituted the new officials and officers of the independent country. Many of these young intellectuals looked outward and beyond Buddhism for inspiration at a time that was globally a fertile period for new ideas and ideologies. These ideas were converted into action and played a defining role in the global upheavals of the time, such as World War One and the Russian and Chinese revolutions. Young, educated Mongols discussed modern ideas and started organizing themselves.

Resistance groups called Duguilans had existed even under Manchu rule: they would quietly and often secretly form to discuss a certain issue, and upon reaching a conclusion, would accordingly petition the authorities. In reaction to the humiliations imposed by Xu and the loss of autonomy, several such groups sprang up, the most famous of which was formed by D. Bodoo immediately after the day of abolition of autonomy. Bodoo was a 35-year-old Mongolian language teacher at a Russian school at Consular Hill who was involved in publishing a journal, was an author and literate in Mongolian, Tibetan, Manchu and Chinese. He was in contact with underground Russian revolutionaries. Another key figure in this Consular Hill resistance group was H. Choibalsan, who was to become an important Mongolian leader two decades later.

Other resistance groups were established in Khüree, notably one founded by S. Danzan in East Khüree to which the famous independence fighter Sükhbaatar belonged and one that was composed of venerable members such as the Dilowa Khutugtu and other high-ranking lamas. The resistance groups were united in their hatred of the warlord Xu and were looking for strong allies to support their resistance. Before 1924 several political leaders, the Bogd Khaan and prime minister Bodoo among them, had approached diplomats from the US in Kalgan and Beijing to solicit recognition and support for independence. The US failed to respond to those messages. The modern intellectuals appealed to the Russian Bolsheviks who, having settled affairs in the center of their country, turned their attention East, brought the whole of Siberia under their control and took over Russian foreign missions and consulates.

The struggle between White Russians and Red Bolshevik revolutionaries within the Russian community at Khüree was settled in favor of the Reds who had gone underground in the period 1918-1920 when White Russians (Semenov's troops) dominated Eastern Siberia and the Mad Baron was running loose in Mongolia. The Bolsheviks established contact with the Consular Hill group and advised their comrades on how to conduct the great revolutionary struggle. As a result, on June 25 1920, the Mongolian People's Party (it became the Mongolian People's Revolutionary Party in 1925) was established at a meeting of the East Khüree group and the Consular hill group in Danzan's ger.

De facto, Mongolia was independent — albeit in close alliance with the USSR — but its status was less clearly defined in the diplomatic sphere. In 1924 China and the USSR signed an agreement establishing mutual diplomatic relations and reaffirming that Outer

Mongolia was an integral part of the Republic of China. However China, experiencing its own revolution, was in no position to enforce its claims.

Just three years after the Bogd Khaan was reinstated on the throne in 1921, albeit with limited powers, he died and Mongolia became a People's Republic. The words "under mysterious circumstances" sometimes follow the account the Bogd Khaan's death. I am not surprised that an overweight alcoholic with a sedentary lifestyle and probably eating fatty mutton three times a day dies at 55. Neither, given the killings that went hand in hand with the power struggles that would take place during Mongolia's maturing into nationhood, would I be surprised to hear that he was murdered. It is immaterial now. Buddhism had contributed to Mongolian independence but the young nation, prodded by its ideological mentor the Soviet Union, turned against religion and the revolutionaries forbade the search for new reincarnations of the Bogd Javzandamba Khutukhtu.

The Buddhists did not agree with the end of reincarnations and in the mid-Thirties a reincarnation was found in Tibet, a boy born in 1933, but his identity was kept secret until after the collapse of the Soviet Union. He was formally enthroned as the ninth Javsandamba Khutukhtu in 1991 in Dharamsala, moved to Mongolia late 2011, and died there aged 79 a few months later. I wonder who is looking for the 10th reincarnation of the Javsandamba Khutukhtu. Shombodon doesn't know, but apparently the ninth Bogd stated before he died that the 10th reincarnation would be identified in Mongolia and will be exclusively involved in religion, not politics.

Mongolia's biggest hero in the fight for independence is D. Sükhbaatar, whose statue still stands in the center of Ulaanbaatar's main square: originally named Sükhbaatar Square, it is now Chinggis Khaan Square. He was born in 1893 and raised in Ulaanbaatar where he learnt some Russian by playing with Russian kids and received an education, a rarity at the time. He was drafted into the first Mongolian army in 1911 and was one of the first Mongolian soldiers to enter the new Russian-founded military school in 1912, where he distinguished himself as a gifted commander. In 1920 he took part in the founding of the People's Revolutionary Party and in 1921 he was the one who smuggled to Moscow the Bogd Khan's letter requesting Russian assistance with expelling the Chinese: the letter was hidden in the handle of his whip and passed the Chinese checkpoints undetected. A historic meeting between Lenin and Sükhbaatar in Moscow that year is depicted in paintings and statues I have seen in various museums around the country.

Sükhbaatar was the commander of the Mongolian People's Army in 1921 that liberated Mongolia once and for all. With assistance from the Red Russian forces, the army defeated the Chinese at Khiagt and captured the Mad Baron who was fleeing north. In 1923 Sükhbaatar died aged 30 of unknown causes. Conspiracy theories being as popular in Mongolia as elsewhere, there are those who say it was poison. His reputation was unblemished at the time of his death and he gained superhero status during socialist times, possibly by reminding people of their even greater superhero, Chinggis Khaan, or because the Communist Party needed a superhero to take the place of Chinggis Khaan in the popular imagination.

The People's Republic of Mongolia

Shortly after the death of the Bogd Khaan a new national parliament, the Ikh Khural (Great Assembly) was formed with the Little Khural taking care of government when they were on recess. In the background, the real power lay with the Communist Party. The new Ikh Khural, composed of 76 delegates, set to work. According to the historian Bat-Erdene Batbayar (known as Baabar): "After the delegates felt they got satisfactory answers to such questions as whether the Bogd Khan's next incarnation was to be unveiled, whether the cattle belonging to the Church [Buddhist Establishment] was to be taxed, the renaming of Khüree, and what the soyombo on the state flag actually meant, they endorsed the constitution."

For those of you who are curious about the meaning of the Mongolian national symbol or Soyombo, it was designed in 1686 by Zanabazar, the first Javsandamba Khutukhtu and symbolizes, from top to bottom: Fire, representing eternal growth, wealth, and success; the three tongues of the flame represent the past, present, and future. The sun. The moon. Triangles represent points of spears pointing downward, representing the defeat of internal and external enemies. The horizontal rectangles

symbolize honesty and justice for the people. The Yin-Yang symbol was reinterpreted in socialist times to represent vigilance because, I was told, it looks like two fish and fish never close their eyes. The two vertical rectangles can be interpreted as the walls of a fort; they represent unity and strength, relating to a Mongolian proverb: "The friendship of two is stronger than stone walls."

Set to work they did, without procrastinating. In 1924 Mongolia's first constitution was passed, a standing body elected for when it was not in session, and a cabinet and a prime minister elected. Niislel Khüree was renamed Ulaanbaatar (Red Hero) to honor the left-leaning freedom fighters, the color red symbolizing communism. The first Mongolian bank opened and in 1925 a Mongolian currency, the tögrög, was established. Based on the experience of having had to refight independence in 1920, the new country also started building a modern military apparatus, replacing the Soviet Red Army's presence. By the late 1920s the Mongolian army had a cavalry of 17,000; 200 machine guns; 50 small field guns; two armored tanks; and four airplanes. The foundations for industrial progress were also laid in the 1920s, notably the Nalaikh coal mine that was established in 1922 and provided coal to Ulaanbaatar about 25 kilometers away and a 500-kilowatt thermal power plant ordered from the German AEG company in the early 1920s.

Outside Ulaanbaatar most people continued to live as they had before — they couldn't have understood Marxism nor fully realized how their traditional Buddhism-inspired life would completely change. They would have heard that the Bogd Khaan wasn't replaced, but what would they have known about the separation of state and religion? They still looked up to the traditional nobles and lamas to whom they paid taxes and owed corvee labor. But those rights of receiving taxes and corvee labor were abolished in 1924, which couldn't have escaped their notice, and other things started to change as well.

A series of social institutions were established in the 1920s to incorporate the people into the centrally planned system and to show them the way forward to modern (Soviet-led) development. Building the utopian communist future was everyone's duty, starting with the children and young people. Consequently, an organization called the Children Pioneers was established in 1925 as per Soviet example. It resembled the Scouting movement: the pioneers wore uniforms, were instructed in sports, outdoor skills, singing, good clean living, marching, nationalism and of course, communist principles. Children typically entered at elementary school until, at 15, they generally joined the Mongolian Youth Organization, also established in 1925. Many people I interviewed had been Children Pioneers and a young woman who guided me through the museum in Choisbalsan, and who was clearly born after transition, said that the Children Pioneers had been a beneficial organization where children learnt important things.

The Mongolian Youth Organization imitated the All-Union Leninist Young Communist League, or Komsomol, of the Soviet Union. Apart from differing ideological details such as invoking Lenin (or the national equivalent of Lenin) instead of God in their promise, the organization was also fashioned after the Scouting movement. Most youngsters joined because it was understood that the organization would help them get access to higher education and jobs as upstanding members of society. The Mongolian Youth Organization quickly became an important radical leftist force in politics.

Traditionally women had been pretty much excluded from positions of political power, which was in the hands of the male religious establishment. Tibetan Buddhism (just like other religions, in my opinion) seems to have had a misogynist inclination. As Baabar explains, Tibetan Buddhist legends recount that virtue derives from a benevolent male monkey-god and evil from a malevolent female demon. It was therefore men who joined the monasteries, received an education, worked in professional fields such as medicine and, above all, held political power. Culture does not change easily and today politics is the only area in which Mongolian women significantly lag behind men. There are surprisingly few women in parliament, ministerial positions and lower-level assemblies, particularly considering their overall high levels of education and labor-force participation.

The emancipation of women was part and parcel of communist ideology: the thinking was that bringing women into the labor force would free them. Pragmatism was involved as well: the young nation needed labor to build the new and improved socialist society. Women's access to education, health services and remunerated employment increased significantly in the years following the formal declaration of independence from China in 1921. That same year, a literacy school for women was established in Ulaanbaatar for 20 students. A decade later, 40 percent of primary-school students were female. Women were also valued as mothers of new generations of loyal party members and builders of the ideal communist future. In March 1924 the Central Committee of the MPRP again followed the lead of the USSR by establishing the Mongolian Women's Development Unit, which became the Mongolian Women's Division in September 1925.

Power struggles

Mongolia did not yet have a unified ideology and identity, and had to settle its internal power struggles if a stable situation were to be created. The main power struggle was, to put it simplistically, between the old power structures of the Buddhist establishment, upper-class military and the nobility in favor of the traditional Mongol way of life on the one hand ("the right"), and young revolutionary intellectuals ("the left") on the other. The revolutionary Youth League embodied the left and had the backing of Comintern, which meant that the Soviet superpower next door would influence the outcome of the power struggle and, for many years to come, define the organization of the new state, its politics, economy, external affairs, and social organization. The old order had perhaps been a bit too closely aligned with the vanquished Manchu rulers to be attractive to the younger generation, and there was no external support for its ideas.

The ideological controversies probably disguised some life-or-death power struggles between dominant males. The losers were executed, among them in 1922 Bodoo, who had been prime minister (possibly because he held the view that Mongolia's domestic affairs should not be fashioned after those of Soviet Russia), Central Committee member Danzan who had accused Bodoo and was accused and executed in turn in 1924, and so on.

At the political level in the annual Party congresses between 1924 and 1928, clashes between the leftists and rightist elements continued to take place, culminating in a leftist victory during the seventh congress of 1928. The left had the strong backing of Stalin, who had gained control of the USSR after Lenin's death in 1924.

Under pressure from Comintern, the MPRP replaced conservative officials with leftists and elevated Choibalsan as head of the Little Khural. Immediately, Choibalsan introduced Soviet-style reforms that were speedily ratified by the Ikh Khural and put into effect. These reforms entailed eliminating the feudal classes by confiscating their properties, arresting, imprisoning and liquidating them. Baabar, in a chapter aptly called "Communist Hysteria Sweeps Mongolia" summarizes the instructions that came from Comintern (1929) to the MPRP Central Committee as follows:

1. Unite private farms.

2. Transfer livestock to state ownership.

3. Intensify the struggle against feudals. Make them jobless in order to exert pressure.

4. Exert all kinds of pressure on the kulaks, as they are petty feudals, and gradually overthrow them.

5. Apply the most aggressive methods in the struggle against religion.

The concepts of "feudals" (nobility with bonded serfs) and "kulaks" (independent farmers) were taken from the Marxist-Leninist political theory in Russia. It didn't fit the Mongolian situation but the MPRP Central Committee figured out what to do with it: the people were divided into commoners on the one hand and feudals and kulaks on the other. The latter categories comprised of all high-ranking lamas, the nobility, anyone who owned property, and, conveniently, anyone who did not agree with those in power.

The People's Republic of Mongolia, copying Soviet-style central planning, swiftly converted these ideas into detailed plans and (Mongols are doers!) did not waste time in starting to build an infrastructure that the centrally planned nation needed. They did not have to invent these institutions themselves, as the Soviet Union was years ahead of them and basically handed them a blueprint of how to steer society towards the ideal of communism. Marxist-Leninist theory underpinned this ideal and was the basis for institution building.

Ethnic minorities

Communist ideology focused exclusively on two classes, those who owned the means of production and those who did not. After having achieved a classless society by annihilating the exploiting classes (capitalists and feudals), further distinctions between higher-level officials and ordinary people were downplayed (although people knew that government officials and other dignitaries were more equal than others) and other distinctions actively discouraged. Accordingly, the Party and government stipulated equality between ethnic groups and the sexes. This worked out well for women, and also for the different ethnicities/minorities who were given equal opportunities with the dominant Khalkh Mongol tribes during most of the 20th century.

The Buriat Mongols became an important ethnic group. Most Buriats, who came from the area around Lake Baikal in Russia, were immigrants. A first wave of Buriat resettlement took place between 1900-1907 and, as a result of the 1921 friendship agreement between Mongolia and the Soviet Union, a second wave of resettlements took place in the 1920s. In 1923 the Buriat-Mongolian Autonomous Soviet Socialist Republic was created and in 1924 the government of Mongolia approved the resettlement of 4000 Buriat households — nearly 16,000 individuals — in Mongolia where they received full citizenship. From 1925 onward, however, the powerful international Soviet-dominated Comintern was against the resettlement practices: resettlement of Buriats was limited by 1930, and then stopped altogether.

The largest ethnic minority in Mongolia are the Kazakhs, who had been living there before independence and gained official residency as a group under the reign of the Bogd Khaan in 1917. Most other ethnic minorities are Mongol ethnicities living in the Western aimags such as the Oirad-Mongols (Uriankhai), Torguud, Durvut, Altai Uriangai, Uuld, Myangud, and Khoyon, who had been living peacefully with each other and spoke only slightly different dialects. The Manchus, their common enemy, didn't differentiate between the Mongol tribes and under socialism these minorities were mostly treated as fully equal nationals. Very few other minorities lived in Mongolia, just some Chinese (including the occasional Uighur), Tuvans and a few Russians.

August 2012. Khovd. Togie, a former colleague of Shombodon and me, knocks on my hotel room door and introduces me to Mr. Aldrach because he thinks his story might interest me. Mr. Aldrach, a large man *in his late 60s, sits down at a table covered with a flowery plastic cloth of the kind I remember so well from the years we worked in Khovd. He states that he is a Uighur, and tells me his story:*

In 1921 his grandfather, an enterprising Uighur from Khotan in western China, decided to pull up stakes and trek more than 1500 kilometers to Khovd Mongolia with his wife and five sons to start growing crops in the fertile valley of the Buyant River. His story didn't include why this Chinese national, at a time when the border between China and Mongol "wasn't peaceful" and the Chinese living in Mongolia were forcefully evicted that very year, made that decision, but he did — and he and his wife never went back to Khotan. I understood that they were not the only Uighurs to end up living in the Khovd region. One of his sons, Kadr, married a Kazakh woman and they had several sons, of whom Aldrach was one. In 1956, inexplicably, when life in Mongolia was becoming better than ever before, a group of Uighurs decided to go back to Khotan. According to Mr. Aldrach, his father Kadr was among those who emigrated back to Khotan: they were Chinese citizens and simply wanted to go back home although they were allowed to stay. There was peace between China and Mongolia and they went back legally because they had understood that China was "socialist and friendly".

The young Aldrach, who trekked back to China with his father in 1956, got into trouble a few years later. China was going through its Cultural Revolution and, in 1962, a whole border patrol that was made up of minorities turned on the Chinese, ransacked their border post and defected to Kazakhstan. After that, all foreigners were suspect and persecuted in China. Aldrach and his brother were imprisoned because they had foreign (Mongolian) passports. He said the Chinese prison was very bad: they were bound hand and foot in metal shackles. Although there was a decree that anyone who had escaped prison could be shot on the spot, the brothers and a friend decided to escape, but Aldrach's older brother fell ill and took at least three months to recover. After that they managed to escape to Mongolia, timing it just right so they could cross the high mountains in summer. It was difficult and risky, but the alternative was being shot.

When they arrived in Mongolia, all three were arrested and put in a prison in Bayan-Olgi while the officials checked their story for three months. Because they were citizens, they were let go in the end. The conditions in the Mongolian prison were much better than in China, and also relatives came from Khovd to Bayan-Olgi to visit them. The relatives also petitioned the government on their behalf. Aldrach was 19 and had been in China for seven years.

Now he is a pensioner. After his China adventure, he settled down and started working for the Khovd Aimag Food Factory and in 1963 he married a woman who was half-Uighur, half-Mongol. His own father had been half-Uighur, half-Kazakh — so they are a mixed family. He worked at the food factory for 41 years, had 10 children and asserts: "I believe in Allah and my kids also believe in Allah." He retired seven years ago and his children are all married. Four live in Khovd, one in Ulaanbaatar and one in Bayan-Olgi. He speaks Uighur, Kazakh, Mongolian and a bit of Chinese and regularly visits his relatives in China and Kazakhstan. He says China is now free and democratic and doesn't require a visa. Then he abruptly gets up and leaves, so I don't get more than the bare bones of his intriguing story.

Mr. Aldrach's story left me to ponder that reading history gives a description of events as general trends, processed by academics who have the advantage of hindsight. I am not always able to fit quirky facts and memories of modern-day Mongols in the general flow of history and cannot explain why some Chinese nationals entered rather than left the country in that momentous year when the Chinese were ousted for good. Maybe the Uighurs didn't consider themselves Chinese. Maybe they had simply heard that there was a lot of good farming land lying vacant after the Chinese who had been living there had been evicted.

The people

In the 1920s, most in the young People's Republic of Mongolia did not understand the new ideas of revolutionary struggle that inspired their more learned and internationally influenced countrymen and could not see into their unimaginable future. How could they? For lack of alternatives, the Mongols attempted to continue living as they had in the past. They planned for positioning their sons in monasteries where they could be looked after and receive education and status in society. Apart from very few small ger-schools for boys who were to become scribes for the Manchu administration, the only education that had been available was Tibetan Buddhist rather than scientific. The shortage of marriageable men, combined with a culture of monogamy, led to a vicious circle in which the large number of boys who became lamas made it difficult for many women to find husbands, resulting in an ever larger number of single mothers deciding to send their boys to the monasteries because they couldn't adequately care for them. As mentioned earlier, fertility in women trumped purity in a society where all additional labor was welcome. In 1926 Shombodon's (single) paternal grandmother sent her only child, nine years old, to religious school to become a lama. There he was looked after by three of his uncles who were lamas, the youngest of whom was mostly in charge of him. Shombodon's wife's grandmother was also a poor single mother who placed her young boy in a monastery.

Whether they had single mothers or not, children and the extra labor they represented were always welcome. It must have been as common for the grandparents to look after their grandchildren while their mothers worked then as it is now. Of the young women who worked for me over the years, many were single mothers: the fathers were out of their lives and the women's parents looked after the children. Typically, grandfather is seen with his grandchild on his lap while grandma is either has a job and/or does the housekeeping. Of course, today's absent fathers are not in the monasteries: they are herding, unemployed, drinking or the relationship simply didn't work out. There is little stigma connected with being a single mom.

The lamasery was well organized and there was quite a bit of traveling between the monasteries, so by the Twenties the lamas must have known and been worried about the anti-religious communist ideology. After all, their own leader, the Bogd Khaan, had not been replaced as head of state after his death in 1924. They were right to worry, as slowly but inexorably people's lives began to change under the new system.

For instance, in 1925 clan names were abolished as being "feudal" and nowadays most people don't know what their clan-names would have been anymore. Since 2000 the government has been trying to reintroduce clan names and use them in the same way as Westerners use their surnames in order to better identify its citizens. The most popular name chosen is Borjigin, Chinggis Khaan's clan name; in fact, so many people have chosen it that a large part of the population has the same surname — rather defeating the purpose of introducing surnames in the first place.

According to Mongolian tradition, you should know nine generations along father's line (like bone) and seven generations along mother's line (like flesh). The abolition of clan names and persecution of lamas and nobility caused a break in traditions, as children might not have been told about their ancestors if those ancestors were politically incorrect at the time. As regards names, Mongols generally have names that symbolize desirable characteristics, usually denoting strength for men and beauty for women. There are also many unisex names that denote auspicious qualities such as happiness, golden or peace. One unusual category is linked to a superstitious belief that giving an unusual name to a child will cause the evil spirits to overlook it. Particularly if earlier children have died, couples might choose names such as Nergui (no name), Munbish, (is/is not), Enerbish (not this one), or Khunbish (not a human being). An ethnic Mongolian colleague explained that he and his brothers had received Kazakh names because boys tend to die young and his parents were advised to give them strange names. The weirdest Mongolian name, however, stems from socialist times: Melscho is composed of the first letters of the names Marx, Engels, Lenin, Stalin and Choibalsan. Needless to say, it has gone out of fashion.

Soon it wouldn't be just their clan names that people would lose, but a much greater part of their traditional identity: their religion and their livelihood as private herders.

5. OBLITERATION OF THE OLD ORDER

The monastery

March 2004. On the road. We drive north from Ulaanbaatar one cold afternoon into white hills with brown patches of frozen larch forest. On our way we stop and stand quietly as we watch a lamb being born. The herder-girl looks on too. Then we pass a big ovoo and our cars gets stuck in the snow. We have to dig them out but all of us are in a festive mood because we, the staff of the Agriculture Sector Development Project, are on an office outing. This is the last time I'll be together with the rest of the team because my input is nearly completed and will leave the country soon (for good, I thought again). It is nearly dark and we are close to our destination, Amarbayargalant monastery. This monastery is one of the few that has not been totally destroyed: its main buildings have survived and been restored with Unesco funds. In the dusk the ochre-yellow, orange and reddish hues of its walls lie peacefully in the cold valley.

We have made reservations to stay at some of the guest quarters beside the monastery and have brought all our food and drink with us. We light the fire in the flimsy wood-burning stove and huddle over the festive dinner with our coats on — but soon we warm up, eating, drinking, joking. During the meal, my Australian boss (he and I are the only foreigners) asks me conversationally which of the long-drops around is the least filthy. At this time of the year the daytime temperature starts rising above freezing point, the stalagmites of excrement in the outhouses start thawing out, and the smell is bad. I ask whether he hasn't been in this country too long — does he consider this a reasonable dinner-table topic? But we are drinking and I gigglingly relent *and tell him my favorite one with its tranquil views. After dinner there are games but I never enjoy these very much and they let me watch. In any case, most of the jokes are in Mongolian. The next day we get a guided tour through the monastery and see the lamas in their bright yellow and red robes sitting in rows on either side of a large round wood-burning stove, chanting. Their bright robes were donated when a movie was made about the monastery. Many of lamas are children — some, I estimate, not older than seven. In my opinion they are too young for monastic life but here they are and I don't know what their lives would have looked like on the outside. There is much I don't know: remnants of Buddhism have hovered just out of reach of my consciousness, specters around the corner, since I have lived here and I never pursued the topic much.*

Religion and communism co-existed uneasily in my mind when thinking about Mongolian culture and my curiosity about 20th-century history was piqued one day when Shombodon casually remarked, "My father was a lama." How could that be? Aren't lamas supposed to be celibate? How does a lama bring up his children within a socialist system? I had heard about purges and the destroying of the monasteries, but hadn't realized the scale on which those had taken place. Nor will I ever know the extent to which it did or did not influence peoples' thinking and feeling. There was definitely a tendency not to talk too much about ex-lama relatives (particularly if they were fathers) in front of the children in order to protect them so much of that knowledge didn't get transferred to the next generation. So what had happened?

Crisis and New Turn Policy of gradualism

After winning the political struggle, the pro-Soviet leftists didn't waste any time starting to work on the creation of a centrally planned economy and society. In 1931 the old territorial administration that divided the country into khoshuus (banners) was abolished and a new administrative system put in its place. The country was divided into aimags (provinces) — originally 13, later subdivided to arrive at the present-day 21 aimags — which were, in turn, divided into soums. The first national Five-Year Plan for 1931-1935 included the confiscation of properties of the feudals, the creation of cooperatives and communes and increased persecution of the Buddhists.

In the countryside people's wealth was mostly measured in the number of animals they owned, which was still the same when I was working there. The national plan called for confiscating animals and other properties and transferring them to the poor, including to the lamas who had been compelled to leave their monasteries and had been put to work in collective farms. There were even attempts to introduce cropping to baffled herders. The immediate repercussions of these unpopular policies were rebellions of monks; people fleeing across the border with their animals; and slaughter and sale of animals. By one estimate total livestock numbers dropped from more than 23 million in 1930 to approximately 16 million in 1932. At the same time trade collapsed because it had been in hands of the Chinese who were ousted in the Twenties. This caused critical food shortages and led the country to the brink of civil war. The revolts that ensued — mainly led by monks — covered the greater part of the country by May 1932 and an estimated 30,000 people fled across the borders. The revolts were brutally put down by the Mongolian Revolutionary Red Army, with some assistance from the Soviet Red Army.

Even so, the Soviet Union's Politburo, in close cooperation with Stalin himself, realized that the precipitous and forced introduction of a Soviet-style economic system wasn't working and that strategic concessions were necessary. These would buy time to plan the purging all potential anti-Soviet, Mongolian nationalist or religious elements in a more systematic manner. In May 1932, the Five-Year Plan was replaced by a more gradual approach, referred to as the "New Turn Policy". The MPRP leadership admitted to having made mistakes and participants in the rebellions were released, with the exception of their leaders. Private ownership of livestock was again allowed and a few years of relative calm followed. Attempts to get the nomadic pastoral population to grow crops had failed and it was decided to establish state crop farms instead. The gradual approach to introducing socialism during this period meant that the herder sector was essentially left alone. A few state farms and only a few voluntary producers' cooperatives were established.

Many households that had fled over the border returned later, but not all. Luvsanjamts of Tsogt soum told me that one of the lamas, Dashtseren Gegeen, who was 12 when he left Tsogt in the general exodus, had lived in China ever since. After transition, Luvsanjamts invited the elderly Dashtseren back for a visit to his home soum to advise him as to where and how to build the small temple that stands just outside of the soum center today.

There was another, less apparent, reason for the New Turn Policy: Imperial Japan, hoping to gain control of a larger part of the continent, invaded and occupied Manchuria in 1931, renamed it Manchukuo and started fueling pan-Mongolian nationalism. This resonated with the Inner Mongolians who, facing the threat of Chinese settlements and control, were trying to preserve their traditional culture and so were disinclined to follow the new revolutionary ideas. They supported their traditional tribal organization identity and princes and drew apart from Outer Mongolia with its revolutionary notions. They had not received Russian support because the Russians were reluctant to antagonize the Chinese. That left aligning themselves with the Japanese and their promises to support pan-Mongolism as a way out. In contrast, the People's Republic of Mongolia was closely aligned with the USSR and realized it was the logical next territory to be invaded by Japan.

The USSR wanted Mongolia to function as a stable buffer state against Japanese and Chinese expansion plans. In 1934, therefore, the Soviet Union and Mongolia agreed on reciprocal assistance in case of further Japanese advances and in 1936 the agreement was formalized by the 10-year Mongolian-Soviet Treaty of Friendship, which included a mutual defense protocol. Soviet Red Army units were deployed to build and strengthen the Mongolian army and military expenditure swelled into World War Two. The number of Mongolian troops rose to nearly 100,000 at its peak. Now a significant number of young men went into the army rather than the monasteries.

Power struggles between the leftists and rightists continued into the 1930s but the latter were never again able to wrest back control over the country. They included not only the religious establishment and old nobility whose positions in society were being threatened, but also educated and nationalist Mongols who wanted to steer an independent Mongolian course, and citizens (many of them herders, of course) who had taken part in the uprisings of 1932. The ideology of the leftists was that beneficial modern development could only be achieved by expunging the old power structure that the lamas, nobles and rich herdsmen kept in place to their own advantage and to the detriment of the poor. Unquestionably, Mongolian society was backward in many ways and did not benefit from modern insights: for instance, there was no medical knowledge of infectious diseases and how to prevent them; there was no universal education; bonded serfs were not counted among the menfolk; women had no place outside their traditional tasks; there was little contact with the modern world. These issues were now being energetically redressed by the government and Party.

Stalin's Soviet Union backed the leftists and played an important role in determining which factions and individuals attained positions of power. Politicians who were against the guidelines that came from Comintern were sidelined or murdered. The New Turn Policy slowed down the introduction of Soviet-style economic structures but persecution of religion continued. At first political anti-religious campaigns and economic methods were used to discourage religion, but by the second half of the Thirties methods became more suppressive and bloody.

Religion purged

The threat of the Japanese penetrating further west from Manchukuo was real, but was also used to eliminate any opposition to Comintern's directives. Opponents of the regime were accused of being Japanese spies and eliminated (often after having been tortured to confess that they were indeed Japanese spies). In 1937 the so-called "great purge" began with, the Little Khural and the council of ministers requesting the Soviet government to send military units of Red Army to counter the Japanese menace. They were directed by Stalin and the Central Committee, who had already decided to kill two birds with one stone and use the Japanese threat to stamp out any opposition to the absolute alignment of Mongolia to Stalinist Russia. Choibalsan, who had shown his worth by being instrumental in the liquidation of some of the politicians who favored a course that was more independent of the Soviet Union — incidentally his rivals — became the person to implement the purges. And so began the blackest chapter in the history of the independent nation of Mongolia.

At the beginning of the 20th century, about a third of the men were lamas — according to one author that had even risen to 48 percent by 1935. So many lamas meant that the whole population had relatives in the monasteries. Being a monk did not mean severing all contact with one's family: families of young monks would live near the monasteries and it was not unusual for monks to visit their families and assist during times when extra labor was needed. Lamas who married were, according to Shombodon, banished from the monasteries, but there were exceptions particularly for high-level lamas (not to forget the Bogd Khaan himself). At the time, the Buddhist religious structure was the most important threat to the power of the Communist Party, as it had been to the Manchus, because it had an organization, a coherent ideology, was held in high esteem and was organically connected to the general population.

Religion had no place in communist ideology and was referred to as the opium of the people in a text by Marx published in 1844. Lenin, whose theories had a more direct influence on politics and Mongolian thinking than those of Marx and Engels, reiterated this point in 1905: "Those who toil and live in want all their lives are taught by religion to be submissive and patient while here on earth, and to take comfort in the hope of a heavenly reward." Marxism-Leninism, being a militant ideology, did not approve of submissiveness and patience and, to this day, neither do the Mongols. The Buddhist power base threatened the new order and had to be eliminated. Accordingly, the eighth MPRP congress in 1930 referred to lamas as a parasitic class of feudal society representing an irreconcilable enemy of the Mongolian revolution.

The Dilowa Khutugtu was one of the three Buddhist leaders with the highest personal reputations at the time and as such he knew most of the important government leaders, referring to Choibalsan as "an old friend". He knew that he himself was a powerful symbol of the old order and consequently next in line to be purged. Well-informed, he was not surprised when, at the end of 1928, a government delegation came to his monastery to expropriate his possessions according to a decree that had been passed to the effect that capital in excess of one hundred bod (a uniquely Mongolian measurement for one's herd, the equivalent of one large or seven small animals) was to be expropriated from high-ranking officials. Shortly afterwards he was summoned to Ulaanbaatar, causing much lamentation among the apprehensive lamas of his monastery. In Ulaanbaatar he went to Gandan monastery where he was put up with a lama he knew. After waiting for some time, he presented himself to the government but was told to present himself to the Party; when he presented himself to the Party, he was told to present himself to the Little Khural. He ended up hanging around Ulaanbaatar for many months, not daring to go home without permission. Finally, in July 1930, he was told to report to the Department of Internal Security where he was questioned nine times over several months, then accused and arrested together with the Mansjuri lama and the Yegüzer lama. It is not clear what they were accused of, but a lengthy trial ensued. At the end of long and convoluted hearings 23 out of 38 accused were convicted, some sentenced to death, and the Dilowa himself received a suspended sentence of five years' imprisonment (according to one source it was 10 years). Early in 1931, on his way back to his monastery, he deviated south from his planned itinerary and crossed the border into China, understanding that it was only a matter of time before he would be arrested again and put to death.

By fleeing he escaped the second phase of the "struggle against religion", the first having been the confiscation of the properties of the monasteries. The second phase consisted of mass killings of lamas and the physical destruction of the monasteries. The struggle against religion took place at the same time as the struggle against the feudals and kulaks (remember that those terms were used for all opposition to the government, including many of the heroes who had taken part in liberating the country and who were its first-generation leaders). The modus operandi, according to Shombodon, was to send undercover provocateurs to the places where they were planning to make arrests to ferret out who should be picked up. This systematic work of arresting people was patterned after the methods of the Soviet KGB and carried out by the so-called "green hats" of Mongolia's Internal Security Agency, who were given quotas for their arrests.

According to Luvsanjamts, the green-hat people came three times to arrest people in his soum, Tsogt. The third time, they had to arrest a quota of 10 persons. They had compiled a list of who to arrest beforehand and went to the soum governor's office to discuss it. The governor had a beautiful portrait of Choibalsan painted on very thin cloth in his office and the visitors asked, "Who has made the portrait of Marshall Choibalsan?" The governor answered, "He is second on the list of people you are going to arrest." The painter was an illiterate lama who had been trained to make religious images of the Buddha. So the green hat man said "I can leave one" and left him alive; he lived long and died a natural death.

According to estimates (sources vary widely on the numbers) there were more than 100,000 lamas in the 1920s and around 73,000 by 1937. At the end of the 1930s about 35,000 lamas were arrested of whom some 15,000 were probably shot; others were imprisoned or became soldiers. The rest went home and were absorbed into the general population.

Virtually all the monasteries were utterly destroyed. Metallic objects from them were taken to Russia and melted for other uses, among them bullets for World War Two. The country was now a clean slate and its population sufficiently cowed to be ready for what was considered to be modern, scientific, planned development, with the assistance of big brother, the Soviet Union.

The minority Muslim religion was persecuted just as Buddhism was, as attested to by a 75- year-old Kazakh I spoke to who was born in 1937, the height of the purges, in Tsengel soum in what is now Bayan Olgi aimag. He told me that the Muslim religion was completely prohibited but that it was practiced in secret. He himself was not brought up very religiously; in any case he lived away from the Kazakh aimag of Bayan-Olgi most of his life and was married to an ethnic Mongol. I gather the only trace of the Muslim religion in his case was that he had learned to wash his hands five times a day, at prayer time (not that I think he prayed), before eating and certainly after going to the toilet. The Kazakhs used to have a special pot of water to wash hands in; they named that pot "human" and it was not used for anything else.

My father was a lama

Before the purges, the lamasery was well aware that things weren't going their way. We saw the Dilowa Khutugtu flee in 1931 and Shombodon told me that in 1935 his father, at 17, was sent home by his lama-uncles taking care of him in the monastery, well before the actual purges took place. Two of his three uncles were later killed and only the older lama-uncle, who was blind, survived. Shombodon's father-in-law, born around the turn of the century to a poor single mother, was a lama who served in the Zuun Choir monastery from an early age where he used to lead the religious chanting because of his good voice. He was about 37 when the police came and arrested his teacher. According to family stories, he angrily kicked the police who arrested him too: he was sentenced to 10 years in prison. Prisoners were useful as cheap labor and he was put to work building the so-called 40,000 living blocks (apartments for the workers) near the state department store in Ulaanbaatar.

After his release he came back to his soum, married a woman with two children and they had four more children together. He was elected bag governor, even though he was illiterate in Cyrillic (of course he knew Tibetan). As Cyrillic had only been introduced in 1941, there weren't many people who were able to use it, so he asked a literate man to assist him and paid him half of the monthly salary of 20 tögrögs he received for the service. Shombodon, who met his future father-in-law in 1969 when the latter was about 70, describes him as a tall and quiet man who secretly held religious ceremonies. There were five or six ex-lamas in the area of Choir and surrounding soums who had served in the Zuun Choir at the same time; they knew each other and occasionally met. He died in 1976 with his prayer-beads wound around his upper arm where his lama friends had advised him to keep them and so he passed away with his religious commitment intact.

In Luvsanjamts' family, religion had also gone underground. His father had been a Geleen, a high-ranking lama in his early 30s when the purges of the monasteries took place. He and his brother, also a lama, decided to flee to China together around 1936 and they had actually reached the border when their teacher told them that their home was important and advised them to go back. The teacher gave them a small picture of the Buddha in a silver frame and another small image of the Buddha to be worn around the neck. So they went home and, to avoid being arrested, they married and had kids.

There are two explanations for the fact that many of the people we interviewed had had fathers who were lamas. First, the more common reason for people born in the Forties and Fifties to have lama fathers and grandfathers is that the lamas who escaped being executed were sent home and subsequently married to avoid suspicion that they might still be hanging on to their religion. It must have been easy for the men who had been removed from the marriage market by entering the monasteries to find wives upon their return. Second, the vow of celibacy for lamas was never strictly enforced. For instance, the 77-year-old Mrs. Lkhamsuren, whom we will meet later, told me she was born in 1935 and that her father, a lama, was taken away in 1937 and didn't come back. She doesn't remember him and doesn't know anything else about him. My guess is that he must have been a high-level lama because they got away with not being celibate — and because they were the ones who were executed during the purges of the 1930s.

∗ ∗ ∗

July, 2012. Baldan Breeven. We visited the partially restored temple complex of Baldan Breeven after a long, slow and wet drive through the fertile green Khentiis — the rains were good that year — heading northeast to Dadal soum. Parts of the old monastery, dating from the 18th century, are being rebuilt. The surroundings are lovely and quiet, an open valley with a tranquil lake and the ruins against the verdant hills with pretty rock formations and larch forests. It is hard to believe there used to be a large town here but there was: I have found photos of the place as it was before it was destroyed in 1937 and was surprised to see that the settlement used to be all houses and hardly any gers; I hadn't expected that as I had found a few telltale stone circles of the foundations of gers around the temples. But the pictures show rows and rows of neatly arranged houses.

There we find Mr. Tserenpil, 77 years old, on active duty as a lama. He has hastened home to change out of his work-clothes and into his bright yellow-orange robes with matching cap when he caught sight of us — I recognize him because of his distinctive tiny white goatee. He tells us that his father, who was born in 1910, and his uncles had been lamas at this monastery. There were originally as many as 8000 lamas there. At the time of the purge there might have been about 3000 left, of whom 202 were arrested: of those, 131 were executed. His father was arrested and sent to serve as a medic in the military during the Khalkhin Gol battle against Japan.

As the son of a "counterrevolutionary" he was not allowed to go to school and became an autodidact who taught himself to read and write in Cyrillic and to do bookkeeping. His father, just like Shombodon's, had not wanted to teach his son Tibetan and he only started learning about Buddhism after the transition. The purges really did achieve the virtual elimination of religion as well as much knowledge and many of the traditions that were associated with Buddhism: medicine, Tibetan language, and access to the body of knowledge that came through Tibet instead of China.

Mr. Tserenpil worked as a herder all his life, became chief of a livestock brigade and later worked in a warehouse brigade and a bookkeeping brigade. He married — his wife passed away in 2005 — and has six sons and three daughters. In the 1980s he started learning about Buddhism and by 1987 he could read Tibetan. Now he is working as a lama in the monastery and living with an elderly lady as his wife.

So many Mongols are struggling to remember their lama ancestors and family members, and the beliefs they stood for. Shombodon's second cousin, Mr. Davagdorj, whom I met when we visited their home soum of Bugat, told me that the family didn't talk about his great-uncles who were lamas, that such things were kept secret in the past. What a loss of stories and of history! I shall leave the writing of a book about how the purges of the 1930s influenced people to a son or daughter of Mongolia — I have seen how deep the traumas of World War Two are buried in my own country.

In the early days of independence, attempts by the left to stamp out religion and to slavishly follow the Soviet Union rather than set out a uniquely Mongolian direction were not fully successful. These attempts, as explained by Shombodon, came in the form of "suggestions" that were given by Soviet organizations such as the Comintern. The early politicians believed they had a choice whether to accept those suggestions. In hindsight, however, the choice never really existed and politicians who did not accept the Soviet suggestions were executed, among them prime minister Genden in 1937 and ex-prime minister Amar in 1941. These politicians had not yet accepted that Mongolia had become a puppet-state of the Soviet Union and were eliminated: After the great purges only two of the 11 original Politburo members were still alive.

Socio-economic development in the Thirties

Due to political infighting and turmoil, the destruction of the old order and the growing focus on strengthening the military in order to confront the Japanese, progress on the economic front was slow. The military budget skyrocketed to 82 percent of the total (meager) government budget by 1939. Young Tsedenbal, who was to become the successor of Choibalsan and the longest-serving Mongolian head of state, took the job of finance minister at just 22 years old, and was in charge of the war budget. Young men, many of them ex-lamas, were conscripted into the military. Kazakhs were granted full citizenship in 1939, an underlying consideration being that they could now be conscripted as well. The Soviets instructed the Mongols to set aside an administrative unit for the Kazakh and the Uriankhai (ethnic minority tribes, including the Tuvans), an instruction that Choibalsan supervised himself. Bayan Olgi became a separate, Kazakh-dominated aimag in 1940.

The herders were basically left alone, so they dedicated themselves to what has today again become the main objective in their lives: enlarging their herds. The vast majority of the population continued to be illiterate — more so after the traditional centers of learning, the monasteries, had been wiped out. There were no health services in most areas and few in the cities. It must have been an unsettled time for the herders, whose lords and monasteries had disappeared together with their source of solace and support when things went wrong. Their ex-lama sons came home traumatized; other sons went to the military. Daughters might not have found husbands to start their own families with and stayed home to help their parents with tasks for which they didn't have enough labor. The population statistics tell the story: in 1930, the population was around 717,000 and slowly grew until 1937 when it reached 835,000. After that it declined for 10 years, reaching a low of 760,000 in 1947/48. Only by mid-century did it start growing again.

Even though the outcome of the power struggles might not have been clear to the people at the time — news spread by word of mouth and was surely embellished in the telling, particularly during the airag season — they had been definitively settled in the late 1920s. The country was going to develop along the examples and communist ideology of the Soviet Union, albeit more slowly than envisioned by the eager youngsters of the Mongolian Youth Organization who had led the struggles and came out as winners. Under the influence of the Soviet Union, western advisers and engineers, among them Germans, Danes and Swedes, were required to leave the country in 1929; Mongolian students were no longer sent to France and Germany. The country was firmly pulled into the Eastern Bloc. Workers were now sent for training to Ulaan Ude in the new Mongolian Workers Facility.

In 1933 the first negdel, or cooperative farm, was established in Alderkhaan soum, Zavkhan aimag, and by 1940 about a hundred negdels were a fact. The first negdels were formed on a voluntary basis. A few state farms were founded as well. More important, the first steps towards industrialization were taken: the Nalaikh coal mine was modernized in 1930 and the railroad to transport coal to Ulaanbaatar was built, laying the foundations for developing industries in the capital city. In 1934, the first Central Power Plant started operation in Ulaanbaatar. The Choibalsan industrial complex in Ulaanbaatar was opened with its own power plant, clothing factories, tanneries and a wool-scouring mill producing blankets, felt, footwear, leather coats and soap. In 1933 the State Trade Organization was established and in 1937 the Construction Trust.

Healthcare started improving in the 1930s as the national policlinic became operational and doctors were trained. Education was deemed crucial and by the early 1940s each soum had its primary school and there were 304 schools throughout the country, of which 209 had own buildings and the rest operated in gers. The printing house upgraded its machinery and by 1936 produced 12 million pages in print, up from only a thousand in 1921. At the end of 1930s, Mongolia had five regular newspapers and seven journals; 13 aimag centers and 20 soum centers had their own radio stations. On September 1 1934 regular national radio broadcasting began.

Western culture was introduced in this decade: foreign classics — Baabar mentions Defoe, Verne, Swift, Poe, Chekhov, Tolstoy and Pushkin — were translated into Mongolian and read by the few who could read; western musical instruments started appearing, many of them used for military-style marching bands; theater and cinema were introduced in Ulaanbaatar; and the western sports of skiing, skating, volleyball and soccer were added to the traditional repertory of wrestling, archery, horse racing and throwing anklebones. Mongolian writers, musicians, dancers and athletes wrote, composed and danced mixing these western imported culture with original Mongolian works. It must have been a heady time for the small urban elite in Ulaanbaatar!

Of course, life was quite different for the 90 percent of the population in the rural areas (mostly traditional herders), but even in the far-flung corners of the country the government made concerted efforts to uplift and enlighten the population. One of our interviewees, Tsevensuren, told us how culture was disseminated in the rural areas: "In the 1930s the Red Gers started. There was education, dancing, songs, lessons on how to make clothes, riddles, legends, concerts and music education. When they got gramophones the Red Gers became most attractive. People could listen to different songs! It was big progress! Some Red Gers were mobile and some soums had their own ger. The Red Gers later turned into 'red corners' in houses (there were 140 of them by 1941) and those turned into cultural clubs and assemblies. Then theaters were established." These are the music and drama theaters we see today in the aimag centers.

In 1940 a new constitution was adopted that took the Soviet constitution as its model. A remnant of the repressive times was that in this constitution "enemies of the regime" were not allowed to vote. The brave new world was a fact and the next excitement of the late Thirties/early Forties was provided by the war that provided an external enemy to focus on.

6. THE WAR AND ITS AFTERMATH

The battle of Khalkhin Gol

Khalkh Gol soum on the eastern border with China was the destination of our eastern trip in 2012 because it is the historically significant location where the battle of Khalkhin Gol took place in August of 1939. In Choibalsan, the aimag capital of the eastern aimag of Dornod, we found out that we should have obtained a permit from the military in Ulaanbaatar to visit the border areas where the battle was fought. We asked for the permit at the aimag military base that covered the eastern area but were denied so we hung out in town until Shombodon met an old friend who had some clout and two days and a few bottles of vodka later, after having respectfully put our request to several sympathetic officials, we received an official permit to visit Khalkh Gol.

24 July, 2012. We arrive at this remote outpost more than a thousand kilometers east of Ulaanbaatar one evening, dead-weary after a long day's drive, and find a mournful-looking settlement that looks as if it had been abandoned suddenly, which is essentially what happened at the time of the transition more than 20 years ago. The old apartment buildings have chimney-pipes sticking out of them because the power company of the soum went bankrupt in 1991 when the old infrastructure disintegrated during the transition, and the central heating system doesn't work anymore. A faded portrait of a dapper Lenin is still visible on the side of the local Khaan Bank branch.

We are directed to ask the museum for hotel rooms: there are a few available at the back of the museum. That is where we are happy to crash, on the thinnest matrass I've ever slept on. The next morning we take our bearings. The Khalkhin Gol Victory Museum commemorating the battle is a dilapidated light-blue building with a heroic frieze depicting victorious Mongolian and Russian soldiers, identified by the hammer and sickle and the Soyombo respectively, both topped by the red star, holding a burning flame and olive branches, against the rising sun and soaring doves. The building is cavernous and surrounded by weeds, an old tank, artillery and a potato-patch. Next to the side-entrance that led to the hotel rooms lies the fuel in the form of a huge pile of dung, which is what the soum centralized heating system has been replaced with. In places like Khalkh Gol, the transition didn't lead anywhere but oblivion.

We are welcomed by the director, Mr. Myagmasuren. A loud and large man with broad cheekbones, looking like a prototype Asian warrior, he is delighted with our visit and personally gives us a tour. He explains that this was a war between capitalism and communism because in 1936, Germany, Italy and Japan decided to fight against communisms and against the rest of the world. This is depicted on a world map with arrows originating in Germany and Japan pointing across the whole world. One of the first exhibits is a small statue of Sükhbaatar meeting Lenin in 1921. Apparently one of the delegation of five Mongols who had met Lenin in Moscow hailed from Khalkh Gol. I remember having seen a small plaque commemorating this meeting at the side of the Metropol hotel in Moscow, which was Lenin's headquarters at the time. Mr. Myagmasuren proceeds to show us the exhibits, maps, memorabilia and a show with light and sound effects representing the battle. At the end of our tour he hears that another group of visitors has just arrived: he goes to host them but tells us to come back the next morning at nine so he can lecture us some more about the soum's history. This he does with vigor, starting his story in the 17th century, relieving me of the worry of writing it all down, the period being beyond the scope of this book.

Mr. Myagmasuren tells us he is planning to research the war stories that are still being told in the area by the sons and daughters of soldiers. These stories are of spies disguised as herders looking for stray animals (of course, they were herders, except they weren't looking for lost livestock); of women catching Japanese spies by inviting them into their gers and entrapping them by plying them with alcohol; of lamas who had studied in a large monastery on the Manchurian side of the border going back and forth as spies. He himself is wondering how come he was born in ger that stood in front of the building that used to be Spy Department #3. His parents never said so, but he thinks that they were working for the spy department.

The week before our visit to Khalkh Gol, we interviewed a man whose father had fought at Hamar Dawa, the name of the small hill overlooking the Khalkh Gol river where General Zhukov, commander of the Mongolian-Russian army, had his headquarters. The father had been in the military for five years and had a lot of medals to show for it. His war stories, as told by his son, demonstrated the mixture of old and new warfare on the battlefield: his unit, handling horse-drawn artillery, was hiding in the tall feather grass to escape the Japanese bomber airplanes. He and his assistant stayed behind to pull out a piece of artillery stuck in the mud with two horses instead of the four normally required. His unit protected them and the bullets zooming around killed one of their horses, but they made it back to their unit where his commander said that it would have cost him his head if he had lost two of his men.

In the years leading up to the Khalkhin Gol battle several Japanese-Soviet conflicts took place on the border between Japanese-occupied Manchuria (renamed Manchukuo by the Japanese) and the Soviet Union. The Japanese also made a number of incursions into Mongolia, at one point in time coming within 70 kilometers of Choibalsan. They bombed the town on July 7 1939 (a painting in the museum depicts the bomb craters) and the very next day the Mongolian troops started their march towards the border. Both sides dug themselves in and started a build-up of troops on either side of the border, the Khalkh Gol ("gol" means river), in preparation for the final battle.

In May the government had already evacuated the civilian population from the area and the entire soum of Khalkh Gol had been moved to the aimag center Bayan Tumen, three hundred kilometers away. (Only in 1962 did the whole Khalkh Gol Soum move back). Many of the men were immediately hired back to serve as scouts and spies and to look after military horses. The town of Bayan Tumen was surrounded by an anti-tank iron fence as a precaution in case of attack, but it was not effective against bombs thrown from airplanes. Khalkhin Gol was one of the first battles that was heavily mechanized, with each side possessing about 400 tanks and 300 aircraft. Horses still played an important role because they performed better in the marshes around the river where tanks and heavy equipment tended to get mired down.

The Japanese Sixth Army was totally defeated in the Khalkhin Gol battle (which they called the Nomonhan incident) and driven out of Mongolia by the end of August 1939. This had far-reaching consequences for how World War Two was fought, as Stalin could now concentrate on the Western front without worrying about his back. Japan had to give up hope that it could push west through Mongolia and Siberia, which was the "Strike North" option that had dominated Japanese strategic thinking until then. This left them the "Strike South" option favored by their navy, involving attacks on the oil-rich Dutch East Indies (now Indonesia), Malaya, Burma and Indochina, while the colonial powers were neutralized or otherwise embroiled in the war. The one thing standing in their way was the US Pacific Fleet based at Pearl Harbor. . . So I learned something about World War Two by visiting one of the remotest places in Mongolia!

Japan's defeat also put an end to any hope of building a greater Mongolia with Inner Mongolia joining Outer Mongolia and possibly Buriatya, as the Japanese had promised. Russia had never been interested in extending its influence beyond the new People's Republic of Mongolia, and the objectives of the Inner Mongols who wanted to preserve their traditional identity, and of the new republic which wanted to build a new socialist society, had diverged.

According to Mr. Myagmasuren, 22,000 Japanese were taken prisoner. Some actually fled towards the enemy, either because they were afraid of being killed for their defeat or because defeat in itself was so dishonorable that it warranted suicide. The Japanese prisoners were put to work on the 40,000 living blocks (just like Shombodon's father-in-law) as well as on the construction of the Peace Bridge and other public works. Mongolia and Japan only established diplomatic relations in 1972, but they are now very close. There is still a cemetery of Japanese soldiers just outside of Ulaanbaatar; the Japanese author Haruki Murakami visited the battlefield and wrote about it in his 1995 novel *The Wind-up Bird Chronicle*

Choibalsan

The town of Choibalsan is named after the most influential Mongolian leader of the 20th century. While hanging around trying to get permission to visit Khalkh Gol, I visited the local museum where two of Choibalsan's private offices are preserved. One is a ceremonial office with the requisite portrait of Stalin behind his chair, an early record player encased in a piece of furniture with ample space for a liquor cabinet, a photograph of Choibalsan posing with wolves he shot, and a smaller, working office. It was here that I found a curious exhibit: some of his ashes, neatly poured into two miniature Buddhist-style stupa-like golden urns about 15 centimeters high. Since his death in 1952, his body had been preserved and been lying Lenin-style in the mausoleum in front of Parliament House on Chinggis Khaan Square, together with the body of the national hero Sükhbaatar, whose body had originally been buried in 1923 and exhumed in 1952 to lie in the mausoleum together with Choibalsan. In 2005, the corpses of both rulers were ritually burned, under supervision of the Buddhist clergy.

Choibalsan was born in 1895 in Dornod aimag to a single mother (not at all unusual at the time, as we have seen) and sent to the local monastery at 13. Five years later he ran away to the capital where he was fortunate to attend the Russian school for translators. When he was 19 he was chosen to attend a high school in Irkutsk, Siberia. He became a member of the Consular Hill resistance group around 1918. As one of the trusted first revolutionaries who was educated and spoke Russian, he was a member of the delegation that traveled to Russia in 1920 to seek assistance from the Bolsheviks. From 1921 onward, he held positions of power, starting as a member of the provisional revolutionary government and political commissar of the Mongolian People's Army and continuing in positions such as head of the commission that confiscated feudal property, chairman of the Central Committee of the Revolutionary Youth League, member of the Presidium of the Central Committee of the MPRP, Minister of War and Commander in Chief — to name some. He was appointed Prime Minister in 1939, after which he held near-absolute power until his death in 1952. He imitated Stalin in many ways, including in the building of a personality cult.

He cannily (and luckily) weathered the power struggles of the Twenties until he was hand-picked by Kliment Voroshilov, Russia's commissar for military affairs, as a useful agent for the Soviet Union to gain control over Mongolia. In the early 1930s, when he was minister of livestock and agriculture, he was taken to Moscow as a suspect in the "Lkhümbe affair" where he was probably turned and ended up participating in torturing his former comrades. Lkhümbe, who had been the secretary of the Central Committee of the MPRP in 1932, was falsely accused of being part of a conspiracy of Japanese spies involving hundreds of people, most of them from Dadal soum, Khentii Aimag and Ulaanbaatar. The affair, officially referred to as "The Case of Counter-Revolutionaries and Japanese Spies", ended up with 56 people executed, 260 sent to prison for between 3 to 10 years, and 126 taken to the USSR (I assume they did not survive their visit). Of the 317 persons prosecuted, 251 were Buriats.

Mongolian Buriats were mistrusted by the Russians because many of them had fought on the side of the White Russians against the winning Bolshevik side and had probably moved to Mongolia to avoid retribution. They might have been mistrusted by Khalkh Mongols as well because they were from a different ethnic group. Baabar states that the Lkhümbe affair was deliberately used by the Russians to thrust a wedge between Khalkhs and Buriats. As a consequence, a disproportionate number of Buriats were accused of being in favor of pan-Mongolism and of being Japanese spies, and were executed during the purges.

After the Lkhümbe affair, Choibalsan was personally groomed by Stalin to be the next Mongolian leader who would do the bidding of the Soviet Union. This involved getting rid of anyone who so much as questioned the official Soviet party line. As was the case with the Ja Lama, myths build around important persons and it is impossible to truly separate truth from those myths. One myth is that Stalin presented Choibalsan with four rifles and 30,000 bullets for the occasion of the 15th anniversary of the Mongolian Revolution and that 30,000 people were subsequently killed.

By the end of 1939 it was decided by Moscow that the purges had served their purpose as Mongolia was now a classless and atheist society. So they had to be stopped and the persons directly involved in them were eliminated, purged in turn. A carefully choreographed national conference was held in which Russian trainers, Choibalsan himself and the chairman of the Central Committee admitted that some zealots had gone too far by persecuting innocent people. The

Special Commission in charge of arrests, show-trials and executions was dismantled and the witnesses and participants in the purges, as well as the last political opponents, were now executed themselves. Only infrequent arrests and executions took place in the years that followed. In 1940 Choibalsan received the Order of Lenin from his friend Stalin.

Choibalsan died in 1952, having been Mongolia's virtual dictator for 13 years. Contradictory ideas and information as to his ideas and role in history linger. He was originally trained as a Buddhist monk (Choibalsan was his religious name), but religion was utterly destroyed under his leadership. He was a slavish follower of the Soviet Union, imposing the Soviet blueprint for society on Mongolia, yet is widely seen as the person who managed to preserve Mongolia's independence in the face of pressure to join the USSR. He assumed the same mystique of a benevolent father as Stalin did, but was responsible for "the great terror". As happened in Russia with Stalin, who died one year after him, Choibalsan's "cult of personality" and "excesses of the late 1930s" were criticized by the Central Committee after his death.

Prevailing Mongolian thinking is that Choibalsan's nationalism kept Mongolia from becoming a Soviet republic such as Tuva Tannu (it probably had a lot to do with the USSR not wanting to rock the boat with China); that he stood up to Stalin on that issue (I have heard that he actually slapped Stalin but that might well be a myth), which led to a falling out with his former mentor. For this reason, and because living standards improved during his rule, many Mongols still consider him a hero despite his role in the slaughter of thousands of Mongols. His life-sized statue still stands at the entrance of the National University of Mongolia.

Once two friends of mine, a husband and wife, both born in the early Fifties and so must have had their information from their parents or their contemporaries, told me: "Choibalsan died before Tsagaan Sar [lunar new year] and we were not allowed to celebrate it that year because father Choibalsan had died. He saved Mongolia from bad things when pressured by the Soviet Union. Choibalsan would visit poor people without letting people prepare for his visit." They clearly had an image of a benevolent and humble "father Choibalsan".

After Choibalsan's death, Y. Tsedenbal became Prime Minister. Tsedenbal had been a close ally of Choibalsan and as such his natural successor; he was also one of the few Mongols known to Stalin. He had spent the decisive part of his youth, from 13 to 22, in Siberia (Irkutsk and Ulan Ude), where he graduated from the Siberian Finance and Economics Institute. In 1940, the year after he came back to Ulaanbaatar, he became the General Secretary of the MPRP at age 23. He was nearly Russian in his thinking, was married to a Russian woman and was strongly in favor of close collaboration with the Soviet Union. He had also been an accomplice (and beneficiary) of Choibalsan's ruthless purges. In short, he was the perfect choice.

Relations with the USSR, Japan and China

One of Ulaanbaatar's many quirky monuments — the arts are held in high esteem by the Mongols and there are monuments, statues and works of art spread through the city — is a World War Two tank said to have been among the first to enter Berlin at the end of the war. Its base shows the route it took from Moscow in 1943 to Berlin in 1945. The monument was benignly moldering away at the far east of town when I first arrived but has since been spiffed up and moved to a more auspicious location at the entrance of Zaizan valley, at the foot of the sacred Bogd mountain, in curious juxtaposition with the ostentatious giant gilded Buddha that was erected in 2006. Apparently some Mongols served in the Soviet armed forces: there are accounts of Mongols entering Berlin at its fall.

Mongolia maintained formal neutrality until the very end of the war while at the same time strongly supporting the Soviet Union. After the Khalkhin Gol battle, in 1941 the Soviet Union and Japan signed agreements to respect the Mongolian border with Manchukuo and to keep a neutral stance towards each other. This enabled Stalin to transfer the brilliant General Zhukov to the Western front where he subsequently became world-famous by winning the battles of Moscow (1941), Stalingrad (1942) and finally Berlin (1945). The agreement brought calm and enduring peace to Mongolia.

Informally, Mongolia wasn't neutral: it supported the Soviet Union by providing funds, goods and financing a column of 53 tanks, the Revolutionary Mongolia tank brigade (is this where the tank as statue came from, I wonder?), and the "Herdsman aircraft squadron". It generously gave horses, cattle, meat, leather, sheepskin and fur-lined clothes, as well as gold and other precious metals (much of it plundered from the monasteries), depleting its national herd from 27.5 million in 1941 to 20.9 million in 1945.

Towards the end of the war, during the Yalta conference of February 1945 between Churchill, Roosevelt and Stalin, the Soviet Union negotiated to preserve the status quo in Mongolia, which to Stalin meant de facto Soviet control. To Roosevelt it meant that Mongolia would be an integral part of China as according to the 1924 Sino-Soviet treaty, but Stalin's interpretation prevailed: China had not attended the conference.

Mongolia moved further under the influence of the USSR. Later that year it followed the USSR in declaring war on Japan and joining its armed forces with the Soviets to invade Inner Mongolia and Manchukuo. Stalin, presumably as a gesture of thanks, dispatched more than 32,000 Japanese POWs to Mongolia at the end of the war to assist with reconstruction projects. These included the National Mongolian Library, dedicated to Stalin, whose statue stood in front of the building for nearly 40 years until it was taken down in 1992, in the early transition days. A statue of the Mongolian scholar Rinchen, who spent time in prison in the 1930s, now symbolizes a new era.

Japan and Mongolia half-heartedly resumed diplomatic relations in 1972, but these only became warm and friendly after the transition of 1990. By the time I started working in Mongolia Japan had become an important donor. Indeed, one of my own projects, the IFC Mongolia Leasing project (2004-2006), was financed by the Japanese Treasury Department. (IFC is the International Finance Corporation, an organization within the World Bank.) I recently came across an article on the internet (http://bit.ly/2zdKZnf) from 2012 about celebrating the 40-year anniversary of the diplomatic relations between Japan and Mongolia. A 94-year old Sharav was featured: he was mobilized into the Khentii tank unit in 1944 and fought against the Japanese 300 kilometers from Yandui monastery in the Tengger desert in Inner Mongolia. From the end of the war in 1945 he worked for the government agency for Japanese prisoners of war until the POWs were sent home in 1947. The article said there were over a thousand Japanese POWs who were put to work on building, logging and brick-making. At the brick-making factory Sharav performed a small kindness to the POWs who did not have sufficiently warm clothes, just the uniform they had been captured with, and intervened with the factory director to allow them to take two hot bricks to bed at night to keep them from freezing. Generally he looked well after his charges even though he was criticized for it by his countrymen. The Japanese responded in kind: on one occasion a Japanese POW approached him while he was sleeping and took his gun. Instead of shooting him, he balanced it against a tree and hung his jacket over the gun to provide shade. Much was made of this little history now that Japan and Mongolia have friendly relations.

In the Sino-Soviet Treaty of Friendship and Alliance of August 1945, the Republic of China, on the brink of its own civil war, agreed to Mongolian independence provided a plebiscite confirmed the people were in favor. This plebiscite was to save face for the Chinese leader Chiang Kai-shek, as no one could doubt which way the Mongols would vote. On January 5 1946, after 100 percent of the 487,400 ballots were cast in favor, China recognized Mongolian independence. The voting process was rigged by Choibalsan to achieve the 100 percent, demonstrating the authoritarian mindset of the regime as well as its lack of political sophistication — the vote needed no rigging whatsoever. The Soviet Union affirmed that it would respect the MPR's independence.

China had more or less recognized Mongolia's independence in the 1946 Sino-Soviet treaty of friendship, but the two countries had no diplomatic relations and China continued to include Mongolia as a part of Chinese territories on its maps — which was only discontinued in 2002. When the Republic of China subsequently had to retreat to Taiwan in 1949, where it resides today, Mongolia expediently recognized the People's Republic of China, its next-door neighbor, with which it exchanged ambassadors in 1950.

Despite agreements affirming Mongolia's independence, Soviet and Mongol troops repeatedly clashed with the Kuomintang forces, consisting mainly of Muslim Kazakh and Chinese troops, over the southwestern border between Mongolia and China. These clashes took place in 1947 and 1948 and were of little consequence because Mongolia, together with its Soviet big brother, was able to maintain its border where it was. The clashes were mentioned twice in interviews when people talked about their parents. Shombodon's father, who was in the military at the time, had had to trek 2000 kilometers in 45 days with horses from Khentii to the border to reach the zone of conflict. This must have been a horrific trek because it took place in late winter: the horses became too weak to ride and the men walked.

The skirmishes took place in a sparsely populated region in the Gobi that deserves the word remote even in the Mongolian context. Shombodon's home soum, Bugat, is there and despite our intentions to visit it years earlier we had never before made it because the high pass you need to go over to get there was snowed under each time we were more or less in the neighborhood — meaning within a day's drive.

Bugat Soum

24 August 2012. We finally get a chance to visit Bugat soum and the road turns out to be good. There is even a new stretch of perfect asphalt from nowhere to the Chinese border, courtesy of a Chinese-owned mine. The drive is spectacular: we pass by the 4000m snow-topped mountain called Suutai Uul, sacred of course, "in front of" (this means to the south of) which Shombodon's father was born; we pass through Tonkhil soum territory where his monastery once stood; we drive by rock drawings, 2000-year-old graves and 3000-year-old deerstones (ancient megaliths depicting leaping reindeer with ornate curling antlers flowing over their backs, found in Mongolia, Siberia and parts of Central Asia); and we find a road down a pass that has been hollowed out over the course of centuries by camel-trains. People have lived here forever! Most colors are represented in the majestic Gobi desert landscapes: black, grey, red, oranges and tans in the mountains with splashes of bright yellow and orange lichens, and surprisingly we also pass by some flat light-green gobis and even lakes and dark-green meadows. At one point we look down on the traces of a large socialist-era crop field where the fragile Gobi ecosystem hasn't managed to recover yet.

We are not sure where the road is and stop at a ger to get directions; there is some pointing and a lively discussion and we are off again. I wouldn't have known how to describe to anyone where to go in that wild empty immensity but Shombodon and Enkhbayar have no problems whatsoever. It is nearly dark so we camp in a cold and barren place; I pitch my tent next to a bleached horse skull close to remnants of old stone buildings or animal enclosures. Shombodon tells me that this is the area where the soldiers, among them his father, were stationed when they fought the Chinese and Kazakhs in the Forties. The next day we visit the former campsite of Shombodon's family high in the mountains. It sits smack in the middle of a field of deerstones and ancient graves. These graves are scattered all over the country, thousands upon thousands of them, large piles of boulders with either a square or circle laid out with stones around it. They were built by the Khunnu (or Xiongnu in Chinese) people who lived in an area slightly larger than modern-day Mongolia from around 200 BC to 150 AD.

What strikes me most in this inhospitable environment is the toughness of the people who live here. Think of the soldiers who trekked across the whole country in winter when night temperatures are usually below -25°C and sometimes dip as low as -40°C, and daytime temperatures only slightly higher. Did they sleep in tents? A friend who used to be a captain in the army told us about learning to sleep out in winter without a tent or sleeping bag: they just dug themselves in. I don't think he exaggerated; he convincingly demonstrated his toughness to me by running the extremely difficult Khovsgol marathon ("Mongolia Sunrise to Sunset") barefoot while smoking a pack of cigarettes. I think about the tough little Mongolian horses as well: although they are much appreciated and loved, they have a hard life. In winter they fend for themselves, now as in the past, and in early spring they are sometimes too weak to ride. One fine spring day I rented a horse but shortly thereafter pitied the thin animal so much that I walked it back to its owners.

We go on over another high pass to the desolate Bugat soum center. The landscape here is shockingly wild and barren with menacing black formations and I marvel at the fact that it even occurred to anyone to build any kind of settlement there. It is nestled in a craggy desert valley of dark black and reddish rock formations, the only green a tiny, square, fenced park between an official-looking yellow building and the pink-and-white-striped museum. It always strikes me how proud the Mongols are of their soum of origin: a museum for this tiny, remote desolate settlement? But here it is and we get the tour. An interview I do with the chairman of the soum council of elders takes place in the soum's hall of fame where there are pictures of the Bugat men (nearly all men) who have achieved something in life. Shombodon's picture is there too. There are large neatly-piled dung heaps in the fenced yards and a large solar panel installation. There is nothing left of the negdel (agricultural cooperative) building or the procurement office where Shombodon's father once worked. Just outside the soum center mud bricks are being made: in this climate there is no need to fire them.

The Cold War

During World War Two Mongolia's undeveloped economy bore the substantial burden of assisting the Russian war effort and maintaining a large army, which delayed its own much-needed economic development. Basically, it exported everything it produced to the Soviet Union, decreasing its herds, in particular its cattle, and had no capital to kick-start their industrial development. After the war, the country, from our western point of view, faded away as it became part of the Second World, as the Eastern Bloc was referred to. To me, the obscure world. The term Eastern Bloc is connected to the period known as the Cold War. By the 1950s the world was firmly divided into the capitalist Western Bloc, led by the United States, and the communist Eastern Bloc led by the Soviet Union. The main feature of the Cold War was the segregation of the two blocs, their intense rivalry that manifested itself in the space race, the race to produce nuclear weapons, and open clashes between communism and capitalism in places like Korea and Vietnam. Within the main blocs, however, this was a period of peace, post-war reconstruction and increased prosperity.

The country became a fully integrated part of the Eastern Bloc albeit a dependent part. It started receiving aid from its Eastern Bloc allies, but those who referred to its economic relations with the USSR as economic exploitation were right. Any and all opposition to the Soviet-style socialist system had been eliminated and internally the country was in peace. Choibalsan's successor Tsedenbal generally continued in the direction set out earlier so politically there is not much exciting to report. The period 1940-1960 was officially referred to as the period of "building the foundation of socialism" by government.

Calm descended on Mongolia as its two neighbors, China and the USSR, fellow communist countries with friendly relations, accepted its independence (under de facto control of the Soviet Union), Japan was out of the picture, and a stable, albeit authoritarian, regime was firmly in control. After Mao came to power in 1949, China recognized Mongolia and established diplomatic relations, quickly followed by economic relations through a Sino-Mongolian Economic Agreement of 1952 offering Mongolia what it most needed: capital and manpower. That year China, Mongolia and the Soviet Union also agreed to build the trans-Mongolia railroad and by the late Fifties tens of thousands of Chinese laborers were building showcase buildings (the State Department Store, a sports stadium, hospital and industrial projects) in Ulaanbaatar.

The Mongolian Border forces were dissolved in 1953 because there was no perceived threat from the southern neighbor and in 1956 Soviet troops were withdrawn from Mongolian territory, presumably for the same reason. By the mid-Fifties Chinese influence was at a high while Soviet influence was lower because the Soviet Union's focus was on rebuilding its economy and dealing with the uncertainty of who would succeed Stalin. Mongolian leaders were temporarily less tightly supervised by the Soviet Union and in 1960 Mongolia even signed a Treaty of Friendship and Mutual Assistance with the Peoples Republic of China. The Republic of China (in Taiwan), however, still influenced Mongolia's position in the world by vetoing a proposal to give it a seat in the UN.

By the mid 1950s the population finally started growing for a number of reasons: there was peace at last, death rates had plummeted as a result of improved medical services, ex-lamas and demobilized soldiers started families, and the hard work of laying the foundations of a modern economy finally started to pay dividends. People had every reason to believe that their lives would continue to improve. There are definite parallels between the general atmosphere of optimism in Europe in the 1950s and in Mongolia. I am of that upbeat boomer generation too. Traumas caused by the terror years (just like the war in Europe) were buried and children were shielded from its knowledge.

None of my interviews or books I read tell me anything about what most Mongols were thinking and talking about at the time but I can visualize how they lived: their primitive small gers with open fires in which they slept on hides on the dirt floor, the young animals taking up half the already cramped living space and filling the ger with the pungent smell of their urine and feces. The older generations had seen great changes in their lifetime: independence and the subsequent chaos in the teens, the extermination of their old religion, the forceful appearance of newfangled political ideas, the battle of Khalkhin Gol and the nation's support of Russia in World War Two. They must have wondered what was to come next, while they were busy surviving, reintegrating their ex-lama uncles, brothers and sons, and trying to understand the new society that was being built around them.

7. POST-WAR PEACE AND PROSPERITY

Education

July 2012. On the road. In the car driving back from eastern Mongolia, I am in a stupor, daydreaming and staring at the ever-changing patterns the clouds make. Mainly they resemble curling dragons. Enkhbayar is driving, David is sitting next to him, relaxed and still like the Buddha, and Shombodon is sitting next to me quietly giving directions from the back when Enkhbayar tries to decide which one of the many faint tracks to follow across the steppe. None of the tracks looks like it is going anywhere at all in the immense landscape and yet we drive right up to the door of the ger of Shombodon's old friend Mrs. Lkhamsuren. The diminutive wrinkled old lady lives in the ger next to her daughter and three grandsons, one of whom welcomes us with a lovely smile, holding the dog. She is avidly listening to the 2012 Summer Olympic Games on the radio when we arrive and is pleased to see Shombodon, who used to work in this area as a young man.

Mrs. Lkhamsuren was born in 1935 and graduated from primary school in 1949. She tells us that Mongolia was trying to become an educated country so all children had to go to school. She describes the one she went to as a house with a stove. Of the 22 children in her grade, 13 were boarding in the two gers that served as dormitories, one for the seven boys and one for the six girls. The gers were heated, they slept on wooden beds, and a cook provided their meals. She lived in that dormitory for three years and liked it: they had good food and it was warm. Breakfast was salty milk tea and cookies. Lunch was usually buuz (steamed mutton dumplings) or khuushuur (fried mutton dumplings). It was good! They ate no vegetables! I have lived in

Mongolia long enough to understand the point she is making: no vegetables means really good! Herder households had to prepare fuel for the school. They did their job well: there were some elm trees by the soum, which were cut and transported by camels to the school. (Here my environmentalist mind whispers: "Cut any of the few trees in this area? You must be kidding me!")

Not only were their basic needs met, but they played chess and checkers (the latter played on a chessboard) and the more traditional anklebones. They also did gymnastics, long jump, high jump, and running, and went on environmental excursions. She became a member of the Children Pioneers in the second grade and they marched to drums, mandolin and accordion, and they danced. The school organized a concert for the New Year and the first of May (Labor Day). Their school had a cultural center called "red corner" and also a silent cinema. At this point she exclaims with wonder that nowadays people have television in their gers! She didn't race horses very often, only twice when she was 12 and 13, because before that the family didn't have many horses to race. She trained yearlings and two-year-old horses for her uncle, as well as one, two and three-year-old camels, mentioning that she was useful to the uncle who had adopted her. I have flashbacks of growing up (in Libya): no television, country dancing, singing, playing chess and checkers, riding the polo ponies of the British officers, Girl Guides, nature excursions, camping out.

Education, considered a key element of building the foundation of socialism, had started to receive serious attention but not all children went to school yet in the Forties and Fifties. Mrs. Lkhamsuren lived in the more developed center of the country only 200 kilometers southeast of Ulaanbaatar and relatively close to the railroad, but the situation was different in more remote parts of the country. Shombodon's former boss, who was born in 1938, told me the next day that schools had not been very accessible in Gobi Altai where his family came from and some herders didn't want their children to go to school because of the labor shortage. His older brother had no schooling, two of his younger sisters went only to primary school and one to secondary school. He himself was lucky because, after his mother died when he was 10, his uncle helped out by bringing him to the aimag center for schooling where he graduated from 10th grade, after which he went to the Agricultural University in Ulaanbaatar.

School attendance had been low through the Thirties and estimates of literacy rates vary from 10 to 25 percent around 1940 because the government had been using most of its education budget for the training of Party cadres. The percentage of school-age children attending school jumped from approximately 10 percent in 1939 to 30 percent in 1940 to 65 percent in 1947. In 1941 the Cyrillic script was formally introduced, albeit slightly modified to suit the phonetics of the Mongolian language, the war delayed general adoption until 1946. By 1950 Cyrillic was the only script to be used for official business.

The first large-scale literacy program was launched in 1947. The government appointed a literacy teacher in each soum and made it compulsory for every organization or enterprise to provide literacy training for its employees. In the years that followed, the government, acknowledging that the country's human resources needed to be developed, allocated nearly 65 percent of the state budget for the years 1948-1952 (its first Five-Year Plan) to education, health services, and social and cultural purposes such as establishing cinemas and libraries. The country's first university, the Mongolian State University, was established in Ulaanbaatar in 1942 with faculties of veterinary sciences, medicine and pedagogy; it had 90 students to start with. Teachers were trained and primary schools became more readily accessible; during the second Five-Year Plan (1953-1957) elementary education became compulsory. By the end of the decade each aimag center had secondary school and around 40 percent of students were accommodated in dormitories. Girls in particular benefitted from the education drive as they were targeted on equal footing with boys — which, of course, had not been the case before.

So the seeds of western science and thinking were planted in the Mongolian mind. The Russian (basically European) school system was transplanted in its totality to Mongolia because there was no Mongolian education system; the latter had ceased to exist when the Buddhist centers of learning were destroyed. My own European primary and secondary education probably resembled closely that of the Mongols of my generation. Mine was old-fashioned but solid (nearly identical to that of my grandparents) and I believe must have been the same as the Russian schools of the period (apart from the

Marxism-Leninism that was presented to the Mongols as the truth and to me at university as a social theory). This enabled me to feel the kinship and communicate easily with the Mongols — to my surprise. Imagine the first time I visited a ger after days of driving through the empty landscape. We waited for the dog to be held and an invitation to come in. I had been instructed on how to behave in the ger and expected the same degree of ignorance about the greater world and the kind of traditional thinking I had found in remote areas of Africa and South America. But no: they asked me if I had brought a newspaper (I had not, to my embarrassment), knew perfectly well where my country was located (try that in a Salt Lake City supermarket!) and the elderly grandfather in traditional deel who looked like Chinggis Khaan's father had studied to be a tractor driver in Irkutsk after completing secondary school.

The socialist system notwithstanding, parents held on to traditional ideas of child-rearing and the need to learn basic life skills such as riding horses, herding and orienting themselves in the immense empty landscape before going to school. Schools were often far from herding camps and six-year-olds were considered too little to live away from their mothers. Consequently, children in rural areas generally started school at eight or nine. Formal education was considered essential for children to get ahead but the Mongols appear to have been more flexible and practical during their socialist past than now: After transition the compulsory school-going age went down to six; at the same time boarding schools became scarce and expensive. As a result, herder households often split up: the women and children live in a soum (or aimag) center while the men are far away with their herds. This is particularly hard on the men who now come back to a cold ger and no cooked food after a grueling icy-cold day out herding. Then they have to perform the traditionally female chores of milking and processing dairy products as well. Shombodon told me that the men also worry about what their wives are up to in town where they don't have to look after the animals and there are opportunities for going out and meeting other men.

Socialist planning

Looking back at what Mongolia achieved in the 20th century, I cannot but admire all that was accomplished, taking into account the extremely low level of socio-economic development at the start.

From the late Twenties onward the government set a series of long-term goals and pursued these through a Soviet-style planning process. Planning was, as the term implies, key to building the socialist "centrally planned economy". The strategy for achieving the ultimate goal of industrialization was to simultaneously develop human capital and increase income for investments by modernizing the livestock sector. The national plans of the countries of the Soviet bloc were generally coordinated with those of the Soviet Union: after its second Five-Year Plan ended in 1957 Mongolia inserted a Three-Year Plan (1958-1960) so that from 1961 its plans would coincide with those of the USSR.

Five-year plans set the overall economic and social goals of the country and these were then broken down by region and sector. In theory, the national planning process started at the lowest level and the plans were compiled, first at aimag level and then at the national level. In practice the process was more top-down: the Congress of the Mongolian People's Revolutionary Party (the only Party, of course) would assess the accomplishment of the previous planning period and set general guidelines and goals for the next five years. The State Planning and Economic Committee and the Ministry of Finance then allocated these goals to relevant ministries, committees and local authorities, who planned their targets and calculated their budgets and then the lower-level plans were compiled into a national plan. The result was the national Five-Year Plan that set targets and quotas for all sectors of the economy, at local, regional and national levels; detailed one-year plans were then based on the overall five-year plan. The system was not just an economic planning mechanism: all aspects of life, social, cultural, health and education, science and technology were part of the national plan. The five-year and one-year plans were then approved by the People's Ikh Khural passing them into law and budgeted for. In the Fifties much of the aid for the implementation of these plans came from China under Mao.

The goal of building a developed industrialized country had been there from the beginning of the People's Republic of Mongolia, but the strategy became more effective after the earlier failed attempts to centrally plan development. The overall strategy, taking into account Mongolia's peculiarity of harboring a small population supported by huge herds of livestock, involved a progression of goals. During the first Five-Year Plan the national herd would be increased in order to export livestock products and raise money for light industries. The second Five-Year Plan, in turn, involved doubling the output of light industry; subsequent plans gradually introduced and developed heavy industry.

Forward-thinking socialists envisaged full collectivization of herding, development of mining, industrialization and introduction of modern crop-farming through state-owned enterprises, as well as building the infrastructure that would connect Mongolia to the rest of the (socialist) world. This meant a radical social revolution, as traditional nomadic herding, the only lifestyle 99 percent of Mongolians were familiar with, was deemed primitive, barbaric, a danger to stability, and an impediment to civilized development.

Physical infrastructure was put into place to enable this industrial revolution. The Trans-Mongolia railway connecting the Trans-Siberian railway with China, which had started from the north in 1947, reached Ulaanbaatar in 1950, the Chinese border in 1955 and Beijing in 1961. Other infrastructure projects of the 1950s included roads, bridges, housing, and electrification. The Nalaikh coal mine, supplying coal to the capital city, was modernized; industrial centers were upgraded. A process of decentralization also started; processing plants for food, wood, leather and felt were established in the aimag centers.

Collectivization of the livestock sector

The ideal socialist economy was to be based on two types of ownership: state-owned enterprises and cooperatives. State-owned enterprises were established in the industry and infrastructure sectors that were to become the mainstay of economic development; and in the agriculture sector as state farms. In contrast to what happened in western countries that became communist, there were no industrial enterprises or companies that could be expropriated and converted into state-owned enterprises. The companies that were established, therefore, started as state-owned enterprises and were dependent on the state budget from the beginning. Everyone else — and that meant mostly the dispersed herder households — would be forced into ("voluntarily") joining the agricultural cooperatives called negdels from the late 1940s onward.

After the war, renewed efforts to implement collectivization of the livestock sector met with more success than the catastrophic attempts that had been made around 1930. The main collectivization drives took place between 1955 and 1958; by the end of the Fifties the process was complete: All herders had joined negdels, turned in their private animals and had been put to work in their negdel. Households were allowed to keep a small number of animals for themselves, according to certain rules. When a negdel was formed in a soum, the process was started off by "agitators", who tried to get support for the whole idea. The word to agitate came up frequently during the interviews — it refers to the practice of using "agitation propaganda" or simply "agitprop" that was used to divulge communist propaganda, ideas and information and get people to subscribe to those ideas. Agitprop started off as a propaganda tool during the revolutionary period and was thereafter used in the Soviet Union and its satellites to consolidate and maintain power by influencing people's thinking and emotions. So the process of forming a negdel started with agitators espousing the benefits of negdels and communal ownership of the means of production — and in Mongolia the means of production were animals.

Herders whose main objective in life had been to grow their herds were generally not very sympathetic to the idea of handing over their pride and joy, not to mention sole livelihood. Nevertheless, amazingly, the whole population joined the negdels in a very a short time, revolutionizing not only the economy, but the whole social fabric as well. I wondered if memories of what happened when one did not agree with Party and government played a role in people voluntarily joining the negdels, so I decided to ask people about it.

10 August 2012. On another grey and rainy day (2012 is an exceptionally wet year) we visit an old friend of Shombodon, Mr. Dugersuren and his wife Barbara — not a Mongol name. She turns out to be Yakut, from Siberia. They are retired and live in a neat red-brick cottage in a lush green valley near the northern mining town of Erdenet, where they grow flowers, vegetables, berries, shrubs and trees on about a hectare of land. We are warmly greeted, taken on a tour of the gardens and ushered into their spotless and inviting home where we drink milk

tea. They demonstrate the easy no-fuss hospitality I have gotten used to in Mongolia where starting a conversation is never an issue.

Mr. Dugersuren commences by stating: "As an intellectual it is pleasant to think and talk history." He and his wife guided foreign participants of a scientific conference around the Western Aimags of Uvs, Khovd and Bayan-Olgi earlier that year. He has written a book about the history of his native Bugat soum, which is also Shombodon's home soum. Mr. Dugersuren, born in 1948 in Bugat soum, explained how the collectivization process took place: "My parents were private herders until 1958 when I was 10. The household had more than 500 small animals and more than 50 large animals before the negdel and then gave 400 small and 50 large animals to the negdel when it joined. That was not nice but people had agitated for joining the negdel and they followed the example of other households. After collectivization the household was left with 100 small animals. My father's brother-in-law had more than 1000 animals and refused to join and moved to Altai soum, which didn't have a negdel yet. When a negdel was established there, he was the last to join. My grandparents and parents also disliked the liquidation of private property."

$$* \ * \ *$$

Other interviewees also remembered exactly how many animals their parents gave to the negdel when they joined. For instance, an ethnic Kazakh, Mr. Stanboul, whom we met the next day told me: "My parents became negdel members in 1958 and gave 258 sheep and our large animals as well to the negdel, on a voluntary basis."

Negdel members could privately own some animals: at first the law allowed 150 per family. Some people initially tried to get away with owning more animals by dividing up their families into smaller households and claiming that each one was entitled to 150. Shombodon's father, for instance, tried to establish a separate household consisting of his sister and his aunt but "government found out and liquidated this new family".

The History of the Mongolian People's Republic, produced by the Mongolian Academy of Sciences in the late Sixties, represents the official point of view at the time. Its 700-plus pages were a bit too much for me. For instance, on the formations of negdels it heroically states (p568): "The fact that the glorious Marxist MPRP, one of the detachments of the world communist movement and the organizer of the Mongolian people's victory and success, steadily directed the question of educating the small private producers and of shifting [them] to the path of a socialist collective economic unit was a decisive factor in our victory." As Dugersuren said, "That was not nice."

On the other hand, by joining the negdels the herders experienced a novelty: they started receiving salaries. During the early years of state and collective enterprises, these were very low, Dugersuren recalled that people earned about 30 or 40 Tögrögs per month, but the money was worth more at the time. Besides, there were just a few consumer goods available in the shops: he remembered flour, rice, matches, tobacco and Russian cigarettes called Papiros. Clothes were still sewn by hand and his mother and grandmother used to make hats and boots by hand as well. Sewing machines only became more widely available in the Sixties and Seventies. Most families celebrated the traditional annual Naadam festivals (without the religious ceremonies but with the sporting events) and the lunar New Year celebrations called Tsaagan Sar at home. Celebrating Tsaagan Sar was frowned upon by the Party and employees of negdels and state-owned enterprises did not get time off — but ordinary negdel members celebrated it anyway. Once in school the children were exposed to Russian culture. The schools and cultural centers organized plays and group-dances.

Mr. Dugersuren gave us a thoughtful answer when I asked whether he experienced hardship when he grew up. He said that herders were well adapted to their lifestyles and didn't think about hardships; they were satisfied with life and had nothing to compare it with. He is right: what are privations if you don't know there is anything you're deprived of?

Rural infrastructure

Over the post-war decades the socialist planning process achieved the objective of shifting the economy away from animal husbandry and towards crop production, industrialization and urbanization. As regards infrastructure, in 1949 the örtö system (pony express), in use since the 13th century, was replaced by a motor-vehicle-based postal system using small trucks called "puluu" that had wooden cabins and could carry one and a half tons.

In order to establish effective control over the country, the government had to put an administration in place that was able to manage and keep track of the population in every far-flung corner of the vast and thinly populated country. By the late Fifties/early Sixties either a negdel or a state farm had been established in each soum. The one case in which one soum contained a negdel as well as a state (fodder) farm became a disaster, as the two organizations clashed over the fact that negdel animals grazed on state-farm crop fields. The soum administration (government) was officially separate from the negdel (cooperative), but of course all structures were part of the overall central plan and more often than not the soum governor and the negdel director were one and the same person. The negdel provided food products and cultural community services for the soum community. In turn, the soum organizations assisted the negdel production activities — hay-making, cropping, building animal shelters and houses, and rearing young animals.

Before 1950 there weren't many buildings in Mongolia outside of Ulaanbaatar; the ones that had existed, the monasteries, had been destroyed. Soum administrations were housed in gers and sometimes moved, as did negdel centers. Shombodon's native soum, Bugat, started with two gers, one for the soum administration and one for the veterinarian. In the Fifties fences and buildings became more common in the rural areas. Shombodon says that in the Fifties Bugat soum had a hospital, a school which was a building and some gers surrounded by a fence, a trade and procurement agency that had an office and shop building and two warehouses, and a cultural center. In 1957 the soum brought at least 10 logs by camel (the thick end of the logs tied to the front hump of the camels and the rear of the five-meter long logs were pulled over the ground). These were used to build the negdel fence and warehouses. At first the negdel was far from the soum center but later it moved closer. It was a good-quality building because the government had a breeding station for sheep in Bugat soum and it produced good carpet wool. That first building later became the soum trade and procurement agency where Shombodon's father worked. None of these buildings has survived and the soum center has since been relocated.

Work in the planned economy was organized through brigades so there were cropping brigades, construction brigades, transport brigades, horse brigades in the military, and so forth.

Negdel herding brigades were allocated herds and pastures and became the lowest level administrative units, which later converted to modern-day bags. These negdel brigades usually had a little center, either in a ger or a small wooden cabin, and employed professional staff such as zoo-technicians, nursing staff, accountants, warehouse keepers. They functioned like rural neighborhoods, geographically large but socially intimate. People knew each other, were neighbors, their kids were in school and youth organizations together, they faced the dzuds together, they intermarried. Government penetrated to the most remote corners through the brigades with the help of social control and agitprop. It is no wonder that Shombodon's father did not get away with claiming that a sister and widowed aunt formed a separate household. The smallest herding units, khot ails, were informal and kinship-based; during socialism, the smallest units were the suuris, officially formed through a decision of brigade management and a part of a negdel. Supposedly not based on kinship, suuris were, however, a lot like the old (and modern) khot ail.

Being a negdel member meant being put to work at whatever the negdel needed at the time. An old school friend of Shombodon told me: "Before they joined the negdel, my parents were herders. After, they came to the soum center and my father did any kind of work in construction, which was not his profession. My mother did any kind of temporary work such as combing goats or as a service worker. Most of the time she spent looking after the household's 75 animals and the children." By 1960 the process of collectivization was completed and 99.5 percent of the herder households had joined the negdels. The advantages of negdel membership also became clear: monthly pay, education, health, pensions, veterinarian services, fodder provisions, consumer goods.

The state supported the negdels in many ways. For instance, in 1955 130 negdel managers were trained domestically, and in 1957 300 were trained in the USSR. Veterinary services were an important part of all Negdels and animals were vaccinated, bathed against ticks and parasites, and the larger animals artificially inseminated. Pasture management was organized by the negdel bosses, the number of animals was kept in check, and care was taken to prevent overgrazing. Water wells were drilled and maintained in the Gobi desert regions. Pests such as mice, grasshoppers and wolves were exterminated through campaigns, often using small aircraft. The government also invested in the negdels by providing larger engineering works such as building dams for irrigation and animal barns, or haymaking and extending low-interest loans with favorable terms. In case of drought or dzud, it would often forgive the debts. In return, the negdels were directed to supply Party, trade union, youth and women's organizations with office space free of charge. Between 1950 and 1960, the number of negdels increased from 139 to 354. Large "scientifically planned" state farms were also established all over the countryside producing fodder, wheat, potatoes, and lamb skins, among other things. The remotest corners of the huge country were firmly under government care and control.

The upbeat Fifties and the cultural campaigns

The economy finally resembled that of the other Eastern Bloc countries in that the people were workers instead of independent operators. The state looked after its workers as best it could, introducing unheard-of services such as a retirement system, paid sick leave and annual leave days. The state enterprises and negdels were separate systems; the former were generally the better place to work, probably because more importance was given to the modern ventures and the state invested heavily in those sectors, with a lot of financial and technical assistance from the more advanced countries.

Mongolia also continued to import culture from Russia: The State Ballet and Opera House was built in the late Forties on Sükhbaatar Square, the center of Ulaanbaatar, as well as the Eldev-Ochir cinema (now the Stock Exchange building). A start was made to introduce culture, as the Russians understood it, to rural areas as well. In 1948 the first rural theater was built in Choibalsan, and others followed. So it was that I saw my very first opera in 2000 at the Opera House. Taking advantage of the few options to go out and relax western-style, those of us who enjoyed the outdoors would often pile into the "Magic Bus" for cycling, cross-country skiing or horse riding. The small bus was owned by a company called Mongolian American Garment International Company (MAGIC) that produced suits for the US market for a few years during the period that the US imposed quotas on imported garments from

China but not from Mongolia. If we made it back in time, we could quickly change and run across the dark deserted square to buy a five-dollar ticket to the opera or ballet and after the performance we would go out to eat and drink. My place in Amsterdam is just a few blocks from the Amsterdam opera house, but do I go there? No, I had to go to Mongolia to get acquainted with that part of my western heritage!

Several of the older people I interviewed were born in the Forties, the most important, of course, being my friend Shombodon who was born in 1947. It was a good period to start one's life in Mongolia: The country was independent and stable; the chaos and fighting of the Twenties was over; the purges of the Thirties were in the past; the war was over. In 1944 the Gandan monastery in Ulaanbaatar reopened, although this was mostly a symbolic gesture. Religion had been wiped out or gone underground. The new ideology of socialist advancement based on modern science brought with it a sense of optimism and enlightenment offsetting the loss of the old religion. Even the older generation would have been relieved that the country was finally peaceful and that that economic development meant less taxation, more food, and better healthcare and education.

The country's leaders believed that the body of social and political theories that were referred to as historic materialism, scientific materialism or Marxism-Leninism was "scientific" and therefore right. Whether those theories were science or a system of beliefs is debatable, but putting them into practice had proved to be effective in building new societies in the Soviet Union and other socialist states. The leaders believed themselves to be enlightened and were committed to bringing progress and unprecedented wealth, health, education and security to the masses by getting rid of the old habits and superstitions that had kept the people in their destitute state. The next point on the program was enlightenment and edification of the masses. The period of cultural revolution and cultural campaigns had started.

August 2012. Gobi Altai is a very thinly populated aimag in the Gobi region. Its capital Altai, with a population of less than 20,000, lies forlornly on a huge windswept, cold and barren plateau of about 2000 meters and emanates a sense of decline. A large industrial area

with crumbling buildings and unidentified rusting heaps of scrap metal that must have been parts of factories is located outside the city center. When working here 10 years ago, the hotel we usually stayed at had a good view of gers interspersed with industrial debris. My room was decorated for typical Mongolian coziness with a carpet depicting Chinggis Khaan hanging on the wall and clean white net curtains between me and the rubbish heaps outside. I used to observe a pair of hoopoes scratching the dirt among the debris, probably nesting somewhere near. The center of town looked as if it hadn't changed much in the past 25 years.

Today the empty streets are lined with low houses with green or red metal roofs, many of them painted in pastel yellow, green or pink, and with charming Russian-style official buildings (museum, opera house) with white pillars and ornamental features. Cottonwoods give the streets a friendly impression, yet the town also feels somehow anachronistic, melancholy, abandoned. We meet Mr. Tseveensuren, the retired father-in-law of a former rural credit specialist, Gaitav, who used to work for me and Shombodon. We have dinner at the home of Gaitav and his wife and they have invited her father to talk to us. He appreciates the fact that I'm doing research for this book and states: "Mongols are patriotic, intelligent and hard-working."

He then tells me about the cultural campaigns: "After the revolution of 1921, the government tried to enlighten the population. To that end, several cultural campaigns were implemented, starting in the 1940s. It was considered crucial to first make the population literate. The first literacy courses were called summer schools and the aim was to cover all school-age children. They didn't always achieve that. All soums had such summer schools. The government, with assistance from foreign governments, prepared teaching staff. Each bag [neighborhood] had a literacy course as well. At the time they didn't have bag centers — the bag governors worked from their ger. In order to implement courses they decided to put up one ger in the warm season for classes. In winter they did homework. That campaign worked for at least four or five years. There were examinations and if someone passed they would receive a literacy certificate. In the beginning they taught literacy in Mongolian script. Then they used Latin script for a year but after that Cyrillic was introduced. When most people had become literate, the temporary courses stopped. Before that, quite a few people had known the old script and also Tibetan. That way many people learned two alphabets and the saying was that 'Mongols had two horses'."

133

Mr. Tseveensuren worked as a literacy teacher himself, after completing the fourth grade in 1944, and was proud to report that about 200 people became literate. Not bad for a 14-year-old! Later he taught Cyrillic and mathematics.

Cultural campaigns were not only used for literacy training: they introduced foreign literature and European culture, including the use of washcloths, showers and sheets on beds, improved personal hygiene, ger hygiene, health and nutrition. In line with the scientific (Eurocentric) ideas about nutrition that were introduced by the Russians, the agricultural engineers started to introduce potatoes and vegetables. Since the time of Chinggis Khaan (and before), Mongols basically ate meat and dairy products, supplemented by wild berries and plants, and occasionally flour made from wild grasses and barley; they did not regard potatoes and vegetables as food. Mr. Tseveensuren himself had been introduced to cropping after he was mobilized in the army in 1950, when he was 20. While he served in Omno Govi aimag on the border with China, his commander gave him a book to read on planting vegetables. In spring, the commander asked if he had read it. The answer was yes, so he was appointed to plant vegetables and potatoes. He had two assistants, harvested three small trucks of vegetables and received 120 Tögrögs, big money for that time. A package of cigarettes cost 1 Tögrög, 2 Mungus. The main campaigns for introducing crops on a national scale were held in 1959: land under cultivation increased by 260,000 hectares in 1959-1960.

The people initially refused to eat the vegetables so the negdels started giving them as part of their salary. The herders just left them to rot at their camp areas when they moved on: they couldn't use them. Undeterred, the government decided to send people to visit individual households in their gers and demonstrate how to cook and eat them. They then provided them for free. They used agitprop. In his own aimag, Gobi Altai, the enterprising boss of the remote southern Bayantur Negdel had potatoes and vegetables planted in the early Fifties. He was invited to the Party conference of the aimag; the crops were displayed and drinks offered to the participants. The conference then asked all the soums to grow potatoes and vegetable and so the new cropping campaign began. By the early Sixties people actually started consuming these things.

When I ask Mr. Tseveensuren why the government wanted so badly to introduce vegetables, he replies, "It was scientifically based: because of the vitamins. Also because of food security. They wanted to diversify human consumption." Being Mongol, he added, "Although meat and milk were sufficient."

In the museum in Choibalsan I found a painting from 1954 by the "Honored Worker of Art", a Mr. Batmunkh, depicting a heroically modern vanguard of agricultural workers weighing the harvest of cabbages and potatoes — in socialist-realist style, of course.

The last cultural campaigns were held in 1959 and mobile groups of representatives were dispatched to the rural areas to enlighten the people: medical staff, veterinarians, apothecaries, artists and performers, and agitprop staff. By 1960 the cultural revolution was fully accomplished. That year the Central National Radio Station, established with assistance from the Soviet Union, started broadcasting 21 hours a day on two channels and provided government and Party with a powerful tool for public education and agitprop.

We say goodnight to the delightful gentleman and the next day we drive off in a pleasant buzz after having drunk the customary vodka with our old colleague Gaitav and a friend at the "goodbye place" just out of town. It brings back many memories of goodbye places. These are usually ovoos either at the edge of town, or many kilometers down the road at a meaningful location such as a mountain pass or border between soums or aimags. It is difficult to get an early start once one has acquired friends in rural Mongolia: your friends will pursue you for kilometers to a suitable goodbye place with a bottle (hopefully only one) of vodka, no matter how early or late in the day. The booze puts me in the overly sentimental mood that mixes the sadness of parting with a vaguely pleasant nostalgia appropriate for farewells. There is fresh snow on the hills around the desolate town: winter is coming.

A more relaxed period started after the collectivization drives and cultural campaigns; everything was under control. I saw a sign of tentative rehabilitation of victims of the purges in the Khovd museum; the last high lama of the yellow monastery (it had stood on the western bank of the Khovd river, opposite the modern town, and was destroyed in 1937), Lama Dambidomi, had been rehabilitated as early as 1962. When I commented on this, Shombodon said, "Yes, long before transition, starting as early as the Forties, the government started to slowly rehabilitate victims of repression." The rehabilitation process had in fact started in April 1939, not in 1990 as popularly believed, but there have been long and short interruptions: sometimes it progressed quickly, sometimes slowly. It has intensified since 1991 after the state broke with its socialist past. In any case, by the 1960s the days of violent suppression of religious ideas were over and memories of the terror years were buried under optimistic belief in scientific socialist progress.

8. THE MONGOLIAN SIXTIES

Hot springs

Charming relics of socialist-era resorts and children's camps, the latter painted in happy primary colors, are dotted all over the country, giving evidence of an innocent era. I have stayed at quite a few, because they are located in beautiful and desirable locations — often at hot springs — and they still function as resorts providing rustic accommodation. They were appreciated as good locations for project training courses and workshops, which is how I became familiar with several of these pleasant but basic retreats.

29 August 2012. We visit Shargaljuut Hot Springs, a typical resort in Bayankhongor aimag, and run into a reporter, Mr. Rentsen, an old acquaintance of Shombodon who offers to give us the tour of the place. As often happens in these interviews, he doesn't stick to the 20th century, introducing the place by telling us that in the 1720s, Luvsandanzan, a Gegeen lama, studied the hot springs and found 108 mineral springs that could heal a total of 164 diseases. Each spring has a specific temperature, ranging from about 20°C to 96°C. You can use the water externally or drink it. The Gegeen studied the mineral formations and was able to see which organs these most resembled. He concluded that the waters of each specific spring were to be used to cure maladies of the identified organs. For instance, there are springs good for the heart, ears, liver, feet, back, female reproductive organs (sit on it like a saddle), lungs (a wooden box was built over that with holes in it through which you inhale the fumes), and so forth. Not long ago the male

organ, shooting water, was broken off by a disgruntled female who had failed to get pregnant. It is lost, but its stump still shoots water.

 At this ancient revered site a state resort was established in 1962 and a negdel resort next to it four years later. The planned capacity of the state resort was 50 people and of the negdel resort 90. They later served more than that: the negdel resort could accommodate 120 in a three-storey building and another 30 in gers and cabins. The Trade Union organized admittance for the state resort: you had to get its permission to go there and it cost very little. The negdels paid for their own members and decided who to send, through the Supreme Council of Agricultural Cooperatives that ran two other inter-negdel resorts. In 1985 both resorts were joined together as a single state resort; in 2005 it was privatized. People still come here for health and healing and each spring has a sign telling us its temperature and explaining its health benefits according to Lama Luvsandanzan. There are also a few bath-gers, each containing a large old-fashioned and inviting bathtub. Water of different temperatures must be mixed manually, in culverts outside the gers.

 After our tour, Mr. Rentsen looks back at the hillside of hot springs, points to the state of the resort infrastructure, and sadly tells us that the paths and rotting wooden walkways were last upgraded in the 1970s. Then it is time for us to take leave and he belatedly remembers his own vocation. He digs a small tape recorder out of his pocket, sticks it under my nose and asks me to give a statement. It is not the only time that a wily Mongol turns the table on me but it is, of course, a fair deal: they tell me about their lives, I tell them about mine.

The Sixties, to those of us who grew up in the West, are left-leaning counterculture, hippies, black power, feminism, anti-war, Cold War, the space race, sex and drugs and rock and roll. Particularly the rock and roll: I grew up in that decade; I remember. Now think of Mongolia at the time. There was no right, therefore no need to lean left, and the happy, optimistic post- purges and post-war era continued. The accomplishments of socialist centrally planned a development were all around for everyone to see. Gers were larger and more comfortable with stoves instead of open fires; consumer goods such as radios, sewing machines, bicycles and motorbikes were more readily available; health services now covered the whole population. Buildings started going up, not only in Ulaanbaatar but also in the rural settlements that had consisted only of gers ever since the monasteries were destroyed in the Thirties. Education, seen as the foundation of socialist development, had been one of the first sectors that the fledgling nation had invested in and this was royally paying off. In 1968 the authorities declared that universal adult literacy had been accomplished. The Mongolian Academy of Sciences was founded by the decree of the Presidium of the Ikh Khural in 1961. More and more young people were able to get work other than herding, and as workers could expect unprecedented benefits. Free education and health care! Pensions! Paid leave! Apartment complexes! Resorts!

Industrial development in the Sixties

The resorts and other benefits were possible when industrial development, supported by the Soviet Union and Eastern European countries, gained momentum. Mongolia's third Five-Year Plan covering the period 1961-1965, focused on increasing the energy supply of the coal-fueled power plants, on mining and on creating industrial complexes. Modern farms, industrial parks, and whole new cities were planned and built forthwith where there had only been open and wild countryside before. Because of the country's perpetual labor shortages, the military assisted in the industrialization drive. One person told me that he had worked in the forest industry in the early Sixties as a junior sergeant in a unit producing wooden parts for the Shariin Gol coalmine, and then worked for a few months in the Darkhan factory producing white bricks. I know those bricks: I immediately picture the dilapidated white-brick company houses along the railroad going north from Ulaanbaatar.

Animal husbandry was still important and one of the largest industries was the Ulaanbaatar meat-processing plant, later called Makh Impex (Meat Import Export). In 2000 I became friends with a Dutchman who buys up cleaned, dried and salted intestines to be processed and sold as sausage casings in Europe. To my surprise, he told me that his father used to travel to Ulaanbaatar to buy Mongolian casings as early as the Sixties from Makh Impex. I cannot think of another product that was exported to countries outside of the Eastern Bloc. Indeed, according to the National Statistical Office, the share of socialist countries in the total exports in 1970 was 98.2

percent and their share in total imports was 99.2 percent. But we got the sausage casings!

The industrial city of Darkhan, the third largest city in Mongolia, was founded in 1961 and built with technical assistance from the USSR, Bulgaria, Poland, Hungary, Czechoslovakia, and East Germany. It is a typical example of a fully planned city that rose from the empty wild steppe adjacent to the main north-south road (the only road that was paved then) and on the railway linking Siberia and China. It was still a wild place: the story goes that when they were just starting to build, a fully-armed Russian soldier was killed by wolves on the hill that now overlooks the city. He faced a pack of wolves and shot them one by one. When he thought he had them all, he prodded the pile to see if they were dead and blood jammed his gun. One of the wolves wasn't dead after all and got him. No Romulus and Remus myth for Darkhan!

The city has been designed in three separate areas: a large industrial area, one for the government buildings, and a separate part of town for the living blocks. At the time, the tallest building in Mongolia (16 storeys) stood in Darkhan. Nowadays the whole town has a faded and dilapidated look about it, with weeds sprouting in sidewalks and roofs. At the same time, judging from the signs and neon lights, it seems to have a thriving nightlife with many pubs, karaoke bars and nightclubs. There are still a number of large industrial plants: a metal-processing plant, sheepskin-processing plant, ceramic factory, white-brick factory and a cement factory.

July 2012. I find snippets of information on the sixties in unexpected places. The night of the first day of our trip to the eastern aimags, we arrive at the Chinggis Khaan monument in the Khaan Khentii National Park, a strictly protected area. At the gate across the track — there are no paved roads in this neck of the woods — an elderly guard with bushy eyebrows, dressed in a camo jacket, a grey fedora and plastic bags wrapped around his shoes as gaiters, collects our entrance fees. He agrees to an interview the next day. Mr. Jamyan lives next to the gate in a tiny log cabin the size of a tent in the lush meadows dotted with larch trees. He is looking after his grandson for the summer.

The next morning we settle ourselves on his bed and he launches into his life's story. He was born in 1930, benefited from the educational system in his home soum of Jargalant in far-away Khovd aimag, and later studied finance and economics at a secondary school in Ulaanbaatar. He graduated in 1960 and got a job as accountant at the Nalaikh coalmine a little to the east of Ulaanbaatar. His ambition was to write, however, and he started writing articles and mailing them to the newspaper anonymously, stealing to the letter box at the post office at night when no one could see him because he was shy of publicity. When the paper started publishing his articles he made himself known and eight months after having started his career as a bookkeeper, he was offered a job by the newspaper. He was put in charge of reporting on trade and industry and worked there until 1970.

At the time, every aimag had its newspaper as a source of news and a tool of propaganda. In 2013 Mongolia celebrated the 100th anniversary of Shine Toli ("New Mirror") newspaper, first published on March 6 1913 in Urga after the first independence revolution of 1911; recently aimags have been celebrating 60th or 70th anniversaries of their newspapers. Shombodon says that before he went to school he knew the 35 letters of the Mongolian alphabet, could count up to 100 and the only word he recognized from the papers was USSR (or CCCP in the Cyrillic alphabet).

The Sixties were interesting times, Mr. Jamyan tells us, because so many industries were founded then — he mentions specifically a sewing factory and a Chinese construction project — and he visited those enterprises, as well as successful labor brigades and voluntary labor divisions. The latter were organizations in which enthusiastic people did additional voluntary work out of idealism. From 1960 education was accessible at no cost for everyone. Literate Mongolians all over the country now had access to newspapers as well as radio and were able to read about these beautiful new accomplishments and marvel at enumerations of heroic production figures.

In 1970 he went to Arkhangai and became the head of a wood-processing brigade that mainly produced ger frames; they produced 1000 frames a year and in 1982 the Central Committee sent him to work as chief of the negdel haymaking brigade and manager of the milk-processing plant. He became a negdel herder in 1986. At privatization he got some animals and continued herding; in 2000 he got this job as security guard for the Chinggis Khaan monument protected area.

This is a typical Mongolian experience. In other countries a guard living in the tiniest of cabins would be illiterate, but here I immediately hit pay dirt: a reporter, no less, who had reported in the 1960s. The interview, one of my first, is unorganized. I am interested in everything, questions remain unanswered, and other information pops up that hadn't occurred to me to ask about. He told us that the Russians influenced Mongolian history but not locally; they stayed at the political level. I understand that he feels they didn't intrude too much at community level. He is critical of the fact that nowadays people accept foreign ideas and use foreign words, and then he starts lecturing me on the history of Chinggis Khaan. He has kept reporting throughout his career and has been writing for radio for 50 years. Nowadays he mainly writes about the bureaucracy and the environment — about forest management, about the loss of springs and streams in his soum, of which there are only three or four left from the original hundred. He still receives letters from his readers.

The Chinggis Khaan monument that Mr. Jamyan guards is the place where Chinggis was voted Great Khaan of all Mongols after having united the warring clans. This took place on the banks of Black Heart's Blue Lake, a small clear lake set among verdant flowering meadows and low hills covered with larches and birches, one of which is Black Heart Mountain. The year 2012 is exceptionally wet here in northeastern Mongolia: the sky is low and grey, the ground squishy, the pastures abundant and the horses fat and healthy. We stay at the tourist camp where the direct descendants of Chinggis who became important monarchs or leaders are commemorated by a large circle of carved poles with a stone monument in the middle, each pole symbolizing one of the Great Khaans. It is a lovely peaceful setting: I understand why, in 1206, the Mongols held their Khural (assembly) here.

We call him Genghis Khan and he is probably the only Mongolian you know by name. He created the largest contiguous empire ever through his conquests. In the early 13th century he struck fear in the hearts of the Europeans when he approached Eastern Europe wiping out all opposition along the way. After his death in 1227, under leadership of his seasoned generals and grandsons, the Mongols invaded Poland, Hungary and Russia where they conquered and famously ransacked Kiev. Why he and his successors didn't conquer all of Western Europe as well is a mystery.

Maybe the Mongol Empire went into decline because of infighting between his descendants; maybe they didn't see sufficient good grazing for their animals.

As the symbol of Mongolia's nationhood (and superiority — Mongols are in no way shy or self effacing), Chinggis, the Mongolian superhero, is important to this narrative. Most Mongols know about his early life through a text called The Secret History of the Mongols which was written some time after his death in 1227 and which had been preserved through the centuries in Chinese-character transcripts, the oldest surviving of which dating from the end of the 14th century. It was transcribed into modern Mongolian around 1915-1917 and became available to western scholars only in the 1940s. During the socialist period Chinggis-worship was strongly discouraged; he was labeled a "feudal", representing the backward society that enlightened socialism was determined to replace. But he hadn't been completely forgotten and the Secret History was appropriately read in secret by a large portion of the now literate population and, as early as the Sixties, he was to play a role in focusing Mongol nationalist feelings against the Soviet-dominated ideology.

Weaknesses of the centrally planned economy

By now the specter of Mongol nationalism was producing inklings of dissent against the foreign-led authoritarian Socialist system. The system was starting to show its flaws despite the great progress that had been made after the war. Under socialism, government and Party tried to control, plan and manage all aspects of people's lives. This required an enormous administration with very long arms. The main weakness of the system was insufficient bottom-up feedback regarding the realities on the ground. Long-term authoritarian governments tend to slowly grow away from reality due to the universal inclination of bureaucrats to present their superiors with inflated figures, and to substitute wishful thinking for realistic planning. In these states there was insufficient freedom to allow checks and balances from below. Risk-averse bureaucrats, who had everything to lose and little to gain, were reluctant to deliver bad news to their bosses and promised the impossible; then they turned around and demanded the impossible from the lower levels, and blamed those lowest levels for not achieving their targets. The decision-makers were far enough away from implementation to see only paper, untarnished by reality. Targets and quotas imposed on the lowest levels — the state enterprises and negdels — were unrealistically high and did not take into consideration the vagaries of nature. A similar thing happened to the budgets that were requested to achieve the targets: in their journey from enterprise/farm to the national level and back, they were modified (cut). In the end what was passed on down the line was different from what was requested, which in turn was different from what was actually needed to produce the planned outputs and quota. Anyone who has worked in a western bureaucracy or large firm will recognize the pattern, although to a lesser degree: the saying "Nothing is impossible for those who don't have to do it" illustrates this. In businesses, profit is an independent measure of success; in government administrations the popularity of the politicians who can be voted out of power checks their tendency to move away from reality.

Of course, the managers of state farms, enterprises and negdels knew how the system worked and budgets were generally estimated too high because everyone knew the administrators at higher level would cut them. Despite that, what the enterprises had to deliver according to the plans and with the available budget was often unrealistic — particularly in the agriculture sector, where harvests and livestock products depend on weather conditions that can neither be accurately forecast nor influenced. In many cases there might be a surplus in one product and a deficit in another. Negdel bosses would therefore travel around and talk to each other and have lively trading going on in their efforts to fulfill or exceed their quotas and earn praise. In the VIP rooms of the negdels, the bosses were served their meat and vodka privately. I can just hear them whispering: "I have more camel wool than I need but insufficient hay. How about you?" Good negdel bosses knew how to negotiate the administrative game, as it was not good for one's image to have to report that one had under-produced relative to the state plan. Those who did well got rewards. Mongolians are a practical people: negdel bosses had wide-ranging authority and were relatively free to find a way to make things work.

Competent negdel bosses who wanted their negdel to thrive therefore went about it in a similar way to private entrepreneurs. At these lowest administrative levels, the administration worked pretty well, because the administrators were close to the people they served and the harsh environment and general lack of surplus kept them focused on progress — as did the general optimistic and progressive social climate. They had learnt about different livestock breeds and were encouraged to experiment.

Shombodon told me some anecdotes about enterprising negdel bosses and their experiments. One boss imported a superior breed of cow from East Germany and saw them weaken and topple over soon after arrival. They finally figured out that the cows had been used to drink from mechanical drinking troughs and hadn't recognized that they could simply drink from the stream at the bottom of their pasture. In another story, a negdel boss wanted to improve his cattle by cross-breeding with yaks and bought a good, healthy-looking yak bull for that purpose. But his plans came to naught as his cows took one look at the weird-looking animal and scattered all over the place. He was never able to get them to accept the expensive bull, and so found out that it was necessary for cows to grow up in a mixed yak and cattle herd to accept yaks as the same species and interbreed. I believe the grandparents of this negdel boss might have known — the gain in scientific knowledge was accompanied by a loss in ancient herding wisdom.

Despite the economy doing well, purge victims slowly being rehabilitated, and children having vastly better prospects than their parents, there were political tensions between the official party-line and people who had diverging ideas, such as Mongol nationalists or those who had some knowledge of what went on the other side of the Iron Curtain. Universal literacy, the cornerstone on which socialism was built, ironically became a threat for the Party hardliners. Dugersuren, whom we met last chapter, told me: "In the early 1960s people started to subscribe to newspapers. The literacy rate was low before that. My own parents couldn't read or write. Information came to them by word of mouth through agitprop, teachers and officials. On certain days, at a specified time in the morning, someone would come and give information. Designated officials also gave lectures on certain topics and each bag had a paid agitator. We received no information about western countries such as America or the Netherlands, only about the socialist countries."

They were given to understand that those countries were of the opposite bloc, meaning they were bad capitalists. However, Dugersuren heard other things as well: "I was a sportsman, a wrestler, and my friends had visited all kinds of countries for competitions. They said development is faster where private property exists. Russia and Mongolia were behind! After the Olympics in 1964 in Tokyo they were particularly surprised: Japan had lost the war but was highly developed! So intellectuals started talking but their criticism was crushed in the Sixties, just like in the Eastern European countries such as Czechoslovakia and Poland. People understood that the time had not yet come to talk about such things."

Chinggis's 800th anniversary

July 2012. We arrive at Dadal soum, a pleasant-looking village of log cabins with white, decorated window moldings, net-curtains, flowers. This is a settlement in the territory of the Buriat Mongol tribe, located in beautiful surroundings of forested hills and pastures in the valleys adjacent to the Russian border. It is a gorgeous day, sunshine and perfect temperature. In the idyllic village we come across a surreal juxtaposition of a Shaman ritual taking place (the village's main street is blocked off all afternoon for that), an old-fashioned marching band practicing in the background, some ugly old buildings with the name of the old negdel on it ("Labor") lining the streets, and the tangible presence of Chinggis-fever. We have buuz (steamed mutton dumplings) at a local eatery, a wooden shack with vinyl flooring, plastic wallpaper and four rustic tables with plastic tabletops, and go to see the sights.

Dadal village, as Chinggis's birthplace, has a museum dedicated to the Great Khaan's youth; it also has a museum with old socialist-era memorabilia but unfortunately both are closed today. Apart from the 1962 Chinggis monument, there is a large ovoo and a stone dedicated to his birthplace on a neighboring hill with a magnificent view of the green valley, the meandering river and the Siberian border. In Mongolia the Great Khaan has conquered and subdued communism, thumbs up. But I am an outsider, wondering who he was and what would have happened if he had pushed a little further west and conquered Europe?

* * *

In 1962, the best-known evidence of friction between a revival of nationalism and the MPRP's ideas of what constituted allowable (Marxist-Leninist) history was revealed around the celebration of the 800th anniversary of Chinggis Khaan. The question of whether and how to celebrate it had been informally discussed among Mongolian scholars and intellectuals, and in the summer of 1961 the MPRP let it be known that a public celebration of Chinggis's anniversary had been approved. Discussions continued to take place within the Party because Chinggis had previously been a taboo subject on account of his important symbolic value to the pan-Mongolian nationalist movement which had been bloodily suppressed only a few decades earlier. Some remembered the not-too-distant decision by the Politburo in 1949 that Chinggis was not an appropriate role model for the Mongols because he was a "feudal leader". In the end, despite misgivings by those who were more fully indoctrinated by Soviet ideology, it was decided to go ahead with the celebration and to erect a monument to Chinggis in Dadal soum, his presumed birthplace. June 10 was set as a date for the celebration.

The Mongols knew that they could not afford to upset their two powerful neighbors, Russia and China, because both had been conquered by the Mongols led by Chinggis Khaan in the 13th century, and both adhered to the Marxist theory based on class struggle and therefore scorned "feudalism". Accordingly, high-ranking historians were dispatched to the neighbors to discuss the matter with their counterparts and assess the points of view of these powerful states. In a political master-move, China decided to celebrate the anniversary itself and so demonstrate that Mongolia and China were one territory. This made it impossible for the USSR and Soviet-leaning politicians in Mongolia to prohibit the public celebrations.

An organizing committee was formed and Chinggis's exact birth date was determined in a uniquely Mongolian manner: science, in the form of accredited historians, and superstition, in the form of astrologers of Gandan monastery (25 years after the great purges!), united to work things out. They came up with May 31 and the Institute of History, which had set the date of June 10, was duly reprimanded for its mistake. As well as the monument in Dadal soum, it was decided to produce a documentary about Chinggis's life, to issue a commemorative stamp, and to hold a scientific conference in his honor sponsored by the Academy of Sciences. An official tribute to the great Khaan was carefully drafted, crafted and fine-tuned by the Politburo.

However, a backlash followed immediately, organized by the opponents of the nationalist Chinggis supporters who yanked the Politburo back into the fold of proletarian internationalism. The scientific conference was criticized by the Russian embassy, an article in Pravda (the USSR's official Party newspaper) attacked Chinggis Khaan and his Mongol-Tatar empire that had oppressed the Russian empire for centuries, and the publication of the conference materials was stopped. The commemorative stamp was not allowed to leave the country. Voices went up to demolish the Chinggis monument and many organizers of the event were condemned for their roles in the celebrations and forced into self-criticisms. The most famous of these nationalist figures was Tömör-Ochir, a prominent member of the Politburo and secretariat, who had initiated the celebration and headed the working group. He was removed from office, exiled first to Bayankhongor aimag and later, after he had illegally returned to Ulaanbaatar, to Turt (Khankh) on the far end of Lake Khovsgol (if you want to know what the word "remote" means, look up Khankh/Turt on Google Earth). His wife Ninjbadgar, who was the nation's number-one astronomer, was asked to stay at her job in Ulaanbaatar but famously asserted that she was married to Tömör-Ochir, not to the Central Committee of the MPRP. She joined him in exile. The Chinggis monument is still there: apparently no one had the heart to take it down.

International affairs in the Sixties

August 2012. The steaming pot has been set in front of us and Shombodon is cutting off small pieces for me to taste: liver, heart, ruminant stomach, blood-sausage, mixed sausage, lung and kidneys. Most of it tastes pretty good, but the ruminant stomach is tasteless and tough. We are sitting in the single cozy and warm room of a log cabin set in a small vegetable garden in the outskirts of Uliastai (the name means "quaking aspen"), the capital of Zavkhan aimag, interviewing a charming couple who have retired from the Border Patrol (now called General Department for Border Protection). Both husband and wife started as soldiers, then got college degrees and continued in the Border Patrol in higher positions. Mr. Dichinsamba, born in 1945, is a trim lieutenant-colonel, quiet with a military bearing. Mrs. Byambasuren, born in 1953, is warm and welcoming, voluminous and voluble, bearing the title of advanced cultural worker. She also writes poetry.

It is a cozy place, basically one low-ceilinged room with a half wall/chimney separating the kitchen from the living area. Embroidered pillows are strewn around and there are pictures and photo-panels on the walls depicting people in uniform sporting a profusion of medals. The large pot of intestines has just been taken off the fire. Mrs. Byambasuren exclaims several times that we are so lucky, so lucky, to arrive just when the pot is ready. Within 10 minutes the bottle of vodka is also on the table. She says we don't have to drink, we can just taste, but in any case she has to offer it. We toast and drink. She talks about their life in the Border Patrol, of which they are extremely proud. They repeat several times that their family protected Mongolian territory; we are shown their military IDs. This is their story:

Dichinsamba and Byambasuren married in 1972 and have five children, four boys and a girl. They used to live in gers and moved many time to various border posts, living in Bayan-Olgi aimag (the western aimag, dominated by the Kazakh minority) for nine years. Military officers had the right to live with their families and wives who weren't in the military themselves (Mrs. Byambasuren was) were allocated any kind of work that was needed, for example milking, laundry, nursing. At one time, she was at a border post when she had to give birth and she had to ride a horse to a neighboring state farm from where they called to the soum center. The veterinarian of the soum came and collected her and assisted her in delivering the baby. She was taken in and given black soup (exclusively meat, considered very healthy for sick people — I have been prescribed it myself) by a Kazakh family because her husband was on duty and did not have time to look after her.

Sometimes they found it difficult to leave the kids at school and go back to the border. But, she exclaimed with pride, their kids understand the border-force and defense; their daughter even looks like a man! They are currently the only "border force family" living in the aimag but have heard that some others are planning to retire here. Most retire in the center of the country — Ulaanbaatar and surroundings.

It was mainly the Chinese border that needed protecting; Mongolia and the Soviet Union were close allies. Tense situations recurred during the Sixties and Seventies. According to Mr. Dichinsamba, there was a serious border situation with China in 1979 when China attacked Vietnam and might have wanted to attack Mongolia. Mongolian defense forces exercised and were ready. As Mrs. Byambasuren put it: "The soldiers were ready and the horses were ready" (she is, after all, a poet). The Chinese exercised on the other side of the border; Russian military forces came to assist. They felt threatened and went into "war-readiness" mode. There were all kinds of signals going back and forth. It was a difficult period in their lives: the kids slept with their clothes on and she sat watch next to them with a gun in her hand.

In 1991 the family moved to the second-level border post organization called Otryad and moved from a ger to a house in a soum center where there were schools. She became a bookkeeper and he became head of supply, including weapons. Now they are happily retired, their pension is sufficient and their children have all graduated from university.

At this point Mrs. Byambasuren deems the interview complete. She digs out her notebook and cheerfully proceeds to extract from me my life's story. Then we look at the family photo albums and part the best of friends after declining an invitation to dinner but having consumed sufficient vodka to go straight to bed.

The tensions at the Chinese border that shaped the lives of the Border Patrol couple were the result of a falling-out on ideological grounds between the two communist superpowers, China and the USSR, between which Mongolia is wedged. This Sino-Soviet split took place in the early 1960s and, while Mongolia had signed a Treaty of Friendship and Mutual Assistance with China in 1960, it stayed firmly in the Soviet camp. In fact, that very year, Mongolia adopted a new constitution that underlined the continuation of the policies of the previous decades, its preamble making mention of "fraternal socialist assistance of the Soviet Union", the guiding principles of the "all-conquering Marxist-Leninist theory" and the "guiding and directing force in society" of the MPRP. The pro-Soviet Tsedenbal continued as the Mongolian leader and relations with China slowly cooled.

China's seat in the United Nations continued to be held by the Republic of China (Taiwan) until 1971 and, as a member of the Security Council, Taiwan had been blocking Mongolia's admission to the UN. In 1960 the Soviet Union applied pressure on behalf of its ally by threatening to block admittance of the African independent states unless Mongolia was admitted. On October 27 1961, Mongolia and Mauritania became the 102nd and 103rd member states of the UN. Shortly thereafter, in 1963, Mongolia established diplomatic relations with the first western country, the United Kingdom, followed by France in 1965. The first UK "embassy" in Mongolia was a room at the Ulaanbaatar hotel in 1966.

In 1962, the year the economy really started taking off, Mongolia joined Comecon (the Council for Mutual Economic Assistance, an international organization under Soviet leadership that served to integrate the economies of the Eastern Bloc), and its ties with the USSR were strengthened politically, economically and militarily through treaties and agreements. In 1966, the Russian leader Leonid Brezhnev even visited Mongolia and signed a 20-year friendship treaty that included a defense clause and generous aid. Relations between the USSR and Mongolia intensified even more during the Seventies; joint Soviet-Mongolian ventures were established and links forged between Soviet research and cultural institutes, government departments, and between neighboring Mongolian aimags and Soviet oblasts (autonomous provinces). Ten years after the Soviet troops withdrew from Mongolia a new Soviet military build-up on Mongolian territory commenced, and a large number of Soviet troops again garrisoned in Mongolia.

Correspondingly, Mongolia's relations with China deteriorated even more. By 1966 Chinese aid to Mongolia stopped and trade decreased. In 1967 China was also becoming more aggressive toward Russia and accused the latter of having betrayed the tenets of communism. It even vowed to return the red banner (of communism) to Red Square in Moscow during the celebration of the 50th anniversary of the October Revolution, suggesting that they would coerce the Soviet Union to go back to its "pure" communist roots. The Mongolians were understandably worried (possibly wondering whether this meant a literal invasion of Russia by China) and most stayed home that day. Shombodon was working in Overkhangai aimag at the time, and had arranged some leave to visit his family starting that day, so he set out and unusually was the only passenger on the postal/passenger truck: everyone else had decided to hunker down. Fortunately, China did not extend their ideological attacks to the military realm and there were no incidents on the anniversary but Mongolia re-established its Border Protection Forces and Shombodon remembers that in 1969, when Karakul state farm moved to Choir, a Russian military division was quartered there, building military defense structures.

By the late 1960s, deteriorated relations with China and the Chinese pullout damaged trade, a series of dzuds caused huge losses in livestock while droughts caused losses in the crop sector. These setbacks caused economic progress to fall short of its goals as set forth in the Five-Year Plans, but the goals had probably been set too optimistically in the first place and people experienced progress regardless.

Childhood in the Fifties and Sixties

The southern border was well protected by people like Mr. Dichinsamba and Mrs. Byambasuren and the clashes between nationalist feelings and socialist ideology had been settled in favor of the latter. Internally, the country was moving peacefully along and most people I interviewed who grew up in the Fifties and Sixties paint a picture of a happy childhood.

✳ ✳ ✳

July 2012. In a wide, lush green valley we stop to ask directions from a herder who is puttering about the orderly surroundings of her ger. There are animal enclosures and, next to the ger, neatly arranged trays of yoghurt drying in the sun and next to that yogurt being drained before drying. A small solar panel sits on top of the ger and a satellite dish leans against it; this is not a poor household. She explains the directions, then candidly points at David and asks how much he weighs — Shombodon, in his capacity as livestock expert, guesses about 120 kilos; David mumbles that might be about right — and invites us in to tea.

Mrs. Munbish is 63 (born 1949), has the weathered face of the outdoors, a wide smile and the warm, easy going and confident manner of the women of the steppes. She is clearly a happy lady enjoying her stay at their summer camp. They are well-off farmers from the soum center where they have a good home; they have more than 1000 animals: 800 small animals, three camels, more than 100 horses and more than 100 cattle, which is impressive. She had been allowed to retire at 50 because she had five kids, according to the law for women who have four or more children. All five (two boys, three girls) are now married. She has a large, well-organized and cozy ger with television and mobile phone reception. On one wall strips of meat are hanging to dry. Her daughter is preparing milk tea on the stove.

She recalls a happy childhood on the Red Star negdel which had been formed around the time she was born, with her father one of its founding members. She was born to a herder family; her father bred racehorses. She used to race horses between the ages of seven and 13: their horses used to come in among the top five and often in first place. She graduated from primary school, but since then she herded and working as a milking assistant. In 1966 she married Mr. Sosor, who is 10 years older than her, and they received a salary herding for the negdel. They also received free schooling and health care and the negdel provided fodder, delivered free of charge right at their ger! She compares this to the situation of their children who have no social insurance and, she thinks, will have problems later on. Two of her children work in Ulaanbaatar as blue-collar workers, one of them a seamstress; the others are herders.

Mrs. Munbish's happy childhood story does not imply that they lived in luxury: she says that children went barefoot and ate exclusively dairy products in summer. They also moved more often before and during the Negdel period, up to 10 times a year, even in winter. They scraped the snow away and put up their ger and slept on skins. Nowadays they move at most five times because "the older people have become weak and the children lazy".

Mongolian kids used to play with whatever they found in nature. One game had to do with creating flocks with colored pebbles depicting the different animals (white was typically for sheep), or constructing the floor plan of a ger, also with pebbles. Shombodon showed me a place near Choir where many such play-gers have been positioned among the rocks, close to a white rock called the Children's Ovoo that is believed to be an auspicious place for children. The ovoo itself is old but most of the play-gers are recent. There were not so many when he worked in that area in 1969-1972.

A distant relative of Shombodon who had lived in the same bag in his home soum of Bugat told me that they collected many white stones for sheep and square stones for horses, and made camels by chipping off shards when they were children. Between the ages of 11 and 16, she and other kids, while they were herding far from home, high in the mountains, used to make stone play-gers and played that the boy was the household head, the older girl the mother and she, the youngest, played the baby. They used to ask each other: "Who will visit these nice gers after we are adult?" Aren't kids are the same everywhere? I spent a lot of time on the beach as a child, drawing play-houses in the sand and using seaweed and "sea balls" (small balls formed by Neptune grass in the Mediterranean sea) as furniture, my brothers playing father and baby and me playing the mother.

In Mongolia, however, it wasn't all play. Children's labor, even that of children younger than eight, was and is valuable to herding households. One woman told me she was so small when she ran with the herd that when her parents looked for her, they looked for the large dog that she always hung on to because she was too small to be seen among the goats and sheep. Herder children were very independent at an early age. Shombodon's parents told the kids to come home at sunset. Of course, there were no watches. Children were trained very early to find their way by wind directions, so all they had to do was construct the floor plan of a ger, duly facing south, and plant a stick in the center that would cast a shadow and show them the time of the day, just as if they were sitting at home in their ger.

The Kazakhs had remarkably similar childhood memories to those described by the ethnic Mongols. The Kazakh, Mr. Stanboul, described the same traditional nomadic lifestyle, though he pointed out some differences: for instance, the Kazakhs used to move out of their gers and into primitive wooden or stone houses they called their "warm gers" in winter. Kazakh gers are normally larger than the Mongolian ones, are more colorfully decorated inside and have a slightly different shape, the roofs having a steeper slant. His parents were herders and from age five onward he was busy tending the lambs and kids. Herders were very busy: women milked and processed the milk, collected fire materials and sewed. Men made shelters, herded animals, made hay and manufactured items for riding

154

horses. When the children had free time they would go to the river to play or to climb mountains. They played with stones and wood and went swimming. They would injure their legs and milk cream was put on it — that would sting and after that they would forget about it and go back to play. It was a good childhood, he said.

Shombodon said that the atrociously cold and long winters were and are hard on animals, the elderly, children (and everyone else as well). The animals still have to be taken out to graze, but in winter this is more a task for strong and healthy adults than for children. His parents settled his grandparents in a "warm winter camp" and took their animals to herd them together with their own. The six-year-old Shombodon stayed with his paternal grandparents. They did not have stoves yet and had to keep the embers of the fire until the next morning, burying them in ashes and putting them in an upside-down iron pot. When the first ray of light came through the ger cover Shombodon had to start the fire from the embers and his grandmother would get up and make tea (salty milk tea, of course) while the ger warmed up. A round iron "potholder" stood on elevated feet over the open fire.

Shombodon's sister Nuurkhu told me that their mother used to make bricks for the negdel and the older children had to bring her baby to her at work for breastfeeding. Father had made a sort of cart to carry the kids in — they didn't have a baby carriage. The children also had to fetch water for the household: the older ones carried ten liters on their backs, the little ones five liters. The metal containers dug into their backs and sometimes leaked and wet their backs. They tried to keep them from leaking with goat fat, which didn't work well. She remembers cheating once: she took the water from an irrigation channel instead of the good spring but her parents weren't fooled and she had to go back for the good water.

They revisited funny stories about their family. At Shombodon's haircutting ceremony, which must have taken place in the early Fifties, the family decided to make it an especially festive occasion (he was the only boy among the eight children) and serve airag. They had never made airag before and, more important, their mares had never been milked before. They found out the hard way that separating the foals from the mares was not as easy as separating lambs and kids from their mothers. The whole family became involved and in the fray an uncle threw a stone that accidentally hit

Shombodon's mother, dislodging two teeth. They made airag that year but decided it wasn't worth the hassle ever again.

Novel items appeared in the stores in the Fifties. Shombodon's grandparents got hold of an exotic clove of garlic and put it in the soup for flavor. They meticulously took out the clove before eating the soup and re-used it the next day, and the next, and the next. After a week or so it ended up in Shombodon's bowl and he ate it: it tasted "something like sugar". His grandparents couldn't find the clove and couldn't believe he had actually eaten it. "That was my first vegetable", he told me. Many elderly Mongols still don't like onion, garlic or any other spice apart from salt, although wild onions are abundant in the steppes and are used to spice up certain types of dried curds called sors. A few stoves came for sale in the 1950s; the household bought their first one in 1957. His father exclaimed: "We have imprisoned our fire!" Nonetheless they liked it because before, when it rained, the materials used for fuel (mainly animal dung) were wet and filled the ger with foul-smelling smoke.

Of course, hidden among the happy memories of the Fifties and Sixties were undertones of a traumatic past. Shombodon once mentioned that, on becoming a member of the Youth Organization, they had to write the history of their previous generations and that he somehow just knew that he should not write about his lama-uncles. Similarly, as a Party member he knew that the subject was taboo. But these memories were fading, dissent was mostly underground, and the centrally planned economy was still becoming more sophisticated. Life was getting better during the Sixties and Seventies.

9. THE SOCIALIST WORKPLACE

Mongolian team building

Summer 2000. *We set out to Terelj National Park, the nearest revered "place of natural beauty" in a rented bus. Our own driver is part of our team and he will drink so he cannot drive. He is the expert at partying and a champion ballroom dancing, which earns him an annual invitation to the President's New Year Party. We make camp with tents, canopies, volleyball nets, a superior sound system blasting Michael Jackson music into the idyllic valley. Food is spread on tarps: cookies and sweets, salads, pickles, dried sausages and beer, wine, vodka. The men start preparing the favorite of all Mongolian meals: khorkhog. It is boiled mutton. A sheep is slaughtered and the meat is divided into chunks. A fire is built and smooth round stones are collected at the river and heated until red-hot. The hot stones are thrown into a milk-can with water in it. The meat and some potatoes, onions, carrots and a pinch of salt are added, the can is sealed with a rag and the lid is clamped shut by weighing it down with a piece of wood held by two people (or by special clamps). The whole thing functions as a pressure-cooker and soon the meat is done. The black, smooth, greasy stones are first extracted and handed to everyone to rub between their hands to ensure good health the rest of the year. They are too hot to hold and have to be jiggled from one hand to another for as long as you can bear it. Mutton fat turns out to be a superior hand-cream with a powerful smell. We will all be very healthy this year.*

Toasts are made, a duty I need to take part in as project manager; I have of necessity become halfway proficient. My German successor was even less adept and my ex-colleagues whispered to me that he didn't like to party! I was present (years after my first job I was still invited to parties of the company we created) when the director, a tall, stately, beautiful Mongolian woman, made her speech, drank half an orange-juice glass of vodka and shouted to the puny German: "Now show you're a man!" He took up the challenge: they were both comatose at the end of the picnic. I assume they bonded as well as I had.

The meat is handed out and cleared off the bone with hands and pocketknives until the bones are squeaky-clean. The shoulder blades have special significance; that meat has to be shared and we are each handed bits of scapula-meat. Everyone is happy and sated and the picnic moves to a next stage of jokes, anecdotes, games and vodka-induced singing. I am serenaded with traditional Mongolian songs that have mother as their theme, appropriate for a middle-aged female. One must reciprocate, so I have memorized a mournful Dutch seafarer's song (lover vanishes at sea while girlfriend waits weeping on the beach). I barely manage to get by and stave off threats that I can buy my way out by downing extra shots of vodka. Late at night we pile in the bus and are driven home and we all love each other very much. I am exhausted.

***Winter 2004.** "Maaike, have you bought your dress yet?"*

"Dress?"

"You know, for the New Year Party!"

Later: "Are you free this Saturday?"

"Sure, why?" "I'll solve your problem for you."

"Problem, what do you mean?"

"We're going to buy your gown together."

I had apparently been underdressed before and wasn't getting away with embarrassing my team the next time round. So it was that at 50 I had my first gown and I went the whole hog: a lilac silk sheath with a low-cut back and with shiny beads sewn all over. I haven't had the guts to show it to my friends and family back home.

Mongolians tend to identify with their work environment and form close-knit office communities that socialize outside of office hours as well. By "socializing", I really mean heavy-duty partying and I have done it all: from drinking sessions at the office to grand gala events with all the trappings: glitzy gowns, profusions of jewelry, over-the-top hairdos, glitter everywhere, elaborately arranged tables, professional entertainers, ballroom dancing. And everything in between: dinners at restaurants (the men take the women out for international women's day and the other way round for men's day), sporting events, karaoke, ceremonial visits to the oldest colleagues during lunar new year, and picnics. I had not realized that partying was part of my job description and it soon became clear to my staff that their manager had insufficient social skills to lead the way; the job was quickly taken over by the project assistant in close cooperation with the driver.

Picnics are particularly popular and organized no matter what the time of the year — and this is a place where the average temperature is minus 25°C in January. In winter only part of the picnic takes place outside and we usually rent a ger to continue partying. Of course, summer is best: the season is short and the countryside turns into a blooming Alpine meadow. A minor picnic involves only the work community; a major picnic involves the colleagues and their families.

Human resources management

Building a strong sense of community at the workplace, by partying among other things, was one of the ways people were encouraged to work together as a team during the socialist system. Its ideals of providing employment for everyone, of treating everyone equally, of paying people according to their needs, and its centralized manpower planning, relied on its own peculiar brand of human resources management. There was no private sector, competition or market; socialist economic structures such as negdels, state farms, large state enterprises (mines, factories) as well as government and party administrations had limited opportunities to, for instance, pick and choose employees — or fire them, for that matter. Human resources management was a joint effort between government and Party-related organizations such as the Mongolian Youth Organization, trade unions and management, and included a wide range of social and cultural services. Incentives to work were provided by non-monetary benefits and perks, honorary titles, and building social cohesion.

Non-monetary-remuneration such as a sense of belonging seemed to work pretty well as incentives for work effort. One thing I never worried about was whether my staff would put in extra effort required to meet deadlines or during periods of heavy workload without extra pay. They did so, unfailingly. Of course, the times had changed by then and I had the privilege of being able to hire and fire my staff.

Other incentives were competitions between work units, titles, medals and awards, and these are still important. There are titles of State Honored Teacher, State Honored Industrial Worker, Red Flag Order of Labor merits, North Star Order, Labor Hero, People's Artist, Honored Artist /Worker (bestowed by government) or Advanced Worker (by ministries) for different sectors, in addition to state order and medals. The government still issues Certificates of Merit; there are youth organization awards with gold, silver and bronze medals; trade union and the women's federation issued certificates as well. Titles and medals were also awarded out of the workplace, for example to encourage childbearing. The Order of Maternal Glory Second Class was awarded to women with five (since reduced to four) or more living children and included an annual subsidy per child (referred to as medal money, it was still a significant source of income for herders in 2006); the Order of Maternal Glory First Class, to women with eight (since reduced to six) or more living children, with a higher annual subsidy per child. Under socialism these medals entitled mothers to inexpensive child-care and two weeks' paid vacation at a hot springs spa resort.

Women achieved a high degree of gender equality during this period: they had equal access to education, health services, and employment because equal rights for the sexes was part of communist ideology. At the same time, their role of mother was held in high esteem as vigorous pro-natal policies of government aimed for a higher population to decrease labor shortages and, presumably, to safeguard sovereignty over their territory (remember that the first uprisings were linked to the fear of huge numbers of ethnic Han Chinese settling Mongolian lands as well as increased taxes) and control over the huge public sector which was still heavily dependent on Russian management and technical expertise. A special tax was imposed on citizens of both genders between 20 and 50 who were unmarried and/or childless (not doing their duty), unless they had the excuse of being a student or soldier.

The Soviet Union, suffering its own labor shortages in Siberia across the border, encouraged and assisted population growth in Mongolia. Women had a role to play in procreation as well as direct labor, and their needs related to childbearing were well catered for: all soums boasted pre-natal rest-homes, maternity-leave was generous and over 90 percent of rural women now gave birth in hospitals, which resulted in steep drops in mother and child mortality. Women were urged to bear many children as a patriotic duty, and labor laws protected mothers by prohibiting dismissal of pregnant women or mothers of infants less than one year old; generous maternity leave of 101 days was granted. Day-care centers, boarding kindergartens and boarding schools for elementary/secondary schools ensured that women could stay in the workforce. Early marriages were not discouraged and students sometimes married while still at university. Shombodon, however, told me that it wasn't allowed in special secondary schools like his in Khovd and that some students (actually four from his class) got pregnant and had to leave school when they were 18 or 19. Contraceptives were not commonly available: in fact possession and distribution of them were among the alleged offenses of Chinese laborers being expelled in connection with the Sino-Soviet conflict of the Sixties. Of course, women's careers suffered with this emphasis on large families, and domestic work was women's work, just as in the West. The one choice that would have been difficult to make was that of not having children.

In any case, girls and boys had equal access to secondary education and a system of boarding schools for the sons and daughters of herders was provided by the state. At the end of the communist period in 1989, the gap between male and female literacy rates (defined in Mongolia as four years of schooling) was less than three percent. It is the reverse now, with female literacy rates higher than those of males.

Industrial development in the Seventies

In the 1970s, the planning process was refined, streamlined and extended beyond the Five-Year Plans. In 1976 Shombodon participated in the XVIIth Congress of MPRP as a student delegate from Irkutsk Agricultural Institute. That congress directed the government to develop "A General Scheme of Development and Positioning of Production Force/Means in Mongolia for the period 1976-1990". The government established a research institute under the State Planning Commission and the Academy of Science to work on that. Projects that formed an integral part of the plan included power-generation plants; housing developments; communications systems; coal, copper, fluorite and molybdenum mines; meat, leather, and wool-processing plants; food industries; and large-scale irrigated farms. Many of these so-called "turnkey projects" (ready-to-go at the end of the project) were financed and assisted technically by the more advanced Eastern Bloc countries. The major mining towns of Erdenet and Baganuur were planned and built.

July 2012. We drop in at the Baganuur coalmine without having made an appointment. The main office building is typical of the utilitarian Soviet-style buildings and looks slightly empty and neglected with a weedy square in front. We ask the guard at the front desk if we can talk to someone about the history of the company and are sent to see Mrs. Kherlenchimeg. She is a gracious host, smiling and enthusiastic, who started her career with the mine 20 years ago as an electrical engineer and has ended up the head of Human Resources. She tells us about the history of the mine:

By the early 1970s a sharp increase in demand for energy in Mongolia's central region prompted exploration for coal and in 1975 coal deposits that could be mined through an open-pit mine were found here. They were under a large pasture area with two deep lakes, one big, one small ("Baganuur" means small lake). Plans were immediately made to build a mine financed with a loan from the Soviet Union. The project included not only the mine itself, but also a railway that connected to the main north-south line, and a whole city with apartment blocks for Russian employees, schools, a hospital and other social services.

The mine was to provide brown coal for a fourth power plant in Ulaanbaatar. (In 2013 it was still the largest power plant of the country; there are plans to build a fifth.) Shombodon recalls being present at the project's opening ceremony, attended by the head of state, Tsedenbal, and other high-ranking officials — it was a big deal. Most of the construction was to be done by Russian construction companies. At the beginning, as a wintry photo shows, the area was just a snow field in which stood two gers that served as offices for the mining operations. Construction of a temporary mine started right away to fulfill the immediate needs for coal. They only started building the town three years later, in 1981. When we visited in 2012, it had about 24,000 inhabitants.

This type of mega-project required a lot of planning, in particular manpower planning. The Ministry of Fuel, Energy and Industry passed resolutions on preparing professionals for employment in the Baganuur mine so the recruitment and training of workers could be included into the National Plans. Education institutes were notified as to the number and types of graduates needed for the different projects. The central government agency in charge of planning and fulfilling labor needs around the country was called the State Labor and Salary Committee: it had to arrange that the human resources ended up where they were needed which was referred to as "organized labor transfer".

Graduates were usually given a limited number of choices of where to work. High-profile projects such as the Baganuur mine were desirable employers because salaries were high and the machinery was new. Graduates considered themselves lucky to get employment there. Sometimes, during the period of central labor force planning, whole classes of graduates managed to get hired as a group. Mrs. Kherlenchimeg makes the comparison with people wanting to work for the present-day Oyu Tolgoi (meaning Turquoise Hill) mine in the southern part of the Gobi desert, one of the largest mining projects in the world. It is financed by the multinational Rio Tinto Group, and an investment agreement between Canadian Turquoise Hill Resources (formerly Ivanhoe Mines) and the Mongolian government. The gold-copper mine combines open-pit and underground mining. It is expected to produce over 30 percent of Mongolia's gross domestic product when it is in full production.

Later I talk to someone who is knowledgeable about the vocational school system of the socialist era.

August 2012. On our way back to Ulaanbaatar we make a stop at Arvaikheer (Overkhangai aimag) and decide to stay the night and have dinner with Mr. Jantsandorj, a retired president of the vocational school in that town. He is a large man with an old-style grey suit jacket over a white shirt and an incongruous white sports-cap on his head. He is relaxed, happy to eat and drink with us, and happy to talk as well. He tells me that a network of vocational training institutes was established in 1962 and that the teachers of those new institutes were trained in the Russian vocational schools network — he himself received his training in Kazakhstan. The vocational schools used to graduate about 500

students per year during socialist times, in subjects stipulated in the Five-Year Plans.

Halfway through our bottle of vodka I ask Mr. Jantsandorj what his opinion is about my observation that Mongols have become very western during the past century through contacts with Russia, eastern European countries and lately the western world. He starts out thoughtfully: he graduated from three Russian schools/universities so it would be impossible to get the Russian education out of his head. But then he rallies, and says that no Mongol would ever sing a song in Russian or English except some opera soloists in Ulaanbaatar; the market economy originated in Mongolia 2000 years ago; Mongolian culture and traditions are immune to outside influences; Mongols protect their environment; democracy was introduced by Chinggis Khaan; and, most important, chess originated in Mongolia (and was introduced to India from there). He is a chess master and still teaches chess. Two of his pupils are currently playing in the Turkey chess Olympics, so he prays for them. I am too sloshed to ask further questions on the matter of western influences and realize that the answers might not be carefully considered either. We part the best of friends and a little worse for the wear.

The city of Erdenet, servicing one of the largest open-pit copper mines in the world, was also created in the Seventies.

* * *

July 2012. *Passing through Erdenet, we visit Mr. Stanboul, an unassuming and quiet retired gentleman who lives in an old-style apartment building, to ask about the history of the copper mine. I briefly mentioned him in chapter 5, in connection with his Kazakh religion, ethnicity, and childhood in Bayan Olgi aimag. His life's story is typical for his generation: he was born in 1937, one of 13 children of whom four died in early childhood. His parents were herders and he was busy with lambs and kids from age five. He started primary school in 1950 and graduated from school when he was 17. Then he herded until conscripted in the army where he served working in the forest industry about 50 kilometers from the city of Darkhan. After demobilizing, he got work at the national meat-processing plant (Makh Impex) in Ulaanbaatar for* *eight years, at a state farm in Töv aimag for two years, and then he went to Erdenet. He arrived in 1974, the year that the government announced the founding of the Erdenet Corporation. He applied for a job and arrived here through the organized labor transfer. First they built the Russian school and kindergarden and then the Mongolian school. They started by building eight wooden houses, three buildings as accommodation for new employees, two shops, a canteen, the administration building and an additional house for administrative staff. These were temporary wooden buildings; only one remains.*

The preparatory work started in 1974; in 1976 the Corporation started its actual mining operations — digging earth and removing copper ore to be shipped to Russia. In spring 1975 Mr. Stanboul was sent to Russia to take a driving course for the big mining trucks called "Bilaz" for a year. He came back in 1976 and worked as a driver of those big trucks for 31 years until retirement. He told me everyone liked to work for a livelihood in order to feed their family: "All Mongolians liked working." The Corporation proposed him for Labor Hero but the government gave him the less exalted title of Honored Industrial Worker in 2001.

Then he wants to talk about his family. He was 40 when, in 1977, he married a Khalkh-Mongol woman who also worked at the mine. She sounds like a typical tough Mongol woman, working as a crane operator before bearing him 10 children, five of whom died in early childhood. He has two boys and three girls left. Four of his children have graduated from university. The eldest did not complete college and married. He has five grandkids and he sees his children and grandchildren regularly. A daughter has been living in Germany for 10 years; last winter she invited her parents there from January to April. She is 27 and single. She doesn't want to get married before she is in her mid-30s, after achieving her goals. He visited Austria and Switzerland during his stay with her. His face softens into a smile as he tells me that he has been living with his family for 35 years now.

He also wants to tell us how very sad he is about environmental damages. When he visited his daughter he saw the level of environmental protection in Europe. It was good! Some say that people in Mongolia care a lot about the environment, but he saw more caring in Germany! Then he says wistfully that Bayan Olgi aimag, where he grew up, has only small spots of forest left in four soums (Tsengel, Altai, Bayanuur and Bugat). Each valley used to have rivers, creeks, springs but now these are dry and even the Khovd River is getting smaller. The five peaks of the Altai mountains where the Khovd river originates used to have snow to halfway down their slopes — now only on their tops. There were many natural beauties — now ex-natural beauties: they had many lakes, rivers, and fish. He remembers in particular two lakes called "sargail" (meaning earrings of a woman) where the fish are disappearing. The vegetation used to be lush, a grassy carpet of flowers. That is now less. He visits home once or twice a year so he sees it deteriorating. Tsengel soum used to be rich in larches but people have cut them for building, it is finished. They also had plenty of wild berries, but now one wouldn't believe there had ever been berries there. It is very sad. Also wild animals grazed there like sheep and goats. Now there is nothing to see. Climate change might influence; but there is definitely the human factor — for instance, cutting the larches. People are destroying nature for money and for bettering themselves at the cost of others.

Yes.

The agriculture sector in the Seventies

The 1979 census showed that more than half of the population was now urban, but efforts to modernize and diversify the agriculture sector were also showing results in the Seventies. The total area of land under cultivation increased to 1.2 million hectares through successful crop-development campaigns; intensive animal-husbandry farms, such as dairy farms and poultry farms, were established near urban centers. These were rapid and profound changes for a country that had not had any type of industry just 30 years earlier and virtually no buildings apart from gers.

Even the unwieldy negdels had become large, sophisticated operations. The negdel headquarters, as well as all main services, were generally located in the soum center. These services would include schools with boarding facilities, shops, a hospital, large veterinary facilities, laboratories and pharmacies for animals and humans, several university-level veterinarians and zoo-technicians, and a host of lower-level "para-veterinarians" and livestock specialists. A negdel might have four or five brigades with at least six households whose members were brigade staff, among them chief of brigade, accountant, warehouse keeper, mail distributor, a para-medical person (something like a nurse-practitioner) reporting to the soum hospital, trade and procurement agent reporting to the soum trade and procurement office, vets and zoo-technicians reporting to the negdel. In summer all milkers (about 20 households) came together in temporary production units, referred to as milking camps. One person would typically milk 20 cows. The milking camps separated the cream from the milk and the cream was sent to a central point to produce butter. One former veterinarian mentioned that his brigade looked after 4000 cattle, 4000 horses and also more than 10,000 small animals (sheep and goats).

Despite — or maybe because of — the negdels being large and complex enterprises, and in contrast to positive developments in the sectors of mining, industry, large-scale farming, and health and education, the animal-husbandry sector struggled. There were severe winters: some people mentioned that the very worst dzuds took place in the winter of 1977-1978, and lagging management skills slowed down production while targets for the livestock sector were continually overestimated. The sector did not receive the same degree of attention as the state-owned enterprises or, more important, sufficient funding. Young graduates and also herders would have tried to get employment in the new projects, or at least in the state farms and get the perks of workers.

In Khalkh Gol, the empty and remote far-east corner of Mongolia more than 1000 kilometers from Ulaanbaatar, where the Khalkhin Gol battle was fought more than 40 years earlier, development only began in the early Seventies when a state farm was established there — and we found one of the early immigrants to the area.

* * *

July 2012. We interview a woman called Khishigt who was born in 1946 in Dörgön soum, Khovd aimag. Mrs. Khishigt is tall with an impassive expression and does not give the impression she particularly wants to be interviewed. During the interview she thaws out, however, and is happy to talk about her childhood and life. I like her. She lives alone in a small wooden house the size of a ger with a neat and clean interior. A wolf-skin is lying on the bed and two of her grandchildren are hanging out with her. She tells us about her childhood and how she grew up on horseback. I image her as a beautiful leggy girl, athletic, taming and racing camels and horses across the western plains.

She started primary school at age nine and graduated in 1959 from the fourth grade. Then her mother took her out of school to help with the chores, although she did well in school and education was free at the time. Now she understands that the problem was that the household lacked labor because her father had died while in the military. The household had two gers, a small one for raising small animals and a four-wall one (the same size as most modern-day tourist gers). In 1956 her mother and grandmother voluntarily became negdel members and the household then got a monthly salary in two parts: a fixed part for looking after animals, and an index-based bonus related to volume of production. She used to work for the negdel herself in herding, construction, building fences, haymaking and whatever work was needed.

She married at 19 and had two children. Her husband found out that the Khalkh Gol state farm was recruiting and made a contract with it before informing her. She agreed with him, though, because she had heard it was a favorable place for herding and liked the fact it has historical significance; she loved coming to live here. The trip took 16 days. They sold some animals, took some and their ger and family and arrived in Khalkh Gol on July 11 1973 with a contract for nine years. They herded until 1994. First they took care of a herd of 200 cows, and then, when their kids were grown, added the care of a herd of sheep as well. Her two daughters used to work as milking-staff; now they are married.

That empty part of the country continued to recruit labor for many years through "labor surges", organized labor transfers planned at the national level.

July 2012. Mr. Myagmasuren (director of the Khalkhin Gol victory museum, whom I introduced in Chapter Seven), tells us that labor for the state farm came from three sources: prisoners after their release; people who had been advised by lamas to start a new life elsewhere to improve on their luck (for instance, after having lost children); and young voluntary enthusiasts. In 1982 he went to Khovsgol aimag to make propaganda for Khalkh Gol, to tell the people that there was good grass for the animals and new buildings. Officially he was well received by the

*aimag and soum governors and told where he could recruit, but behind
his back soum governors were making counter-propaganda. Labor was
still the most important input for any development and the negdels and
soums did not like to see households move out. He managed to recruit 15
families and took them to Ulaanbaatar where they were received at the
Ministry of Agriculture with a little ceremony, then on to Dornod aimag.
But that year there was a dzud and the grass was not tall as described
and the people caused him some major headaches by complaining,
drinking vodka and making trouble en route. Finally they arrived and
saw the nice new buildings. A welcome ceremony was arranged and each
household received a new ger and a small radio. They were happy. He
says these early immigrant families were in good shape and owned many
animals when the state farm fell apart after transition, but most of them
went back to Khovsgol aimag when the jobs in Khalkh Gol disappeared.
Only now in 2012, after 20 years of depression, the soum again needs to
attract labor. I suggest importing some people from Inner Mongolia as
labor because it is just across the river, but he shakes his head: "We
don't want them. They eat Chinese vegetables, not meat like we do."
And that is that. No meat, irrefutable.*

* * *

During the next labor surge, around 1986, the State Farm recruited
60 "mechanisators" (tractor drivers/combine operators).

* * *

*July 2012. We meet one of them, Mr. Enkh-Ochir, who was 30 when
he relocated to the Khalkh Gol state farm. He lives in a dilapidated
building stemming from the time when the soum was flourishing because
of the state farm. The stove is in the kitchen with the pipe poking
through the roof — it was originally a centrally heated apartment block.
He welcomes us with a charming smile and tells his story. He was born
in 1956 in Erdenekhairkhan soum, Zavkhan aimag, more than 2000
kilometers to the west, where his parents were herding for the negdel. He
has good childhood memories of living in a gorgeous soum that combines
forest-steppe with dry Gobi. They used to make four seasonal moves,
traveling 100 kilometers in summer and twice that in winter. They
moved without carts, everything on the backs of camels. The small
children were put in square willow baskets on the back of a camel. Due*

to health problems he only started school at 10 and the next eight years he spent the winters in school dormitories at the soum center. He tells us that it is pleasant to remember that time.

After school he was conscripted into the army and served in a motorized unit in Sükhbaatar aimag. When he came out he went to a vocational school to learn his trade of mechanisator after which he worked in Töv aimag until he heard that the Khalkh Gol state farm was recruiting. He was hired and met his wife.

How was he to know that the successful state farm would collapse soon after the transition of 1991? Or that there would even be such a thing as transition? Khalkh Gol soum, in the heyday of the state farm, had 9000 inhabitants: when we visited in 2012 it had only 3200.

Socialist organizations

Organizations such as the Mongolian Youth Organization, trade unions and the less important Women's Organization played a role in organizing labor and providing social services. The politically powerful Mongolian Youth Organization was heavily involved with preparing young people for their place in socialist society and imbuing them with revolutionary fervor and progressive ideas. It was "voluntary", but one really had to become a member if one wanted to get a good position in life. It was also a centrally planned organization that connected remote soums with the Party in Ulaanbaatar. Just like the MPRP, it was an initiative of the superhero Sükhbaatar, and its flag displayed three orders, indicating high-level awards given to it: Mongolia Red Labor Valor Order; Mongolia Order of the Red Banner of Military Valor; and, in 1981, the Sükhbaatar Order.

Most people I interviewed grew up before the transition and had been members of the Youth Organization. As a former soldier put it: "Where there was youth, there was the Youth Organization." He served in the military for three years and when he became sergeant he became the head of the Youth Organization of his military unit.

July 2012. I hear a bit more about the youth organization when I visit Galshar soum where I meet the energetic director of the modern soum

cooperative that succeeded the old negdel when it collapsed. When he hears I am interested in stories of people who are old enough to remember the socialist period, he rounds up two brown, outdoorsy types, Mr. Agwandorj and Mr. Arsojan, to tell me about it.

Mr. Agwandorj, born in 1959 in Galshar soum, became a herder in 1974 because the Youth Organization wanted him to, though he wanted to himself and was a good herder. Each brigade had a Youth Organization unit, a voluntary organization of members between 16 and 28. They did a lot of work, such as haymaking (soldiers also pitched in), building animal shelters, milking cows (normally women's work), drenching animals, constructing wells, liaising with vets and animal breeders. They had a checklist of things to do in May called the Thirteen Tasks of Spring: these related to livestock after wintering and preparing for next winter, and included animal health examination, vaccination, purging, selecting animals by their quality, separating sick and old animals, planning repair of animal shelters and so on. The soum had a youth committee headed by its secretary who was elected by its members. In most cases soum youth accepted "suggestions" from aimag youth committee regarding their elections

It wasn't all work: At night they partied and danced to electronic music with their girlfriends. There were two bands of electronic musicians in the soum. The youngsters also went around the countryside to serve the brigades with portable showers and cinemas. They generally had a good time and sang during their monthly and quarterly meetings. I ask Mr. Agwandorj and the more reticent Mr. Arsojan, who was a tractor driver in the same negdel, if they studied Marxism. They say, no, they studied Leninism: there was a "Lenin examination" every three years on a book by Lenin that young people had to study. They laugh about this: "Mongolian herders don't need Marxism." I ask whether they knew about the West but they only learnt about socialist countries, they understood capitalism was not very good but never knew much about it.

* * *

Trade unions in the Soviet Union — and therefore in Mongolia — were not independent organizations but were controlled by Party and government just like everything else.

∗ ∗ ∗

August 2012. In Erdenet we invite a friend and former classmate of Shombodon to dinner in the dark restaurant of our hotel. Mr. Terbish has a slightly formal manner at the start of the conversation — he is clearly used to official occasions — but thaws out when talking about his personal career. Like Shombodon, he graduated as a zoo-technician from the agricultural secondary school in Khovd, and had a career with the trade unions. He was hired because one of his former teachers was a member of the aimag Party committee and advised him to apply for a position with the Khovd aimag trade union council. His teacher then recommended the union to accept him because of his education and maturity (he had served in the military). He became the head of the two-person Division of Culture and Livelihood of the Trade Union Council, which had connections to the Housing Council.

Apartment blocks with central heating, electricity and hot and cold running water had sprung up everywhere in the provincial capitals and around industrial towns. These apartments were much sought after and had to be distributed in an equitable way. This is the way it worked: each enterprise or organization had its own trade union committee and housing council that made a list of people who needed housing. The aimag trade union's Housing and Livelihoods Unit collected lists of housing applications from different organizations, analyzed and prioritized them, and made suggestions to the Housing Council, headed by the first vice-governor (responsible for planning), on how to distribute housing. The council then prepared a final proposal for the distribution of the newly built apartments which was submitted to the aimag Planning Commission.

The trade union councils also occupied themselves with direct labor issues such as safety and security issues, access to resorts, support for the Children Pioneers, social insurance and with organizing socialist competition among labor collectives. Trade unions from Leningrad, East Germany and Poland helped Mongolia organize its unions.

Mr. Terbish's dream, when he came out of military service, was to get a higher degree and in 1975 he noticed an opportunity for one person to study in Leningrad. The criteria were that the person was working in cultural and public services, passed exams in Russian language and social sciences, and was under 28. He was the only candidate and after passing the exams at aimag and national level, he was accepted at the Trade Union College in Leningrad, but had to take a one-year Russian language course first. He received his Master's degree in 1980.

Russia paid foreign students stipends, accommodation, trips to other cities and to resorts. Students were also eligible to buy discounted tickets to go home or to visit other countries. He had a wife who was the head of the aimag bookstore and two children (aged two and three), so he went home during his holidays. Mongolian students in Russia were often homesick but usually went home twice a year, in summer for two whole months. I ask him what subjects they studied and he says, History of the International Trade Union Movement, History of the Soviet Trade Union movement, Provision of Public and Cultural Services.

Then we talk a bit about the changes after transition and he says: "Like other organizations after transition, the trade union movement needed to be restructured. Previously, government used to pay for resorts, Pioneers Children's camps, social insurance, etcetera. According to the restructuring of the economy, there was a loss of tasks [no more need for socialist competition, housing privatized] and the trade unions cut staff." He accepts the transition as a necessary step, but says it is sad that all the services previously provided by the unions that went to the government have now collapsed or were privatized. He isn't happy with current government budget allocations, thinks insurance premiums should accrue interest and be used for the intended purpose, but the government uses it to cover budget deficits. I can only tell him that Mongolia is not the only country where that happens.

The centrally planned economy and society had its own structures and organizations to ensure law, order and compliance with the national planning process. I found someone who could shed some light on this in Bugat soum.

26 August 2012. In Shombodon's soum of origin we meet Mr. Gombo, born in 1940, who has been the chairman of the soum council of elders for the past 21 years. Dressed unassumingly in grey with a flat cap, a shirt without a tie and a sporty jacket, he sits at his desk and offers us seats at the table placed perpendicularly to the desk as is the custom

among officials. He started working for local government in 1960 and retired in 2002. Most of his career he worked for an agency called the People's Inspection Committee, created in the early Seventies. The way I understand it, the Inspection Committee combined tasks of auditors, ombudsmen and secret police. He is pleased to talk about the olden days, a vodka bottle is produced, and this is what he tells me:

He was born in a herder household and, after having graduated from seventh grade, herded until he was 20. He was then employed in the soum trade and procurement office as shop assistant for two years, after which he became the secretary of the Soum governor's office. Then he studied at the "Party High School" for two years in Ulaanbaatar, as apparently he had been identified as cadre material. Back in his home soum he became the chairman of the People's Inspection Committee (PIC) where he worked until it was abolished in 1992. The PIC, according to Mr. Gombo, was a very nice organ: it inspected the implementation of legislation, ensured fairness between citizens, inspected whether local government legislation was in line with the law, whether people worked in a disciplined manner, and protected public property. At soum level the committee had only one salaried staff member (Mr. Gombo), between five and seven committee members and also, at brigade level, a small group of three inspectors per brigade. The PIC worked for fairness and for governance for people and connected people with government and had the right to take certain measures. It could simply signal that someone wasn't doing his job efficiently, require the negdel to discuss cases of low performance, or even impose a monetary fine in cases where communal property was lost or damaged.

He makes the point that finding violations was not his task but prevention was; the PIC would try to solve problems before they had to be handled by the police or the courts. For instance, he would plan to inspect the soum secondary school at a certain time and let them know in advance. He acknowledges that, although the committee worked in favor of government and individuals' rights, people were to some extent afraid of him and sometimes tried to hide things from him. He gives an example of his work: a brigade bookkeeper conspired with a local para-veterinarian to transfer 43 healthy animals to the vet care station and then write out certificates that those animals had died. The PIC revealed this and ordered them to repay these animals. The bookkeeper could have been committed to four years in prison but Mr. Gombo advised the court that the animals had been repaid, so would they please remand the case to negdel authority. The negdel removed the man from his position and he became a herder. Later, after privatization, he became a skilled herder with over 1000 animals. (Herders with more than 1000 animals are held in high esteem.)

Apart from the planned inspections it carried out, citizens could address the PIC at any time with complaints and he would conduct an investigation. The committee received about 10 letters of complaint a year. For example, someone complained that the negdel hadn't paid him his monthly salary for the past six months. The PIC hired an accountant, found out it was true and ordered the negdel to pay the plaintiff.

At soum level the PIC was independent because it reported directly to the aimag PIC, which in turn reported to the national PIC. The soum-level PICs worked closely with the soum Party organization and were represented in the local Khurals (assemblies). They inspected the work of the soum government, its civil servants, the negdel administration, brigade managers and specialists, or even individual negdel members. Regarding preparations for winter, it monitored what decisions were made by the soum government and if these were in line with the higher-level plans, then it went to bags and households to see if they implemented the soum governor's decisions, for instance if they had prepared so much hay and repaired so many fences.

Mr. Gombo is one of the few people I met who was negative and resentful about the transition. He tells me: "Senior people don't like transition and the measures taken during transition. They used to have independence, freedom, democracy, and socio-economic issues were resolved and people's livelihoods increased. The country developed on a planned basis. There was no unemployment, no poverty, no crime. Now people's lives have been badly affected. Criminal cases are increasing. Previous achievements have been destroyed, state farms, fodder farms, cooperatives, big factories. I can't accept it. Now they are trying to rehabilitate the economy. There are many poor herder households. Government couldn't even deal with the 2010 dzud! Life is OK in the big cities but not here."

Then he gets going about the youth nowadays: "It is Mongolian tradition to respect senior people and follow their advice. Young people didn't smoke or drink when around their elders. Now that has become common. Mongols respected people — they were quiet and just. Not any more. There is AIDS, drug use and prostitution. They didn't have that, so I cannot accept it and cannot agree with those things. At soum level *they don't have these things, but people drink a lot." (This doesn't surprise me as he is pouring us shots of vodka at nine in the morning.)*

The PICs at the different levels — soum, aimag, and national — may have been a genuine attempt to create some checks and balances, fight corruption, give people a voice and generally ensure that the massive state administration, the most defining characteristic of a centrally planned economy, didn't derail through corruption, laziness and incompetence, and so ensure that the plans were implemented correctly. They also functioned as an additional instrument for the Party to control society to the lowest levels. Probably a bit of both. The lines between state and Party were blurred, with the official state organs formally in control but the single political Party the puppeteer. The Party formed parallel structures to those of the official state apparatus, and was heavily influenced by the official Party line of the USSR. The relations between the formal power structure and the Party wielding de facto power were complicated and made it nearly impossible to analyze decision-making processes, but it is clear that the Party's power amounted to totalitarianism disguised as the reign of "the people".

In 1990 the Ikh Khural abolished the PICs. Their functions were taken over by the National Anti-Corruption Agency and the National Audit Office, but these two agencies do not have much depth: at aimag level only the latter has representation. In the Seventies, however, as the socialist system reached maturity and had its own organizations in place, things seemed to be humming along quite nicely.

10. FINAL CHAPTER OF THE SOCIALIST ERA

Socialism's maturity

Who of us, in the 1980s would have predicted that the USSR would disintegrate, the Wall would come down, communist systems cast off? Not I, immersed as I was in my own petty life: graduation, unemployment (I wondered briefly whether our own capitalist system was breaking down), first job in the Third World (Ethiopia with its famine), marriage. No, it never crossed my mind that the Second World would disappear. The Iron Curtain seemed a given and hadn't I myself inspected the Wall in Berlin from both the western side and the eastern side? It seemed permanent to my generation, even in its weirdness. While I had visited Poland and what was then Yugoslavia, I didn't know much about the other side and certainly nothing about the USSR's far satellite, Mongolia. Whatever was brewing out there was invisible to most of us, but it was nevertheless fermenting like good strong airag.

Neither would the Mongolians have predicted the impending implosion. Their lives had only improved in their lifetime and they were proudly taking their place in the wonderful socialist new world. In 1981 they even had the satisfaction of seeing one of their own in space! Mr. Gürragchaa, born in a rural soum in lovely Bulgan aimag, studied aerospace engineering in Ulaanbaatar, joined the air force and was recruited by the Soviet Intercosmos program to train as a cosmonaut. Mongolia had come a long way: anything was possible. A child growing up in a ger in bucolic Bulgan, who liked catching and looking after horses, went on to become a cosmonaut! In 1981 he and a Russian colleague orbited the planet 124 times, docked with the

Salyud 6 space station and carried out experiments in the earth sciences. They landed safely a week later and Mr. Gürragchaa became an instant Mongolian superhero.

Indeed, it looked as though the developments of the previous decades would continue virtually unchanged. Industrialization and urbanization continued to fuel rapid economic growth. The centrally planned economy increased geographical as well as social mobility, with its centralized labor force planning aimed at filling all jobs with qualified workers. Labor productivity was increased and full employment achieved; at the same time the principles of free will and material interests, right to work and free choice of occupation were pursued. Education continued to be a priority, and ever-increasing numbers of Mongols studied at the 40 vocational training institutes in the country and abroad in the Soviet Union and other Comecon countries. Working conditions were better than they had ever been and the Labor Law, emulating the Soviet Labor Law naturally, provided for eight-hour workdays (less in the case of minors or arduous working conditions), eight public holidays, 15 days' paid annual leave days, compulsory state social insurance, retirement age of 60 for men and 50 for women, paid training courses, and generous provisions for pregnant and nursing women and women with children. As a result, female labor force participation was close to 50 percent by the late Seventies.

More than half the population was now living in urban areas, many of them still in gers, but utilitarian centrally heated apartment complexes served by shops, schools and playgrounds were rapidly being built to accommodate the increasing number of industrial workers. The rural areas were not as luxurious or advanced — most people still lived in gers as they still do — but state services covered many of the needs of rural communities.

The transport sector illustrates this. The public auto transport sector that replaced the pony-express in 1949 had reached a high level of development, with 40 auto-transport hubs distributed over the country and specialized routes and vehicles for transporting different goods, for example, fuel, post/passenger, consumer goods, fodder, logs, seeds, fertilizers. Most trucks were utilized both ways, transporting consumer goods from the urban centers to the rural areas and livestock products — wool, hides, skins and meat — in the other direction. For harvesting and transporting crops, the government established a powerful special commission that included representatives from different ministries to manage all the logistics involved. By the late Eighties, Mongolian Airlines, the national air carrier, used its aircraft not only for passengers, freight and mail transport, but also for crop dusting, pest control, fire patrols, and air ambulances. In cases of extreme dzud, Soviet and Mongolian military helicopters assisted in transporting animal fodder and relocating households. Before the transition, all aimags had two 11-seater Antonov-2 aircraft for passenger, freight and mail (except Selenge: located on the main railroad and north-south road, it needed only one). The mail flights on Tuesdays and Fridays would usually continue on to the more remote soums after arriving at the aimag centers from Ulaanbaatar. Larger Ilyushin 14, later replaced by the Antonov 24 that were still flying when we arrived, were operated from Ulaanbaatar airport, particularly for longer flights.

While the contribution of agriculture to the national income had dropped to about 18 percent in the 1980s, it still employed about a third of the labor force and supplied nearly 60 percent of Mongolia's exports. The most common professions were still related to animal husbandry: veterinarians, zoo technicians specialized in the different animals, herders.

✳ ✳ ✳

July 2012. Choir. We visit Shombodon's sister, Mrs. Nuukhuu, who is a veterinarian. She is an energetic woman with the red cheeks that demonstrate a lot of time spent outdoors. Inviting us to lunch in her apartment in a typical Soviet-era block, she beams and giggles, clearly delighted to see her older brother and nephew, and is more than happy to tell her life story. Fifty-six years old, she is actively retired, following courses on different subjects and growing vegetables in greenhouses. She opens a bottle of vodka and pours, while her story pours forth as well.

After graduating from the Zaizan Agricultural College in 1985, Mrs. Nuukhuu went to work for the Dornogovi aimag Livestock Procurement Office. At the time the aimag had 13 soums from where herders trekked their animals to the soum centers. Livestock procurement was done locally, with assistance of the soum and bag governors. The livestock purchasing process started in the soums at the beginning of May. Each soum had a trade and procurement office that purchased animals (from negdels, mainly), organized the herds and hired local herders. Purchases were based on the live weight of the animals and there were certain standards for health, age and weight; mostly healthy male animals were purchased. The veterinary office inspected them at the livestock station that had facilities such as animal fences for different type of animals, scales and an office.

The Livestock Procurement Office then recruited drivers, herders and organized herds, transferring them to the "livestock trekking expedition" where Mrs. Nuurkhuu worked. There was one herder for 400 small animals or for 150 large animals, e.g. cattle. Each herd consisted of 1200 small animals or equivalent, and was handled by three herders. The herds were trekked to number 14 livestock herding station (between Choir and Ulaanbaatar) from which they were transported to Ulaanbaatar by railroad. The livestock trekking expedition at aimag level was managed by a mobile unit made up of a chairman, a university level veterinarian (Mrs. Nuurkhuu), a para-veterinarian, an assistant, a driver and a trade agent. The whole process took many months and ended on December 15 when the animals were sold to the national meat-processing plant. The aimag People's Monitoring and Inspection Committee oversaw the process. The purchasing process was monitored in the soums. One person monitored three soums and made sure that herders didn't exchange healthy animals for weak animals, and that false certificates about animals dying weren't made up. The committee was a powerful institution that was independent of the Party and protected state property. The inspector was paid for by the trekking expedition and had responsibility to monitor it.

Mrs. Nuurkhuu worked there for two years and four months, after which her father advised her to quit because she was on the road all the time and he didn't consider that suitable for women (he was an elderly ex-lama born in 1917, a different time). Also, she has walked with a limp since she was seven or eight after a fall from an animal fence which the siblings kept secret from their parents for some time, probably worsening her condition. So she found work as a veterinarian in Ikhkhet soum center, where their brother-in-law was negdel director and soum governor. In 1990 she came to Choir to work for the coal mine as the veterinarian at the company's livestock farm for three years. Then they promoted her to the manager responsible for supply (trade, canteen, hotel, livestock, services — everything except coal mining itself). Like Shombodon, she is looking back on a typical Mongolian career.

Shombodon and his family

In 1960 Shombodon's father decided to move his family from Bugat soum to neighboring Tugrug soum because he wanted his only son, Shombodon, to go to school there. Bugat had only a primary school with grades one through four. The young Shombi completed fourth grade in 1959 in Bugat and then enrolled in the fifth grade in Tugrug soum where there was an incomplete secondary school (grades one through seven) attracting children from neighboring Altai, Tseel and Bugat soums. His father applied for a travel certificate but the administration refused to let the family go. In sparsely populated rural Mongolia, labor shortages were bottlenecks for economic development and in any case the centrally planned political system was not partial to people freely moving around when and where they wanted to. People lived and were registered in a certain soum and needed permission to move out, needed travel papers to move and needed to register in the next soum. It was important to be registered somewhere in order to receive benefits such as child support. People who moved illegally could be checked by police at any time and required to move back or punished. That said, most soums welcomed newcomers if they behaved well, and because of the labor shortages newcomers usually found employment. The family moved: Bugat negdel sent a car to Tugrug to fetch them back but Shombodon's father was a hot-tempered and stubborn man and they didn't go back. One-zero for Mongolian-style nomadism versus Soviet-style red tape!

The issue with documents wasn't resolved, but the family moved again a few years later on temporary travel papers issued by the Tugrug soum administration. In 1961 the oldest daughter (Shombodon's older sister) had been officially transferred to work at Arkhust state farm a little to the east of Ulaanbaatar, approximately 1400 kilometers from Tugrug soum. Her reports on the area of Arkhust were favorable, saying the place was greener and more fertile than their own Gobi region, and her sister and brother-in-law, who were herders, decided to move there. In 1963, they took jobs trekking locally purchased animals to the Ulaanbaatar meat factory, which took them three months. From Ulaanbaatar they went on to Arkhust state farm. A year after that, the parents with the rest of the children left their remaining 40 animals and two gers behind and moved to Arkhust; in 1966 Shombodon's uncle followed.

Shombodon's sister Nuurkhuu was eight when the family moved from Tugrug to Arkhust. She remembers it well: they traveled in a postal vehicle, a Gaz 51 truck that could carry between 25 and 30 passengers — all 12 of them traveling together, the parents, eight children, their maternal grandmother and a son-in-law. The trip took long because there was an outbreak of bubonic plague in Arkhangai and Bayanhongor aimags and they had to wait at least 10 days before they could continue. At Lun soum, where the road crosses the Tuul river, the vehicle had to refuel and the passengers were asked to get off and walk. There she found baby frogs — the first frogs she had ever seen. coming from an extremely dry and rocky area in the Gobi — and showed them to her mother, who threw them away and said: "You shouldn't pick up frogs with your hands."

The family had a hard time in Arkhust at first. They had left behind their large six-wall ger in Tugrug soum so strangers had to take them in, and the large family was at first distributed among other households. Father started to work as a watchman for the auto garage and mother was unemployed. The next year the family got hired as herders, were issued a small ger from the state farm, and had to move out of the soum center. Nuurkhuu, who was 10 by then, had to go to boarding school in the soum center and was homesick for her family the first year.

Shombodon joined the family in 1968. Between his graduation from the Khovd Agricultural Secondary School in 1966 and moving to Arkhust, he worked for one and a half years for a negdel in Overkhangai aimag as a zoo-technician. There he worked mainly for the "Guchin Tav" (the name means 35, for the 35th anniversary of the revolution) brigade that had originally been a separate soum, but was now integrated into a large negdel. The brigade was subdivided into eight sub-production units, each with more than 20 suuris, each of which in turn consisted of one or more herder households, and had almost 20 staff including the head of brigade, an accountant, a warehouse keeper, two para-veterinarians and a junior vet technician, a zoo-technician, eight heads of the livestock sub-production units, a trade agent, a post man, two medical staff and a watchman. The medical and veterinary offices and trade agents reported to the relevant organizations in the soum and others were paid by the negdel.

Shombodon's job was mainly to perform artificial insemination. It was a good job: in winter he was not very busy, sometimes giving some advice to herders, and it paid quite well. He could buy at least four or five sheep on his monthly salary — these cost 80-100 tögrögs each and he earned 500 tögrögs per month. In comparison, in 2012 he could buy only two sheep on his pension. The negdel used to pay out 70-80 percent of salaries and kept the rest for bonuses at the end of the year if they had a good production index. This was the same for herder households. They were rich by the end of December or early January. They didn't have big New Year's parties like they have now and Tsaagan Sar (lunar new year) celebrations were also very limited. The government allowed nedgel members to celebrate these traditional festivities but not employees of state farms; in fact, they specifically made sure that employees worked during those periods.

College graduates normally got a choice of several positions; Shombodon simply chose the position in the direction of where his family had moved to and in 1968 he took the bold step of simply moving to Arkhust to try his luck there because he wanted to live with his family. There was no job opening in his field at first so he was initially put to work in the heating installation of the mechanical workshop for agricultural equipment, shoveling coal. After a few months he got a job in his profession. The whole story demonstrates how the centrally planned economy worked — and how it didn't work. To me it also demonstrates that the Mongols retained sufficient flexibility to make it work.

The Arkhust state farm mainly raised Karakul sheep producing lambskins for military officers' hats in the USSR and Mongolia. The lambs are slaughtered three to five days after birth to get the good fur. Karakul hats have a long history in Central and South Asia: Muhammad Ali Jinnah, founder of Pakistan, made the style popular among Muslims of the Indian subcontinent; and the kings and later presidents of Afghanistan, such as Hamid Karzai, liked wearing one. Politburo members of the USSR used to favor the Karakul hat: the fur is called astrakhan in Russian. But I digress.

The state farm had three production units, two for Karakul sheep and one for cattle. In addition, it had three cropping sections and a haymaking brigade in Arkhust. During the milking season temporary dairy units were established. Milk trucks visited twice a day (morning and evening) and transported milk to Ulaanbaatar. Shombodon's sister and mother milked cows during milking season.

In 1969 the government moved the state farm (except for its dairy unit) from Arkhust to Sumber soum near Choir, which was a different aimag (Dorngovi — later to become the separate aimag of Govisumber), and changed its name to Sumber state farm. The whole family moved to Choir, where their first period was particularly difficult: Shombodon's sister and father were looking after Karakul rams in the new area that they didn't know very well and 20 rams were killed by wolves. The family was held responsible and had to pay for the loss. Fortunately, Shombodon, his father, three sisters and two brothers-in-law were working as herders for the same farm and the family was able to compensate the state farm within a short period of time. Their registration problem was still unresolved so they didn't receive the child support allowance. Only in 1970 was Shombodon able to resolve the paperwork for the household: he managed to get the family de-registered in Bugat soum and they became legal residents of Choir.

Shombodon told me, "In 1970s, many changes occurred in our family life. First, I met Togtokhbuyan, my wife, just after the state farm moved to Choir in September 1969. She was a local young lady and her smile was attractive to me. She was an assistant herder at the time. Soon we became friends and got married." They held the wedding in the countryside outside Choir, "just like herders". Her parents provided the ger-frame and his parents finished it, as was the custom. Their ger was set up next to his parent's household. Shombodon was away a lot: it took 10 days to do the rounds in the section allocated to him. He was responsible for the whole livestock production and pasture management, and the management of the suuris. Every month he counted all the state-farm animals to make sure everything was right with the herds. He made plans for each suuri and monitored their implementation; he calculated the monthly salary for each herder. In summer, he organized herders' movement for fattening animals and haymaking. In autumn, he conducted artificial insemination of sheep and in winter and spring, he gave instructions to herders on how to herd, feed, water and take care of animals. He had a busy job compared to his former easy job on the negdel.

When we visited Choir in 2012, Shombodon introduced me to his former boss Mr. Baanchig, who had worked for the state farm for 30 years until he retired in 1992. His parents and parents-in-law had originally moved from Gobi Altai to Arkhust through an organized labor transfer, more conventional than Shobodon's family. Mr. Baanchig had also worked as a negdel boss for a few years, so I asked him what the difference was between a negdel and a state farm. He said negdels were based on collective property, were self-financed and paid taxes from their profits. State farms were state property, depended on the state budget and were directly controlled by the government. For instance, all the operational costs of state farms were allocated by the Ministry of Finance and profits went to the state budget. Arkhust state farm made a loss for 15 years and only became profitable in 1970, after it moved to Choir. Most of the profits came from Karakul lambskins, of which they produced between 15,000 and 19,000 per year.

Meanwhile, the young couple started a family and tried to get ahead. Shombodon became a member of the Party in 1971 and the next year Togtokhbuyan took a short training course in Ulaanbaatar to become a cook and started working for the state farm hotel. In 1973 Shombodon took advantage of an opportunity to go and study in the USSR, the intention originally being to specialize in Karakul sheep in Tashkent, but instead the Ministry of Agriculture decided to send him to Irkutsk to specialize in dairy farming. Including the preliminary Russian language course, he spent five years at the Irkutsk Agricultural Institute. When he went, they had two children, their three-year-old daughter Enkhmaa and Enkhbayar, a ten-month-old boy (who later worked as our driver). His marks were all excellent so he was rewarded with a special stipend named after Sükhbaatar — 90 rubles per month instead of 60. This enabled him to support his wife and two children and send them children's clothes and toys.

After graduating from the institute in 1978, he was recruited by the Central Committee of MPRP. "I was selected for its Agriculture Division. That is how I was promoted from the farm level to the decision-making level. The division had over ten staff including a head and a deputy head and instructors including an agronomist, an agricultural machinery engineer, a water engineer, two zoo-technicians, etcetera. I worked there five years and was responsible for intensive livestock development policy, dealing mainly with state farms. At the beginning it was not easy for me to communicate with the Cabinet of Ministers, the Ministry of Agriculture as well as the State Planning Commission and aimag governors' offices, sometimes state farm and negdel directors. I participated in developing many policy documents, but I am most proud of the approval of two joint resolutions of the Central Committee and the Cabinet of Ministers — one on strengthening mechanized dairy farms and another one on improving and regionalizing animal breeding in the country. The latter was even discussed on the agenda of the Central Committee of the Party before approval of the resolution.

"In autumn of 1978, we moved from Choir to Ulaanbaatar and lived two years in our ger, after which we received a two-bedroom apartment. When we arrived in UB, my wife started work as a cook for the Central Policlinic till 1986. Then she was a senior cook for a kindergarten in Sükhbaatar city till 1989. After that she worked as a senior cook for the airag sanatorium, then for the national tuberculosis center till her retirement in 2004. She was awarded with the title of Advanced Worker of the Ulaanbaatar health system."

The "airag sanatorium" is an unexpected Mongolian twist that airag gives to an otherwise perfectly ordinary health institution. Just as in Europe, tuberculosis was a serious contagious disease in Mongolia and was dealt with — apart from the airag — according to the available medical knowledge of the time. As early as 1924 the government established a division of tuberculosis, then an anti-tuberculosis department in 1931 and the first three sanatoria in 1934. The airag sanatorium was established in 1946 with 15 beds and was operational till 1994, nursing patients who had been treated in special hospitals back to health. At that time, the sanatorium had about 40 staff including five doctors, six nurses and six junior nurses, and eight staff in the canteen. It could serve about 70 patients in one shift. It had its own dairy cattle and horses, and was almost self-sufficient in milk and airag.

Shombodon's stories are the ones I am most familiar with and I can relate to the warmth and closeness of family they exude. I picture the snugness of a ger in winter, a fire warming it up in the morning, grandmother making tea. I think of the extended family trying to milk the unruly mares. I see how the family stuck together during difficult times, how they traveled halfway across the country to find a better life. I imagine the girl's smile that captivated the young Shombodon. I see Shombodon and his generation wondering about their lama relatives and what they had gone through. And I see how life seemed predictable through the Fifties, Sixties, Seventies, and Eighties, and how things were improving bit by bit — until they didn't.

Hidden things

Beneath the surface of predictability, undercurrents were subtly changing direction, despite the fact that dissident voices of the Sixties had been silenced, despite the visible economic progress that was going on, and despite the normalcy of daily life. As early as the Seventies, hidden things wanted to surface.

August 2012. Mr. Luvsanjamts of Tsogt soum (see Chapter 2) tells me that he turned 12 in 1970, an age when children understand more than their parents give them credit for. It is difficult to keep secrets in a ger: children are sleeping while adults conduct their business — or they are pretending to sleep. Mr. Luvsanjamts, whose father had been a lama, remembers that a relative, the ex-lama Baanchig, came to their ger once with something concealed in a sack announcing: "Older brother [this must have been how lamas addressed each other], I have brought this hidden Thing," But father was angry and asked: "Why did you open this Thing on your own?", so Baanchig took the Thing back. Some time later Luvsanjamts and his brothers were in bed while his father and uncle Purev were discussing what to do, thinking the kids were asleep. Baanchig had opened the Shutèn (a sacred object of adoration of the monastery). It was the Divanger Burkhan, an image of the Buddha, the most sacred image of the monastery — the monastery that had been destroyed more than 30 years earlier. They discussed what to do now that the Shutèn had been uncovered.

Some time later, when he was in grade seven, the relatives started preparing a ceremony. His mother said: "Don't open your mouth, this is a celebration for animation of the Shutèn." It was the celebration of Aravnalaikh (consecration), a religious ceremony in which the Buddha comes alive. A new ger was erected and food prepared. One evening three lamas came on horses and each brought a saddlebag; the next day three more came, and then another three. In the end there were nine lamas and they started the consecration. On the fourth night they held the Aravnalaikh until four in the morning to animate the Shutèn. So the Shutèn was accessible to people from the end of August 1972. During the ceremony the children stood watch and had to notify the adults if anyone came.

Later Mr. Luvsanjamts heard the nine lamas openly discuss politics and what to do regarding religious issues. The religious ceremony had been good for them: they were less afraid after that and talked as if they believed times would change for the better. The young Luvsanjamts was drawn to the old religion and gained the trust of several of the ex-lamas. So it was that some of them entrusted small objects, such as small Buddha-images that are worn around one's neck and, more importantly greeslels (riddles or clues referring to religious affairs), among them encrypted instructions as to where some other religious objects were hidden. Inside the Buddha-image he inherited from his father — the one his father had received from his teachers when he turned back to Mongolia halfway through his intended flight to China — there was a greeslel that said: "Time will change". It also explained the hiding-places of several religious objects, so he received clear instructions on what to do when times would change: find the hidden things. These were Buddhist artifacts buried by desperate lamas during the purges of the 1930s. He was still digging when I met him in 2012.

Perestroika Mongolian-style

By the 1980s political change started happening in the Eastern Bloc. Invisible at first, these changes were moving inexorably toward a tipping point. In 1984, in a Soviet-inspired move, the Politburo of the MPRP forced the elderly Tsedenbal to retire from his positions of general secretary of the Central Committee and president of Mongolia. Taking into account that he had become general secretary and the nation's number-two leader at the party's Tenth Congress in March 1940, he had held high power for 44 years, 32 of them at the very top, and was considered a staunch ally (some say puppet of) the Soviet Union's previous leader Leonid Brezhnev. As usual with dictatorial leaders, Tsedenbal had nourished a personality cult. He was married to a Russian woman who was close to Brezhnev and whom some saw as the power behind the throne. The 68-year-old was vacationing in Moscow when a Kremlin doctor diagnosed him as suffering from overwork (burnout, we would say) and the Soviet leaders summoned two of the top Mongolian leaders (J Batmönkh and D Molomjamts) to tell them that he could no longer serve. He never went back and spent his retirement years in Moscow in a modest apartment, his health slowly failing until he died in 1991, the first year of transition. Batmönkh, a former economy professor who had gone into politics in 1973, became the new head of state. His focus was economic development, in particular energy and mining, and his major accomplishment would be to abstain from using force against the demonstrators who clamored for him to resign in 1990 (he later published a book called Never Use Force).

In March 1985, Mikhail Gorbachev, at age 54 the youngest member of the Politburo, was elected general secretary of the Communist Party of the Soviet Union and thus became the de facto leader of the USSR. Gorbachev realized that profound political, social and economic reforms were needed to revive the stagnating Soviet economy. Interestingly, he started with an anti-alcohol campaign (leading to a loss of an estimated billion rubles for the state budget). This must have been a shock for the Mongols as well as the Russians! Gorbachev's reforms, the most famous of which were called perestroika (restructuring) and glasnost (openness), were designed to improve the workings of centrally planned economies by introducing market-like reforms, lessening the tensions of the Cold War, allowing more freedoms (such as freedom of religion and freedom to express previously banned ideas), multi-candidate (though not yet multi-party) elections, and allowing state enterprises to respond to demand rather than being limited to fulfilling state orders. The reforms designed to make the existing socialist system work more smoothly opened floodgates of pent-up frustrations, nationalist movements and repressed opposition, eventually leading to the dissolution of the Soviet Union. A similar thing was to happen in Mongolia.

The relationship between Mongolia and China, which had continued to deteriorate during the Seventies, reached a low point with the expulsion of some 1700 Chinese nationals in 1983, many of whom had arrived decades earlier to work on construction projects. (Ethnic Chinese Mongolian citizens were not expelled.) By the mid-Eighties tensions between China, the USSR and Mongolia started to ease. In 1986, after an important speech by Gorbachev in Vladivostok in which he initiated détente with China, the Russians withdrew troops from Mongolia, and Mongolia and China re-established diplomatic relations. Mongolia continued as a satellite state to the Soviet Union and tens of thousands of Soviets and East Europeans were living in Mongolia in the 1980s, working as technical advisors, trainers and professionals.

Despite the rapid growth of the past three decades, Mongolia's economy, just like the Soviet Union's, had started to reveal more of its inherent inefficiencies and weaknesses. Politicians and bureaucrats overrode the more scientific opinions of scientists and engineers. In the cashmere sector the price per kilogram is highest early in the season, when the first cashmere is offered for sale, and drops as greater volumes become available. This led the bureaucrats and politicians, unencumbered by reality and focused on increasing profits, to force the negdels to start combing the goats at ever earlier dates. Cashmere should be harvested when the goats start shedding their downy undercoat in April/May. Combing the goats before the cashmere started getting loose made them cry piteously and went against the better instincts and knowledge of the herders — it visibly pains Shombodon to remember it. The animals are weakest in spring and need protection against the season's blustery weather with its accompanying extreme wind-chill factor. Every year many animals (and a few people) die, even when the winter is not defined as a dzud. But if a committee in Ulaanbaatar set a date for starting to comb the goats, that was when the negdel boss had to do it.

Something similar happened with wheat. The dates on which to start the different agricultural activities were set at aimag level. Töv and Selenge aimags organized consultation meetings in which weathermen, agronomists and other scientists would discuss the conditions and propose a date to start planting. In autumn, ministry officials and experienced specialists visited the crop fields by helicopter to propose harvesting dates. Higher-up accountants and bureaucrats would regularly override the scientists when they thought the prices would be better if the crop were to be harvested at a later or earlier date. Their foolish disregard for the fact that there are factors beyond human control influencing harvests often resulted in the opposite of what they intended.

From 1978 to 1983, Shombodon worked for the Central Committee as advisor responsible for intensive livestock development policy, mainly related to state farms. He was involved in preparing resolutions for the Central Committee and government on issues such as upgrading dairy farms or introducing new breeds of goats and sheep that yielded finer wool. In 1983 he was sent to the Moscow Academy of Social Science to work on a doctorate degree on the modernization of the livestock sector (the subject of his dissertation was "Socio-economic effectiveness of specialization in the livestock sector in Mongolia"). The prestigious Academy reported to the Soviet Central Committee, so Shombodon had a front-row seat in Gorbachev's theatre of change. His new ideas were avidly discussed and the Mongolian students resolved to introduce similar changes at home.

Economic development had stagnated by the end of the Seventies with actual production lagging behind planned production, and many highly educated Mongols were disillusioned with the antiquated system. Influenced by perestroika, Mongolia adopted a program of economic reform in 1986 that was to accelerate development through increased use of science and technology, management reforms, improved planning, more freedom for individuals and generally by striving for a better balance between private and collective interests. In the next two years, a thorough reorganization of top-level state planning committees and ministries took place, streamlining the planning process.

The government's economic reforms meant that "private interests" were to be taken into account, i.e. to give workers a personal stake in the production process instead of assuming everyone would to their level best for woolly concepts such as "the people", "the collective" or "glorious socialist progress". The term "private interests" did not mean the same thing as when we in the West talk about the private sector because there was no private sector as we know it: all production was state-owned and/or state-controlled.

As Shombodon explained: "In 1986, after having completed and defended my PhD thesis, I was appointed chairman of the Agricultural Management Board and vice-governor in Selenge. Because of where I had studied, I had a certain understanding about perestroika in Russia and tried to do my best to hold the course plotted out by the Party and government. We, the Agricultural Management Board, started restructuring economic and financial mechanisms of the state farms [Selenge had 16 big state farms and no negdels] by introducing a new, more detailed system of budgeting and monitoring at the level of production units of state farms, limiting government investment and making them more efficient. Agreements were made with state farms employees, crop and livestock producers, encouraging the private interests of the employees [linking their performance to their rewards] and so increased economic effectiveness of the state farms. The contracted primary producers received up to 50 percent of the saved production expenditures and the amount of products produced in excess of the production plans as economic stimuli.

"This paid off: Selenge produced and sold to government over 100,000 tons of wheat, 5000 tons of potatoes and 2000 tons of vegetables, which was more than the targets stated in the production plans for the years 1986-1988. In 1988 our agricultural management board was recognized as the second-best among the 18 aimags and we received a reward from the Ministry of Food and Agriculture. During this period, we could build a new office. I never worked there; in fact, I disliked this job and always asked to resign. In June 1989 I left and became a researcher at the Research Institute of Animal Husbandry in Ulaanbaatar."

Similar changes were implemented in other sectors. For instance, a process of restructuring the negdels had started in 1987, when the responsibility for production was gradually shifted to the herders, first by agreements and then in 1989 through a lease system where the herders weren't paid by the negdel anymore but generated their own income from collectively or state owned animals. Another example of attempts to incorporate private interests to make the centrally planned economy work more efficiently comes from Tosontsengel's wood-processing plant.

August 2012. Tosontsengel's Skyline Hotel in a rehabilitated old building is furnished according to Mongolian taste: gold wallpaper, silver curtains and radiators, ornate crimson bedcovers. There is no water: they are having some trouble but will bring us water to our rooms. The outhouse is in the back. Shombodon works his network to find someone

who will talk to us and we are invited over to a relative's ger to meet Mr. Dashtsend. He is a tall, handsome and distinguished-looking gentleman who first of all wants to know if the book I intend to write will be translated into Mongolian. I say that a friend has offered to have it translated and published in Mongolia and he graciously tells me his life's story:

He was born in Tosontsengel in 1948 and attended school from 1958 to 1968. His parents were living in the countryside, so he lived with his grandmother while going to school. He interrupts his rather formal recitation with a soft smile: "Now we are grandparents ourselves!" He says his parents, like all parents, loved to send their children to school. They went six day a week in shifts because there weren't enough classrooms. The high-school kids went in the mornings and the little ones attended the afternoons. He loved to study and loved sports, playing volleyball and basketball in school and he wrestled — "Mongolian boys always wrestle" — when out of school. Their teachers also taught skating and skiing, often using homemade skis and sleds. He tells me with regret that physical education received more attention in the past than nowadays. He was also a member of the Children Pioneers in grade school and then joined the Youth Organization. He was one of the young people who was absorbed by the industrialization surge and did not continue herding as his parents had done. We are invited to eat khuushuur: our hosts offer two khuushuur to the altar as well. Then we talk about his career.

Mr. Dashtsend worked as a driver for the wood-processing plant, received the status of "champion driver" many times at the enterprise level and even once at the national level. Just before the transition, they established a "self-financing transport brigade" with 11 heavy trucks — each truck had two drivers — plus three technicians for the whole brigade. He was head of the brigade. "Self-financing" didn't mean that the employees actually financed the trucks and operations themselves, but that the brigade managed its own budget and they got to keep savings and excesses over the budget allocated to their production. The employees received financial benefits from performing well. The self-financing started in 1988 and ended in 1991 at transition. He was responsible for their expenditure and he had to make sure that the brigade achieved high productivity. It was collective work: each person was responsible for the collective and vice versa. They became close like brothers and still keep in touch. The administration announced competition among the brigades, and incentive money was distributed according to performance. Thanks to that money, labor heroes from Tosentsengel became famous.

As an afterthought he says that people used to be enthusiastic, working in three shifts in the plant. They weren't worried about frost: they worked outside in winter when the temperatures dipped to between -45°C and -50°C (Tosentsengel is said to be the coldest town in Mongolia; temperatures of -40°C are common in winter). He sounds nostalgic for those times past when employees were taken care of: "The plant used to pay attention to social issues. They had a hot-springs sanatorium with a capacity of a hundred persons. The sanatorium had two hotels, five standard gers and one big ger, some houses and a restaurant. Employees went there to restore lost energy. Sometimes they stayed there for one or two weeks and went to work from there during daytime. The plant owned animals — sheep, cattle, and a few horses — and provided the meat needed by employee restaurants and the sanatorium. There were greenhouses at the plant as well. When they were transporting the logs there were certain eateries along the way where they could eat at discounted prices. Ex-employees still visit each other and talk about the good old times."

The good old times, however, were inexorably coming to an end, for better or for worse. Initially it was for worse.

11. TRANSITION

And Then Everything Changed

August 2012. Shombodon's vivacious cousin Tsengelmaa, who had told me about the ceremonies surrounding births and haircutting (Chapter 2), also talked about transition. Born in 1969, her childhood and adolescence were the typical preparation for a useful career in the centrally planned economy. After eighth grade she went to Khovd Agricultural secondary school (Shombodon's alma mater) for four years (1985-1989) where she lived in dorms. Students were used as extra labor during harvest time from mid-August to late October: she worked two seasons on Baruunturuun and Tes state farms in Uvs aimag. One season she practiced in Erdeneburen soum (Khovd aimag) for a month in spring, staying with a young couple who had five boys. They treated her like a daughter. She rode a horse and looked after animals — when these gave birth she had to bring the kids and lambs home. It wasn't easy to put the newborns in a lamb-bag on her back or on the horse, as she wasn't very tall. If there were more than six, it was difficult to load them all on the horse — she had to climb on a stone to reach up high enough. One time she had to do this in a snowstorm.

She graduated from Khovd with excellent marks so she was offered an appointment to teach at the agricultural vocational school in Shamar soum, Selenge aimag. She did not go because she didn't want to be apart from her mother who still had two small children at home and her brothers were in the military. So she requested work in her own soum and was appointed to work as a para-veterinarian in a brigade (bag) and was housed with a young couple. Herders would come on horseback or by camel to ask her to come and see sick animals and she would go. She liked the birthing season! There was no doctor or nurse so herders

195

asked her to do injections. So she treated the herders as well as their animals and learnt a lot about human medicine! After a year she requested a transfer closer to the soum center where her mother lived. But that bag also moved — to the other side of the Altai range. It was difficult. She did artificial insemination of sheep in at least three artificial insemination stations. While riding horses and camels and doing her work at the brigade, she met her husband. She got pregnant, married "with her son in the belly", and then everything changed — but not because of the baby:

"After my first birth, perestroika started. Our soum had a veterinary and zoo-technical division of twenty staff. After transition all except two, the chief veterinarian and the pharmacist, were fired. My husband was a herder, so I moved to herding. Our new household cooperated with my husband's parents' household. I milked cows and goats and trained camels and horses. I also assisted my husband with horse-racing; I hadn't raced when young but had learnt after graduation.

"I could sew deels and other clothes and do embroidery. My mother owned a Russian hand-sewing machine and bought me a sewing machine as a present during my wedding ceremony. I made clothes for the children. The local people and the parents-in-law appreciated me — I was good at producing milk products, including good quality milk vodka made from airag. I still know how to do it, but don't any more now that I am living in the aimag center. I am now a laboratory analyst. Herding was not easy and I had given two births in two years. My husband looked after the big animals and I had to look after the small ones with my two children on my back! The beginning of the transition was hard for rural people. They had no access to flour, which was rationed at two kilos per person per month, and nothing to mix it with. People say 'the shops only had salt'. Around that time I had access to border trading and traded skins and hides. Trading made our life easier; we did that for five years. Then we lost our ger in a fire caused by an electric short and we moved to the aimag center and I continued studying at the Agricultural University. Since 2006 I have been a veterinary analyst. My profession used to be para-veterinarian and now I have graduated as a full veterinarian. I like my current job. The Ministry has recognized me as an Advanced Agriculture Worker, for which I received a certificate."

I ask her views on government: her parents were party members and she supported that. Personally she is not interested; besides, she is *not allowed to be politically active as a civil servant. Then Tsengelmaa wants to tell me about her mother of whom she is so proud. I find it endearing that several people I interview about their life let me know towards the end of the interview that they also want to tell me about a cherished family member, such as a wife, brother or mother. This is what she tells me about her mother's childhood and family:*

She started to go to school in 1977, aged eight. Her siblings were already staying in dormitories but her father always said he would set up a small ger and look after her himself. Unfortunately he died a few months before she went to school, so it was her mother who came with her, put up a small ger in the soum center and looked after her. She worked as a watchwoman for a bank branch on a schedule of 12 hours on, 24 hours off. She owned a rifle and about five bullets. After work she sewed and cooked. She also managed to complete seven complete gers for her seven sons' marriages, as was the custom, as well as giving presents to her daughters and daughters-in-law. She survived her husband by 36 years and passed away when she was 76. She sure sounds like a tough old lady, worthy of pride.

I have not done Tsengelmaa justice: she must have bubbled and blurted out at least three times what I was able to capture through Shombodon's interpreting — he couldn't keep up with her excited deluge of words, jokes and fits of giggling, I have notes such as: "Now people are fat and lazy — they use cars instead of camels!"; "Human doctors treat people; vets treat mankind!"; "Nurses can't find veins, but I can!" She lives with her husband and four children: the boys are 22 and 23, the girl 17, and the youngest three. She is so proud of her parents and siblings who are well educated and achieve their objectives.

✳ ✳ ✳

Halfway through many of the interviews, the story changes: "And then everything changed. . ."; "Then perestroika started. . ."; "Then transition started. . .". Transition from socialism to capitalism, Mongolia's third revolution of the 20th century, changed everything for everyone, instantaneously. The centrally planned economy was resolutely dismantled and quickly reduced to ashes, to be replaced by a market-based economy — but capitalism rose only slowly from those ashes. It is always easier to tear down than to build.

The reforms introduced in the late Eighties as part of Mongolian glasnost and perestroika, although they seemed to have worked reasonably well, were all too little, too late. The global winds of change swept away the centrally planned system in the Eastern Europe and the Soviet Union, and Mongolia's economic and political system ended up being blown away as well, erratically in different directions, like tumbleweed over the autumn steppe. The country had revolved around the Soviet Union until that was no more; suddenly the Mongols were on their own, unprepared. Democracy replaced the authoritarian power of the MPRP. A wave of foreigners arrived from unfamiliar countries with foreign ideas. From the inside hidden things were emerging, among them Chinggis's spirit.

When exactly was the tipping point that made transition inevitable? In December 1989 small-scale protests started occurring in favor of following the Soviet Union in its policies of perestroika and glasnost. The formation of a Mongolian Democratic Union was announced by a young leader of the protest movement called Ts. Elbegdorj, who was later to become the president of Mongolia. In the deep-freeze cold of winter these protests gathered momentum as rallies, demonstrations and hunger strikes were organized and people started waving the Mongolian flag minus the star that symbolized socialism and holding up portraits of Chinggis Khaan. The power structure that had been in place since the early Twenties simply gave way and Batmönkh, chairman of the Politburo, dissolved the Politburo and resigned on March 9 1990.

In May that year, the government made the important decision to amend the constitution and end the MPRP's monopoly of power; other parties were allowed. A law was also passed banning parties from operating within government organs and requiring civil servants to drop their party affiliation. Opposition parties were promptly formed and in July 1990, for the first time, the former communists of the MPRP competed with the new pro-democracy parties for seats in the Ikh Khural. These first free elections were won by the MPRP by a landslide (85 percent of the 430 seats of the Ikh Khural) because it alone had a strong political infrastructure — and in the rural areas, the only political infrastructure. The swiftness with which the system that had taken more than half a century to build disintegrated must have taken everyone by surprise — at least, everyone who was not close to the protests in the capital. Mongolia was the first country outside Russia to form a Communist Party and embrace the communist ideal, and it was the first country to drop it. That's Mongolian decisiveness for you.

Dropping the communist ideology included expelling most of the Soviet professionals and technicians, which they started even before the one-party state was abolished. Shombodon, as deputy governor and director of Food and Agriculture in Selenge aimag, was involved in evaluating the efficiency of all Soviet consultants in agriculture sector and reported his findings to the Party committee. By the end of 1988 there were more than 40 Soviet consultants working in the Selenge agricultural sector in 16 state farms. At first he asked his staff to prepare a paper as well as the consultants themselves, but he didn't like the quality of either paper. He then requested a livestock specialist with a PhD to assist him, and together they produced a pretty good paper. After that, in a meeting to which all Soviet consultants were invited, the conclusion was reached that the consultants didn't work very efficiently and should go home. This decision was accepted by the Ministry of Food and Agriculture. Most didn't want to go back, including the two who were working for the Selenge Agriculture Board, one a 60-year old Ukrainian, the other a Tatar. The former Soviet Union, at the time, wasn't a place one wanted to go back to.

A month later the Soviet embassy in Ulaanbaatar organized a similar meeting with Soviet consultants in Mongolia and also concluded they were working inefficiently. They were sent back as well. In the coalmining town Baganuur, the Russians were replaced by Mongolians in 1990. In the Choibalsan museum, I came across a photo of Russian troops saluting their goodbye in 1990. Apparently they had received orders to leave the country within 24 hours. The Mongols say: "They left their apartments with everything still in it and the television still on but the wives were allowed to go and pick up their cats." It probably wasn't altruism that they were allowed to take their cats; Mongols generally don't like cats, for what reason I don't know (the cat-lover in me speaking here). They have a saying that "At night a cat goes round her sleeping owner three times to make sure that he or she has died, while a dog does the same, but to make sure that he or she is alive."

Democracy and freedom

In 1999 I arrived in a democratic country and didn't give it a thought that that in itself was noteworthy, that for the Mongolians democracy was a novelty. Granted, I had other things to worry about (a new job, a husband down), but I was embarrassingly unaware of Mongolian history, even very recent history. Democracy had occurred without major upheaval or bloodshed. When the first demonstrations took place there were a few voices in government in favor of forcefully repressing the demonstrations, but those opposed to violence (among them president Batmönkh, who decided to step down instead) prevailed. Shombodon adds that there really weren't many reasons to use force against the demonstrations because the Mongolians were well aware of perestroika and what was happening in Russia and other Eastern Bloc countries.

The constitutional amendments that ended the one-party monopoly were deemed insufficient for building the new Mongolia. In November 1991 the Ikh Khural began discussing a whole new constitution which, in accordance with the Mongolian tendency for decisive action, entered into force on February 12 1992. In addition to establishing Mongolia as an independent, sovereign republic and guaranteeing a number of rights and freedoms, it restructured the legislative branch of government, abolishing the Little Khural and creating a unicameral legislature, the State Ikh Khural, and stipulating that the president be elected through popular vote rather than by parliament.

A confused period followed the landslide win of the MPRP in 1990. The first presidential elections of 1992 produced the first win for the opposition, ironically because the sitting president from the MPRP, P. Ochirbat, had become too progressive for his party and stood for the opposition. There was a divided government with an MPRP-dominated parliament and an opposition president.

By the mid-Nineties people took to the streets again to protest corruption and demand higher wages, because wages had been hollowed out by inflation. In the elections of 1996, the land slid another way: this time round the opposition, having finally organized themselves and formed a Democratic Coalition, won the majority in parliament. In 2000 the landscape changed again and the former communists, who had by now embraced democracy and market economy, won. The back and forth between opposition and MPRP was to continue into the 21st century, where it is no longer the concern of this book.

The political turbulence was caused not only by people jockeying for positions of power and trying to take advantage of the situation, but also by people genuinely trying to understand what the western-style democracy, designed through the post-transition constitution, meant. In a 2013 study, a wide range of interpretations are linked to the word "democracy": freedom from oppression, freedom of speech, independence, human rights, justice for all, dignity, self-determination, equality, to name a few. Mongolia's transition wasn't just towards a market economy but also towards a democracy that embraces human rights such as freedom of speech, freedom of religion, and freedom of assembly.

Possibly the most valued element of the new democratic society is individual freedom — an idea that certainly appeals to the Mongols. People are happy that they now have access to different news sources and opinions, that they have freedom of speech, and, even more important, that they can come and go as they please. Before transition, the system kept track of all travel and vehicle movement through travel papers and checkpoints. This had been doable when the only vehicles around were official — after all, in every country there are systems of keeping track where government vehicles go to prevent abuse. Around 2003 the government tried to regain control and reintroduce travel permits and checkpoints for all vehicles. For a short time we had to fill out forms and experience delays when leaving Ulaanbaatar for work. This was soon abolished because such a level of government control could not be maintained in modern times: it was seriously detrimental to business and deeply unpopular besides.

Russia's influence rapidly diminished after transition, but there is an interesting small parallel between Gorbachev and president Elbegdorj: both incorporated campaigning against alcohol into their reform programs. Alcohol abuse has been a bigger problem in the former Eastern Bloc countries than in the West and socialist governments have been struggling against alcoholism for a long time. (as attested to by the many entertaining Soviet-style posters against alcoholism that can be found on the internet). In recent years, befuddled Mongols and expats alike have been faced with days that you can't buy a bottle of wine in your supermarket and restaurants don't serve alcohol. In Russia, Gorbachev's campaigns were unpopular and eventually abandoned: we shall see what transpires in Mongolia. Why alcoholism was so prevalent in the communist bloc is not clear to me: I have seen communist movements that were idealistically straight-laced, and anti-alcohol attitudes in western countries. Possibly it functioned to make the unpalatable possible: a Russian colleague once told me — under influence, naturally — that he had been recruited as a KGB agent while consuming several bottles of vodka with his recruiter.

Democracy and freedom do not solve the problem of how diverse cultures should live together in one country, as we from the West know well. Mongolia is a very homogeneous country but even it has a few ethnic minorities. For the Kazakh community the transition has been an unsettled period in view of the Mongol nationalist feelings that emerged. The subject is pretty much officially taboo, but there are feelings of them (the Kazakhs) living in our (Mongol) territory, particularly in far-western soums where the Kazakhs, with a higher birthrate, are changing the demographics in their favor. Younger Kazakhs told me that they experience discrimination, finding it hard to compete for jobs with ethnic Mongols.

The Kazakhs experienced their own surge of nationalist feelings after transition. By late December 1991, when Gorbachev declared the formal end of the Soviet Union, the reality was that the Union had already lost the last of its republics, Kazakhstan, which declared independence in 1990. Its government immediately promised citizenship to the Kazakh diaspora and in the months that followed, many Mongolian Kazakhs answered the call for Kazakhs all over the world to come home, in some estimates as many as 62,000 of them. Many returned to Mongolia a few years later. The exact numbers are not known as there has been quite a bit of back and forth after transition. In the process some Kazakhs who emigrated and lost their Mongolian nationality subsequently renounced their Kazakh citizenship and are now back in Mongolia, effectively stateless. They are, at the time of writing, still trying to get their Mongolian citizenship back.

Market economy

Mongols are not given to indecisiveness or procrastinating. In total contradiction to the method I employed when working in other developing countries, giving very specific orders and following up whether the responsible staff was "on it", I had to learn to be careful what I said as a manager in Mongolia. If I mentioned that it might possibly be a good thing to do something, my staff would come back a week later and report proudly that they had done what I wanted. Without discussing how to do it, without checking whether it had priority or not, without meticulous planning. This was exhilarating but caused me stress as I am afflicted with a detail-oriented and risk-averse personality. Similarly, once the decision to transit to a market economy had been made, the Mongols went all the way, immediately. They dropped the five-pointed red star that symbolized international communism from their national flag, eliminated price controls and rushed through privatization of state and collective assets (three quarters were privatized within a year) — and all this before there was any infrastructure to replace the socialist system.

There were no (or insufficient) laws to regulate the market economy; the banking system was inadequate; there was a lack of modern management experience in both private sector and government. Not that officials weren't trying hard: I was heartened to see a State Secretary in the ministry I was working with engrossed in reading Management for Dummies when I came in for a briefing. The dissolution of the Soviet Union meant an abrupt end to the Comecon markets and an end to the aid Mongolia had received from the USSR and its allies. The Soviet and Eastern European advisers left. All this led to a catastrophic collapse of the economy, starting immediately after transition in 1991. The currency devalued steeply, the cost of living skyrocketed, per capita income nosedived, food shortages led to rationing through food stamps, and barter became common. The Gross Domestic Product shrank for 1990-1993. Crop production was halved in the first four years; industrial output declined by a third. Negdels fell apart and state farms were left without budgets. What good does a combine harvester do with no capital to buy fuel, labor or seeds, and no spare parts because the Russian manufacturer has ceased to exist? Applications for large loans to finance such operations were approved by inexperienced bank staff unfamiliar with the concept of due diligence. Many of these loans were not repaid, leading to a collapse of the unsteady new banking system. Unemployment shot up and looting and stealing of state properties took place nationwide in the absence of effective state control.

Amid this collapse, a group of young foreign-exchange traders gamely gambled away half the national treasury, US$82 million, through currency speculation. The fact that these traders were somehow affiliated with the opposition Democratic Coalition increased popular misgivings about the country's new direction: it had plunged the economy into a crisis that left many people penniless and, for the first time in their lives, facing a very uncertain future. The currency gamble wasn't the only thing that went catastrophically wrong: a huge embezzlement case was uncovered in the country's largest income-earner (and taxpayer), the Erdenet Mining Corporation, a joint-stock company owned by the governments of Mongolia and the Russian Federation. The lack of tax income from the Erdenet mine caused such financial ruin that Prime Minister Enkhsaikhan of the Democratic Party stepped down. The subsequent audit of the company's books revealed that taxes, royalties and other income due to the government had been diverted to the private accounts of directors of the company. The English-language Eagle TV station aired a six-part series on the affair, Swindle of the Century, in 2000. Everywhere state-owned companies collapsed: for instance, Nalaikh Mining stopped operating in 1990 after a methane gas explosion that killed 21 people, putting 1500 out of work: its properties were plundered.

In some cases, fortunately, the infrastructure basically stayed intact. The Baganuur coal mining company, essential for heating the city of Ulaanbaatar, was restructured in 1995 and became a stock company: it is owned 75 percent by the government and 25 percent by private persons. From 1998 to 2000 a World Bank project assisted in modernizing the company: it still uses Russian digging equipment, but transport equipment is from Komatsu and Caterpillar. Some of the systems of the planned economy persisted for a short while after transition; for instance, state allocation of labor was still functioning in 1992, according to Mrs. Kherlenchimeg, whom we interviewed at the Baganuur mine.

The economy as a whole started recovering during the latter part of the decade after the first confusion was over and it became clear who were the economic winners and losers of the transition. Recovery of the banking system, the first priority of the government and the technical-assistance programs of the international organizations and western countries, enabled the private sector to utilize some of the privatized infrastructure and take advantage of a well-educated work-force. Western aid agencies poured in huge amounts of aid. Free trade after many years of shortages fueled the economy. International mining companies started coming in to explore Mongolia's mineral wealth and found huge deposits of copper, gold, other non-ferrous metals, and coal.

Surviving transition

The transition disrupted everyone's lives, regardless of whether they eventually came out on the right side or on the wrong side of the new-fangled rich-poor divide. The chaos and confusion of this period created opportunities for getting ahead, often at the expense of others. For instance, when the currency was devalued by 50 percent in 1991, private savings were protected by doubling them. So it was possible to take a loan, spend half of it and put half of it in a savings account so it would double and pay back your loan after devaluation, and those in the know did exactly that. Prices of everything in the shops doubled on January 16 1991; the shops were swamped on January 15. Many government officials (probably everyone in the Ministry of Finance) had prior knowledge of how and when the devaluation would play out, and many profited greatly. Such practices contributed to a sense of unfairness among the general public. Mostly, people's careers and lives were cut short and thrown into disorder.

2012. In Khovd we hook up with one of the people Shombodon and I worked with in 2002-2004, Mr. Togtogbayar, who reported to us as one of our five rural credit specialists. Because of our closeness to him, I shall call him by his nickname, Togie. Togie, who was based in Khovd, is a Torguud Mongol (a minority Mongol tribe) with an engaging smile, a sense of humor and a caring personality. I remember him knocking on my hotel room door one icy night with a pot of hot water, which the hotel couldn't provide, so I could wash my hair. (I didn't, because it had a film of mutton fat floating on top, but I appreciated the gesture.) Togie's

career during the transition period demonstrates the confusion of the times:

He was born in April 1963 in a place called Sharkhulst in Bulgan soum, Khovd aimag. His father worked as a herder and the household also planted grain, mainly barley. Togie is the youngest of eight, of whom two sisters and a brother passed away in childhood. He and two of his brothers got Kazakh names because boys tend to die young and his parents were advised to give their children strange names; they elected to give them Kazakh names, with which they were familiar because most Kazakhs live in the western aimags.

He started to ride from when he was six and looked after lambs and kids. He rode his horse to primary school in his bag center every day, about 15 or 16 kilometers. He liked riding, couldn't ride slowly and made it to school in 20 to 30 minutes. At the time they didn't have manufactured schoolbags: his parents sewed bags for textbooks. They dissolved some sort of powder to make ink. In the winters, father was away with the animals and mother lived near the bag center. After third grade he went to school in the soum center. When he was eight his father passed away and his mother a year later, so they were taken in by his brother-in-law's household. He had excellent grades and graduated from grade nine in the soum. Bulgan soum's school had 10 grades but he relocated to a school in the aimag center when his brother-in-law was transferred to the aimag Party committee.

In 1981, after graduation, he enrolled in a contest to enter university, which consisted of three exams. He did well and was accepted for the University of Science and Technology in Ulaanbaatar. He did well there too and he went to Irkutsk in 1984 where he worked in construction, laying foundations. There he graduated in 1986 as construction engineer for civil and production construction. He was assigned to work for the General Committee of Mongol Bank — at the time the only bank — at its branch in Khovd. He started as the engineer responsible for investment, monitoring the progress of construction until 1991. During that period he attended a two-month course on banking at the university.

In 1991 the whole banking system was restructured and a two-tier banking system was introduced. Togie was transferred to the Investment and Technological Restructuring Bank that was established in 1991 (and was bankrupted in 1996). Then he moved to Ardeen Bank, which had been separated from Mongol Bank as the first state-

owned commercial bank. The general director of Ardeen bank, A. Tserendorj, who hailed from Bulgan soum — though he didn't actually know him — had been instructed to recruit Togie. A messy period ensued in which successive governments, each with their own political agenda, moved the banks around like chess pieces: A year after Togie was recruited, Ardeen Bank was declared bankrupt by government and in its place the Reconstruction Bank, Savings Bank and a Collection Center for bank debts (based on Ardeen bank assets and debts) were established. Togie was assigned to work with the Reconstruction Bank. The aimag branch where Togie worked decided to take collateral for all the loans that had gone bad: animals were all some people had to give. This move was dictated by the Collection Center — no doubt prodded by the burgeoning number of foreign banking consultants that flooded the country at the time. Togie, two economists, and three accountants found themselves drawing up a schedule for who was going out to look after the bank's animals. For several months they herded in shifts as there was no market to sell the animals. He continued to work for the Reconstruction Bank after its official bankruptcy in 1998 — until 2001 when he was laid off.

I asked him how he got those successive jobs and he said that he had wanted to go to Ardeen Bank (I gather someone must have talked to the bank director on his behalf), but that all his other moves had been decided at the national level. Individuals had no control; some staff lost their jobs and others were moved. He knew how to keep books and when he worked for the banks he did every single job except cleaning and being the director. Togie ended up being unemployed for six months, after which he was recruited to work as rural credit specialist in the program that Shombodon and I ran. He worked the full five years for the project and then got himself a job at the aimag Department of Land Relations and Public Buildings, where he was happily working when we visited him in 2012.

And that is how one Mongol weathered transition.

∗ ∗ ∗

August 2012. The younger generation knows about socialism and transition from their parents. In Altai we met Ms. Basentseren who is Shombi's third cousin. Born in 1984 in Bugat soum, she was the fourth child of seven. She remembers little of life before the transition, only that her father worked as housekeeper for the school and her mother as a junior nurse/cleaner for the hospital. Their jobs disappeared at transition but they received a little over 100 animals (a little below the bare minimum if you want to make a living) and started herding. She liked herding: the household had cattle and it was pleasant; mother milked while she held the calves. The grass was good and she ran without any shoes on. That happy time was short-lived, however, as to continue her education she had to spend eight years in a dormitory in Bugat soum center. It was difficult because there were 16 people in the room — four boys and 12 girls and no heating. The school provided wood for their stove, but they just had the fire on shortly in the mornings before classes. Breakfast was one slice of bread. For lunch they had a first and second course (e.g. soup and a main dish and tea) and in the evening just a main course — it was OK.

According to her father, who had become warehouse keeper in the soum center, the food was worse than when he was young. He tasted it and said it had been better before transition. Before transition they used to have sweets on Wednesdays but after the transition only grains — no sweets. Parents paid two sheep annually per child as a contribution to food. The school had a herd, which a relative of her mother looked after. The rooms where the kids lived were organized per bag. Usually boys and girls lived separately, but brothers and sisters usually lived together. There were only 12 beds for the 16 kids — four pairs of siblings shared beds. The room was improved by the parents of the children with carpets, TV, gramophone-player. Each bed had a front-curtain. The parents paid for that. There were about 80 or 90 kids boarding.

The stories illustrate how people just had to make do during transition, particularly in the rural areas that were forgotten while changes were engineered (muddled through) in Ulaanbaatar.

Transition and life in the soums

The soum centers were important links between government and people in socialist times: much of the rural infrastructure was located there. When that infrastructure collapsed during transition, the soum centers went into decline and their water systems and sometimes even their power plants stopped functioning. Khalkh Gol is an example of a prosperous soum based on a state farm that spectacularly failed during transition. After privatization of the state farm, somehow four large private companies and 30 cooperatives emerged. The four companies ended up in hands of, respectively, the state farm's former director, its chief agronomist, its accountant, and the animal husbandry specialist. The cooperatives all went broke in the first two years, and the last of the private companies was bankrupted in 1998. Two people who had transferred to Khalkh Gol through organized labor transfers when the thriving state farm needed labor told me about transition (Mrs. Khishigt and Mr. Enkh-Ochir, both of whom I introduced in chapter 9).

July 2012. Mrs. Khishigt, who moved to Khalkh Gol as a young bride in 1973, tells us about the difficulties of transition. When the state farm was divided into private companies, she and her husband lost their salaries and didn't get a pension. After transition — she was 46 at the time — the government retired her early with a small "compensation", but the compensation was insufficient. Before transition, they rode horses and herded animals; after transition they had to survive by knitting and processing milk products for sale. She is still making a living from her dairy products. They decided to stay in Khalkh Gol because of the kids. Her husband died in 2005 of liver cancer. She has 13 grandchildren (two of them were hanging out in her house) and even a few great-grandchildren.

There is no work. Two of her five children are unemployed and looking for temporary jobs; these are hard times. Previously the bosses would say go there, do that. Now there is party discrimination: the soum governor is Democratic Party while she and her children are People's Party. If the People's Party would win, they would not discriminate, it would be different. (The soum governor had just proudly shown us a reward, signed by the Democratic prime minister, because the soum had created 500 jobs in 2011, so I assume other households are more upbeat.)

Mrs. Khishigt's sister still lives in Durgan soum (Khovd aimag) and last year she was able to visit. When they were working for the state farm they used to visit their home soum nearly every year in their holidays, by plane to Khovd. Just after transition there was hardly any transportation available any more. Last year she went home and tried to convince family members to move to central Mongolia or Ulaanbaatar, but they did not. I tell her life isn't necessarily good in Ulaanbaatar; I once did some research in the ger districts of Ulaanbaatar and was shocked at the poverty, insecurity and filth I found there.

The next morning Shombodon and I receive a bottle of milk-vodka, aaruul (dried curds made from sour milk) and a letter containing two poems. It is from Khishigt: she is excited to be in the book! We are moved. Both poems are typical for Mongolia, about the beauty of the landscape. One of her poems is nostalgic and yearning for Durgan soum where she grew up and one is about Khalkh Gol, the empty country to which she was transplanted. Although they do not translate well into English, they demonstrate her deep love for the country: its mountains, lakes, rivers and springs, wind-swept meadows, flowers, dunes, birds, and her connectedness to her present home saying "the lonely steppe is mine". This is indeed a lonely place and it has become even more depopulated after transition. In the heydays of the state farm the soum had a population of 9000; now it has only 3200.

Mrs. Khishigt was not the only one who had fallen on rough times after the collapse of the state farm. Mr. Enkh Ochir, the "mechanisator" who had moved to Khalkh Gol in 1986, was able to continue working in one of the four private companies that emerged from its ruins — until it too went bankrupt in 1998 and he lost his job. He and his family are struggling but at least he receives a small pension derived from the fact that he had worked for the state farm for 12 years. He is 56 old and his wife 54; she will retire next year (they only have two children, so she couldn't retire early). The family survives by baking bread and they also own a small tractor that they mainly use to transport wood for the bakery. In summer they sell more than 30 loaves per day because during the cropping season people need bread in the fields; in winter they only sell about 10. There is no market for products because since 1990 two thirds of the population has left the soum. The crop sector is being rehabilitated, but he is not happy with the achievements of the modern farms: last year they harvested 1.5 tons of wheat per hectare but in state farm days it was 2.2 tons per hectare. The transition worked out badly, he says, especially for the cropping sector. His family did not get any animals at transition; they weren't interested in that because they were working with crops.

* * *

Khalkh Gol's future, however, looks brighter than these stories suggest. The Ministry of Food, Agriculture and Light Industry, together with the Korean International Cooperation Agency, plans to establish a large modern farm here to produce for the Korean market. This empty corner of Mongolia is close to densely populated Korea; the Koreans have already leased 20,000 hectares of what used to be the state farm for food production, which will certainly revitalize the soum.

In some cases, if a strong cooperative was able to form that could maintain some of the infrastructure that had been there in the times of the negdels, a whole soum could benefit, even if the cooperative was run by one family. I saw this in Galshar soum, where the local cooperative performed useful services in marketing raw products, buying inputs, financial services, consumer shops, slaughtering, haymaking, veterinary services and running other businesses such as operating a fuel station and a bottled-water plant. More than 200 members receive monthly salaries and dividends at the end of the year, and the cooperative pays a substantial amount of money in taxes. The soum looked more prosperous than most.

A soum with a decidedly less rosy future is Kukhmorit ("blue horse") in the northwestern corner of Gobi Altai aimag. In this northern band of the Gobi desert the process of desertification, probably a result of climate change combined with overgrazing, threatens to literally submerge the whole soum under sand dunes. This graphically brings home to me a subject that many elderly Mongolians bring up: they worry about the environment, particularly about climate change, pasture degradation, desertification, forests disappearing and streams drying up.

* * *

August 2012. Kukhmorit. There are heaps of sand swept in piles against walls and fences of the buildings in the soum center. We visit a delightful friend of Shombodon, a classmate of his from the Agricultural secondary school in Khovd. Mrs. Myadagmaa is a comfortable-looking smiling lady in western clothes and a headscarf. We meet her at her house which, she explains, she bought eight years ago after her husband died; they had always lived in a ger. Although it has radiators, she uses it as a summer house only. In winter it is warmer to live in a ger and she uses less fuel to heat it. One of her five daughters and a grandson live with her. She also has three sons, and, she laughs out loud when telling me she has 18 grandchildren. The room is neat and cozy: white net curtains, a few potted plants, knick-knacks, a carpet used as wall-hanging with a panel of the family's neatly arranged medals pinned to it.

Shombodon and Myadagmaa both graduated in 1966 (she was born in 1946). She laughs warmly at him and says that Shombodon was the smallest of the class and they all loved and protected him! She herself had nearly been expelled from school because of angina and joint pain for which she was lengthily hospitalized, but because of her embroidery skills — she used to embroider illustrations for certain school subjects that were used by the teachers — she was allowed to stay. She busies herself with preparing lunch for us. We eat meat, boiled potatoes and carrots, and locally made cheese and drink vodka. She asks me if I believe in God. I say no and we bond over the fact we are both atheists. She shows us her photo album: one photo shows her and two friends as teenagers looking quite European in western dresses with old-fashioned headscarves like my mother used to wear when she was young.

She started her career as a livestock specialist, married soon after graduation and moved back to Kukhmorit soum where she was from. While she was in second grade at the agricultural college of Khovd, she had met her future husband when she was back on holidays in her home soum. He had worked as a teacher in the soum for 30 years when he died. He started teaching in 1962 when the school had four teachers and was just a primary school. Now there are 25 teachers and nine grades (primary and secondary). The soum has a dormitory capacity of 120 students but there are currently about 100 kids in residence. In 1968 she started work as a human resources development specialist, or "head of cadre". She worked there until 1992 after which she was promoted to vice secretary of the Party unit within the soum. She used to be responsible for employment and social issues of the more than 1000 negdel members. Even children after graduating from grade four could become members; if they didn't continue school, they would become negdel members. The negdel name was "Thirty-five Years" which was the name of a bag that came from a neighboring soum and refers to the anniversary of the 1921 revolution (so it was established in 1956).

At the beginning people who came to the soum were simply registered as negdel members. Later when people came in, they had to put in an application. You didn't have to become a member of the negdel. The main difference was in the number of animals you could own privately: in the Gobi region, if you worked for local government, you could own up to eight animals; if you worked for the negdel, you could have up to 16, and if you were a member of a herder household, you could have up to 75. She occasionally traveled officially for her work and has visited five aimags and twice went to the USSR for short training courses; once to Irkutsk and once to Yakutsk, where she had to use interpreters.

Like many other people I interviewed she let me know, without going as far as stating that she doesn't approve of the market economy or that she wants to go back to socialism, that the process of privatization was botched and implemented without oversight. She points out that some people had more access to assets than others, and the latter became poor. At least that is how it was in her soum. She says that the negdel used to work well and was beneficial to the negdel members. The only problem was that members expected too much from the negdel and were waiting for it to provide ready-made things.

Before we leave, she changes into a new powder-blue and gold deel to pose for a photo and gives us a present of bags of two types of hand-milled grasses and tells us of their health benefits. Despite the piles of sand outside her home, she has managed to plant some pretty purple cosmos flowers.

12. THE 21ST CENTURY

Adjusting to the capitalist world

During the years that I was involved with lending to small businesses and agriculture-sector borrowers, I experienced time and again how unfamiliar, more than 10 years after transition, the private sector still was to those who had never really experienced it. Government itself presented many challenges because officials were used to having considerably more power in the socialist era than is possible in economic systems that are based on the private sector. The power structures in the rural areas had not changed as much as in the capital, as we found out.

2002. Our Agriculture Sector Credit Program is based on the principle that commercial banks borrow funds at a preferential interest rate from the Asian Development Bank and on-lend these funds to borrowers in the agriculture sector. Twenty percent of the loan funds have to be provided by the banks themselves and any profits or losses are carried by the banks. The design of this program is based on decades of experience with donor-funded credit programs worldwide: studies of the successes and failures of credit programs everywhere clearly indicate that it is crucial that they are run by specialized private-sector financial institutions that have a stake in loans being repaid as well as in assisting the beneficiaries. If loans are not repaid, credit operations peter out for lack of funds. It is that simple.

At issue in our project is that government officials want to have a say in deciding to whom to lend money. They argue that the Asian Development Bank loaned money to the government for the project and that therefore the loan decisions are to be made by the government. In fact, the project document stipulates that the commercial banks (private sector) are to make the loan decisions because they risk losing funds in case of default — but that is not commonly understood.

The regional directors of our project are themselves government officials and have not clearly understood that the credit component will be managed by the commercial banks, with training to bank staff and clients the only assistance from the project. Politicians and government officials have made propaganda for our project thinking they will get to distribute loans. In one case a project director has received a big pile of proposals from hopeful applicants before it is clear to everyone that these ought to have gone to the banks directly. He makes a selection from the proposals and sends a list of 50 "best applicants", on project letterhead, duly signed and stamped, to the bank director indicating support for these enterprises and individuals. He proudly reports this to the credit consultants (Shombodon and me) as proof of hard work. The bank director agrees that the list is a valuable help to her as she is not familiar with many of those businesses and does not have the means to go out and visit the ones in the outlying areas. It comes as a surprise to both of them that the credit consultants object to the practice.

Unfortunately for our regional project director and the bank director and fortunately for us, this first batch of loans has a higher percentage of problem loans than the loan portfolios in other regions, a fact that I carefully research and document. One of the problems is that the government, trying to govern the way it did during the socialist era, has proclaimed a Year of the Cooperative and suggests that cooperatives will receive preferential treatment, including government-sponsored loans. Consequently, there is a proliferation of "cooperatives" that are, in fact, disguised private companies. In some cases neighbors' names appear as cooperative members without their knowledge, and fake minutes of founding meetings are submitted. It isn't always malicious intent: I believe that many of the borrowers, 15 years after transition, genuinely don't understand the fundamental difference between a cooperative and a company.

Collateral is also a problem in a country that has no history of private ownership of real estate and where everyone agrees that a ger can't be taken as collateral because it is essential for survival. In our first non-performing co-operative loan I was told that the chairman of the remote co-operative died and that "the co-operative died with him". The loan officer then told me what they had confiscated as collateral: the list included several concrete beams, two Russian-made safes, 55 kilos of animal oil, a toilet bowl, a weighing scale, 50 light-switches, 50 scythes, a stove, and the promise of 24 kilos of cashmere after the combing of the goats. For each of these items the bank staff had to establish if they could find a buyer, estimate a price and take the time to sell it and I appreciated how hard they worked to recuperate some of their losses. I also have to admit to having had a thoroughly unprofessional giggling-attack when they arrived at discussing the toilet bowl out there in the empty nowhere.

In any case, I have earned my giggle after having been yelled at by angry officials and summoned to the governor's offices to explain personally why I thought that he did not have a say in the loan decisions; after all, he makes a Five-Year Plan for the development of the aimag and it is the duty of the private sector to support his master plan. And why I am agitating against government policy to support cooperatives? (I wrote and distributed guidelines on vetting cooperatives for authenticity.) Shombodon and I are having a rough time of it, this first year on the job, Shombodon more than me — I am a bloody foreigner while he is portrayed as working against the interests of his own people. Our project directors eventually come round when I explain that I am an adviser only and that they make the decisions; moreover, I have been a technical advisor for many years and am therefore used to my advice not being taken (at this point, fortunately, one of them starts laughing). I also point out that I have my professional reputation to protect and that I retain the right to put my professional opinions in writing to project management so that I won't get blamed if they do not take my advice. Furthermore, they have to take the issue up with my boss and their bosses in case of conflict. They do take it up with the bosses and find out that Shombodon and I have their full support. We are able to cooperate just fine after that, and the credit component is doing well.

Not only did the role of government change fundamentally after transition, but the very nature of Mongolian identity also became an issue because it couldn't be derived from their proud place in the Glorious Socialist World anymore. During Mongolia's transition to a market economy, alliances were forged with countries other than Russia and China. The Cold War had been winding down; diplomatic relations with western countries had been intensifying since the United Kingdom first established relations in the early Sixties. In 1987 even the leader of the Western Bloc, the USA, established diplomatic relations and in 1990, US Secretary of State James Baker visited Mongolia and again a year later to address and congratulate the first democratically elected parliament. Foreign aid started pouring in from what formerly had been the politically incorrect capitalist countries and from international organizations such as the World Bank, International Finance Corporation, Asian Development Bank and UN agencies. International NGOs such as the Red Cross, Asia Foundation, Soros Foundation and a variety of missionary organizations (the most important of which was the Mormon mission) also came in. These replaced the Soviet-led Eastern bloc on which Mongolia had depended, reflecting the global power shift.

Relations with China also shifted. Since Mongolia's second independence in 1921, these had been fully dependent on the Soviet Union's relations with China — as befitted a satellite state. Since transition, trade on Mongolia's southern border intensified. At the same time, Mongols tend to be uneasily distrustful of the Chinese, acutely aware that not only Taiwan but also mainland China still think they have claims on Mongolian territory stemming from the era of the Qing dynasty, and that Inner Mongolia is forever lost to the Mongols and has become a part of China. Occasional outbursts of nationalism and xenophobia are directed first and foremost against the Chinese.

Mongolia has a wealth of natural resources, the most important being gold, copper, molybdenum, uranium and coal, and its economy will increasingly depend on these going into the 21st century. Understandably, with the important role of the foreign aid community, its economy's dependence on foreign mining corporations and the foreign provenance of the new ideas that are molding the new Mongolian society, nationalist feelings are emerging more strongly. During and after transition nationalists have been attempting to recreate their unique Mongolian identity, often by highlighting the break with their socialist past and many youngsters talk about the bad old time. People started to focus on the fact that Mongolian symbols, culture, religion, and history had been repressed during the socialist era. But the elderly have a mixed view. Mr. Tseveensuren, who told me about the cultural campaigns in Chapter

7, said: "Now people criticize the socialist system a lot, but there were good results combining livestock with crops. Socialism liquidated the differences in wealth. Stoves, radios and bigger gers were introduced. It was good. Soum and bag centers were established. Equipment with high capacity was introduced, as well as good professionals who knew how to use the machines. Any good economy cannot survive without agriculture and during the socialist time Mongolia was self-sufficient in grains and vegetables. The country even exported those. After transition harvests went down. Only recently things are getting better. Agriculture is being rehabilitated due to the new crop campaigns and high-yielding techniques are being introduced. I hope it will be better. Also, the country is getting assistance from international and national experts. At the beginning the transition and privatization was done with no preparation so many soum centers and bag centers collapsed, losing hotels, public baths and cultural centers. Local government is now trying to rehabilitate those. Destroying is easy; creating and re-creating takes time."

Mongolian identity and symbols

The most powerful symbol of Mongolia always was Chinggis Khaan and he came back with a vengeance — not that he had ever been truly forgotten. The airport has been renamed Chinggis Khaan. Ulaanbaatar's main square has been renamed Chinggis Khaan. There is a huge statue of Chinggis Khaan erected on the steppes to the east of Ulaanbaatar. His name is used to sell beer and vodka, to advertise hotels, guest houses, clubs, travel companies and all sorts of other businesses. A large part of the population has chosen his clan name as their own last name. I wonder whether it is prudent to pin all one's pride and ideal of nationhood on a figure who lived seven centuries ago. Doesn't that imply there weren't any other worthwhile Mongols during more recent centuries?

While unique, Mongolian identity never existed in a vacuum and Mongols have absorbed foreign influences since time immemorial. Chinggis Khaan famously invited representatives of different religions — Christian and Muslim missionaries, Buddhist and Taoist monks — to discuss the merits of their belief systems in front of him. Modern Mongolians are still figuring out their post-socialist cultural identity. Immediately after transition, interesting questions were raised by some parliamentarians such as, in view of Chinggis Khaan's multiple wives, whether to introduce polygamy. A female parliamentarian countered that, since men and women are equal, women as well as men would have to have the right to marry multiple partners. According to Shombodon, those who raised the issue "were uncomfortable at home and criticized by their wives". The issue was dropped. I assume there are enough smart Mongols to recognize that the 13th and 21st centuries require different societies. I certainly wouldn't want to live a 13th century life in the Netherlands!

The Chinggis symbol conjures up the romantic idea of what is to be a Mongol — to freely roam the steppes that are open and available to all. Private land ownership didn't exist before transition. In the socialist period all land was owned by the state; before that, territories were ruled over, allocated to groups as pastureland, but not privately owned in the modern sense. Although all land, with the exception of small urban private lots, is still public nowadays, the concept of freely roaming the steppes clashes with the reality of the 21st century and the market economy.

But the idea is powerful. Nostalgic city-dwellers, confronted with horrendous pollution and traffic jams send their children to the countryside in summer — there is nothing more glorious than the short Mongolian summers! All the same, I don't believe the urbanites fully appreciate the harsh realities of poor herders who face the winter; face having to live apart from their spouses; cannot afford the same quality schooling they themselves received; lack healthcare; cannot afford all the modern technology (televisions, mobile phones, appliances) considered normal by their brothers and sisters in the city and by the few rich herders; would gladly take jobs in other sectors if these were available. Their lives have deteriorated since the time when workers on state farms could afford to visit their home aimag once a year to visit family — by airplane, no less!

The only monastery that was allowed to exist under socialism, as a living museum rather than an independent religious entity, was the Gandan Monastery in Ulaanbaatar. It is currently trying to take the lead in reintroducing Buddhism to the population. Times have changed, however: while there are still many elderly Mongols who are the sons and daughters of ex-lamas and are searching for what they have lost (religion, identity, knowledge, wisdom, spirituality), it seems unlikely to me that the younger generations, the modern urbanized professionals I worked with, would be inclined to go into monasteries, learn and perform lengthy medieval Tibetan chants, or call in a lama instead of a doctor.

Ovoos are one manifestation of Mongol culture that fell into disregard during the socialist era; predating Buddhism, they are cairns of stones or wood signifying a sacred place or landmark. It is customary to circumambulate an ovoo thrice and preferably add some stones or other offerings while doing so. When one is in a hurry, one can suffice by tapping one's horn while driving by — if you make sure the ovoo is to your right as you pass it (as if you are circumambulating it clockwise). Traditional celebrations, such as Tsagaan Sar (lunar new year), which had been discouraged or at least played down in the socialist era, also experienced a revival and became public holidays; Naadam festivals became bigger.

Nevertheless, Buddhist and pre-Buddhist superstitions and customs are common, such as believing that there are auspicious dates for certain activities such as starting a trip, marrying, or moving to a new place. There is no longer a strong Buddhist power structure or body of knowledge, and many modern-day lamas play to these superstitions. The Mongolian nouveaux riches are happy to construct or rehabilitate temples and statues of Buddha, but these are lifeless manifestations, a shadow of the religion it once was. Or they are tourist attractions whose function is to earn income. Foreign Buddhist organizations are active in trying to resurrect the religion: the Dalai Lama, despite vociferous opposition from China, has paid the country several visits with the same objective.

The work of the State Commission on Rehabilitation speeded up during the first years of transition: in the period 1990-1993 nearly 23,000 purge victims were rehabilitated (exonerated from accusations of wrongdoing), three quarters of them lamas. Tömör Ochir of the Chinggis anniversary was among them. The state has formally apologized to the victims and their families. Between 1939 and 1990, rehabilitations had not been very high on the agenda and the Commission had managed to exonerate only about 4000 persons. Psychologically, the rehabilitations make a difference to families that have repressed the memories of persecuted relatives.

August 2012. I visit the Memorial Museum of Victims of Political Persecution in Ulaanbaatar. It is housed in a shabby old log building in the center of town, with its paint pealing off, set in a weedy lot. Contrasting oddly with the high rises around it, the forlorn setup announces that the past is of less concern than the future. It was open but the caretaker had to be found. I bought a ticket and wandered through the dusty old building without understanding most of it, though some of the exhibits (photos and texts written in the old Mongolian script) had explanations in Mongolian and English. There are smudgy photos of high-level lamas — including a youthful Dilowa Khutugtu — and politicians, many of them freedom fighters who had been persecuted and executed. The office of Prime Minister Genden, who tried to resist Stalin's plan to exterminate the lamas and was executed in Moscow in 1937, is displayed. One display case contains a heap of skulls in front of a blown-up photo of the location where they were found in 2003.

Mr. Luvsanjamts, whom we met in Tsogt soum, is trying to reinstate ancient traditions and true religion by performing Buddhist ceremonies and explaining their content to the people of his soum. After transition he left his job as driver for the Party's ideological secretary in Ulaanbaatar and decided to rebuild the temple in his home soum, find the objects hidden by persecuted lamas, and become a lama himself. He nearly left his family as he became deeply engaged in the endeavor and there was no time for family — but he didn't leave. When I visited his ger in 2012 his wife cooked us dinner and large photos on the wall showed a happy family. They were doing grandparent duty, lovingly looking after a delightful infant.

In 1995 he organized the building of the new temple. He has collected sacred objects, participated in religious ceremonies and learnt to read religious texts in Tibetan. He has also been instrumental in sending a young local monk to study in Daramsala, where he has lived since 1998, periodically visiting Tsogt soum on partial sponsorship to serve the people. It is likely he will take responsibility for rehabilitating religious heritage in the soum. He has received support for his Buddhist initiatives from the Citizen's Council: these councils are made up of people who originate from the soum and represent its interests politically; well-to-do members often finance charitable causes or religious projects).

Mr. Luvsanjamts explained that his father, who had been a high-ranking lama, believed that a time would come when Buddhism would be restored and had instructed him as follows: "Our previous generations strived for: 1. Humanism (oneness of self and others, altruism and mutual assistance). 2. Enlightenment (education, respect for previous generations, and striving for perfection in all things). 3. Respect for nature and economical use of natural resources. 4. Preservation of our cultural traditions." He added that these four key values of the Mongolian nomadic civilization were virtually wiped out last century and he wants to bring them back. One important tenet of Mongolian Buddhism is respect for nature, so he is trying to clean up the open garbage dump that is polluting the river (water is sacred) and contaminating ancient graves.

Some of the objects he is looking for are hidden in the ground and some are in the hands of people. When the lamas hid items underground, they packed them well, first in deeply smoked felt (waterproof felt from ger covers, meaning it was smoked over an open fire) and then in camel hide or goatskin. Then they marked the spot with burned wood or a mark on a stone. Mr. Luvsanjamts shows us some objects that had been hidden underground by his father and that he was able to recover because his father had told him their location. There were offering bowls, butter lamps, texts, faded khadags and a stick with a small silver bell on it and a sharp point to call to fortune. A lama giving a reading would stick its sharp end in a shoulder blade and turn it clockwise like a rattle with the right hand while holding the front leg of a sheep by the hoof in his left hand. This would summon prosperity.

Much has been lost. Cultural heritage is normally passed from one generation to the next but the repressive period broke the chain of learning and only a few people are left who are able to teach the younger generations. Nevertheless, many traditions have (partially) survived: they are being rehabilitated and performed. Mr. Luvsanjamts, together with a local schoolteacher, have in their possession the texts of more than 250 Mongolian long songs, some written in old Mongolian script, some in Cyrillic, which they plan to revive. Old people still know the melodies of many of them; they would like to record those songs, both in written form and in sound.

He and his fellow Mongolians have entered the 21st century with a mixture of nostalgia and optimism. New-found freedom allows resurrection of old traditions, but not many people are genuinely interested: they are simply living their modern lives as best they can. But Mr. Luvsanjamts is still digging. . .

Back to traditional herding

In the countryside the gradual process of incorporating market reforms into the negdels and state farms was abruptly halted in 1991 as transition happened. Exactly how the process of privatization took place is unclear, but I know it was messy. Restrictions on the number of animals any one household could own were lifted and the previously state-owned livestock was distributed among households according to family size and length of time they had belonged to the negdel. The animals represented real value to the rural Mongols, who still knew how to care for animals and who, all through socialist times, related to their salaries in terms of how many sheep they could buy with it. Other negdel assets stayed under control of negdel management and, in the confusion of transition, often became the property of private companies created by negdel ex-cadres. Most of these new companies failed because the whole marketing and banking infrastructure in the country had collapsed.

Many households ended up with only their ger, personal possessions and their small allotment of livestock. They became the new poor. Quite a few moved back to their ancestral soums where they still had family. I have met plenty of herders who told me they had trained as tractor drivers, accountants or nurses, or had college degrees, but went back to herding when their jobs disappeared, living without the services they had come to expect during socialism. In the centrally planned economy, the rural areas had probably been subsidized by income generated in other sectors such as mining; after transition there was no more money flowing towards agriculture and the rural areas in general.

The negdels with their economies of scale and government support had been able to herd the different animals separately (only goats and sheep are herded together), forming specialized brigades for each of the herds. Individual households now have a hard time juggling their labor to be able to manage the separate herds, even though small groups of households still live together in certain times of the year, in an encampment that is usually based on kinship, to pool labor. They have to pay for fodder, hay and veterinary services and are dependent upon the prices of cashmere, skins, meat, dairy products and upon private traders who buy their products and sell them groceries and other necessities. Water wells that were previously maintained by the negdels have fallen into disrepair.

Services have to be paid for now, the most important being health and education. Some new herders are inexperienced, because they had been working in other professions and might have grown up in a household with a few private animals, but the traditional knowledge of their grandparents has been long lost. Particularly worrisome is that school dropout rates have been increasing in the rural areas, particularly for boys who are considered more important for herding than girls. Poor rural households cannot afford boarding schools and need the additional labor. This leads to a vicious circle because those herder children do not learn any other vocation than traditional herding and cannot escape. There is insufficient work in other sectors to absorb them, so they herd and survive at subsistence level.

One researcher gives an example of the unintended consequences of dropping central planning: a medical doctor she interviewed in 1999 explained that maternal mortality had increased after transition because in the socialist time "area leaders" were responsible for knowing everything that was going on in their neighborhood, including all pregnancies, which were announced in public. Consequently, women were sent to the soum center approximately three months before they were due to give birth to prepare for it. Nowadays there is such a thing as freedom and women elect not to announce their pregnancies and to stay at home in the herding camps (of course, partly because they cannot afford to do otherwise) where the risks of dying in childbirth are higher.

Since transition, then, the traditional nomadic pastoralist livelihood has been functioning as a safety net for the people who were left behind during the abrupt and disorderly transition to a market economy. The safety net prevents people from dying of starvation but otherwise lets them hang, unable to claw themselves out of the net. Those who can, move to the city. The pace of urbanization increased rapidly as people were not only free to move to the city and aimag centers in search for a better life but were forced to leave the rural areas as their quality of life plummeted.

Urbanization had been an objective during socialist times, but it had been controlled and planned; now it just happens.

The typical answer to the question of why people are herding is that have no other profession or do not know how to do anything else: they hope their children will get ahead through a good education. Families are proud when their children manage to make a living in Ulaanbaatar and don't come back: they are disappointed when they do. The vast majority of herder households do not have herd large enough to generate the cash needed for expenses such as veterinary services, hay and fodder to get the herds through the winter, good-quality animal shelters, and quality stock for breeding. Most herder households survive because they have some other source of income in the form of pensions, child support, disability payments, "medal money" for having many children, and remittances from family members living in other parts of the country. They make use of free natural resources (pasture lands, dung for heating their gers, water sources) and hope that they will escape the next dzud, that their animals won't contract any contagious diseases, that the cashmere prices will be high. The only way poor herders can get ahead is to utilize to the maximum the country's communal and free resources, and increase the size of their herds as rapidly as possible. Economic necessity, supported by a culture that highly values large herds, is therefore leading to overgrazing and severe degradation of pasturelands, particularly near rivers and lakes and in the surroundings of soum- or aimag centers where herder families choose to live to be near the service centers. The number of animals rose from around 20 to 25 million, where it had been maintained during the socialist era, to about 30 million by the end of the century and over 40 million by 2008.

Within the herds, the number of goats, valuable because of their cashmere that provides a large portion of the household's annual cash income, has increased disproportionally, leading to increased tearing up of pasturelands. Now that everyone is free to choose where they live, households move to desirable places where competition for pastureland leads to neighborhood squabbles as well as erosion and desertification. The simple fact is that there are too many animals, too many subsistence herders and, for the first time, insufficient jobs to absorb the excess labor. Poverty is here to stay for the time being.

So that is the back story to the charmingly picturesque herder encampments that delight tourists in summer, giving them the impression that the Mongols have uninterruptedly lived their romantic nomadic life since Chinggis Khaan's days and before. I shouldn't just talk about tourists; I suspect that urban Mongols who visit their rural relatives in the summer months also want to believe that the Mongol way of living — roaming the endless steppes and cavorting in colorful, sweet-scenting meadows — still exists and that herders choose that great lifestyle. And who is to blame us harried professionals for romantically dreaming of an unfettered life, herding our flocks, riding our horses across the open steppes?

AFTERWORD

The future's not mine to see

The transition stories I have collected tell a bit of a one-sided story, not only because of their rural bias: the last decade of the 20th century was a confused period of economic depression. Interviewing more of the urban middle class and elite would have shown a more upbeat picture. Many families tried their luck in the cities after transition, often because they saw that the chances of getting an education for their children lay there. These new immigrants initially had a tough time of it and scraped by on the worst of jobs. One was the woman who cleaned our stairwell when we lived in the center of town from 1999 to 2001. The apartment building had clearly been built for the socialist high society. The apartment itself was pleasant, roomy and had high ceilings, but what these buildings lacked was a lobby or any kind of pleasant entrance. The entrances to the stairwells were typically at the back of the buildings where they faced inner courtyards with charming playgrounds for children. I don't know how it had been in socialist times, but when we lived there the entrance was dark and creepy, and the stairwell horridly filthy because the main downstairs entrance door didn't lock and the light fixtures had been torn out of the walls. Another foreigner and I had the lights fixed twice and tried unsuccessfully to keep the door locked (the teenagers living in the building didn't lock the doors). In winter there were drunks huddled on the stairs and you had to be careful not to step on broken bottles or slip on used condoms, frozen urine or vomit. You get the picture.

The cleaning lady assigned to the stairwell had what I considered to be the worst job in the world. Trained as an engineer, she relocated to Ulaanbaatar to give her children a better life. Terry befriended her and was instrumental in getting her a better job cleaning the apartment of another foreigner. Later she managed to get a job in a modern store and we lost touch with her until she sought contact on Facebook and now I see a smiling, well-dressed Duya on my screen who clearly has help communicating in English. She has made it through!

Most of the professionals I worked with had a middle-class urban lifestyle not unlike that of white-collar workers in richer countries. They are well-educated, live in apartments, work hard, juggle two careers and kids (often with assistance from the grandparents), go to the gym and eat at restaurants.

Although Mongolia is still ranked low on the list of GDP per capita, its economy became the fastest-growing in Asia around 2011-2012, after which it slowed down. It is driven by the mining industry; the country has huge mineral resources and huge coal deposits, and some oil. About 10 percent of the world's known coal reserves are found in Mongolia and its neighbors, particularly China, are hungry for it. It also has huge copper and gold deposits. The Oyu Tolgoi mine alone is expected to account for over 30 percent of GDP.

In anticipation of immense riches to flow in, Ulaanbaatar has become a congested, hectic modern city with expensive cars — Hummers in particular are popular — clogging its roads. One man bragged how easily Mongols use modern machines "as if they are riding horses". (Terry used that same expression rather less admiringly when he mentioned the Ulaanbaatar traffic: "Mongols herd their cars along as if they are horses — with the difference that horses think for themselves and know when to swerve.") High-end shops such as Luis Vuitton in the center demonstrate new wealth; the many glitzy eating and drinking facilities — including Irish pubs, beer gardens, a profusion of nightclubs — attract well-heeled foreigners and Mongols alike. All this has happened in the 21st century.

The century I wanted to talk about has passed. I can't keep up with what is happening and how the Mongols are (re)writing their own history. Reminders of the socialist era are rapidly disappearing. The statue of Stalin in front of Ulaanbaatar's main library had already been removed before I arrived and now serves as a decorative piece in a night club.

I have tried to give an idea of what the 20th century was like in Mongolia. A whiff of the socialist past still lingered when I was there because the socialist system ruled the country for most of the century and formed its people, whether they acknowledged it or not. To what extent will the importance of those who influenced the 20th century be forgotten, just as the physical manifestations of socialism have disappeared? Will Sükhbaatar be forgotten? Will Choibalsan be portrayed as villain only, and not as instrumental in keeping Mongolia from joining the Soviet Union? Will the last depictions of Lenin be painted over as if he never existed? Will Chinggis take over all?

I have left the country and written up memories of a place I never knew, 20th-century Mongolia, and of a place I did know but it too has already vanished. What stays with me is a sense of common humanity. When a Mongolian senior citizen points out that modern life is easy and people have become soft, I hear my own father talking about the younger generation. When a colleague talks about his mother not being able to care for herself but refusing to leave her ger in South Gobi saying she was going to die looking out the door of her ger at her herd of beloved camels, I think of how my mother wanted to keep driving and living in her own house when it was becoming difficult. Mongolians are very close to their families and very much attached to their ancestral soums. I can relate to that too. They are refreshingly direct in their communications — not that that was always pleasant but I appreciate knowing where I stand (admittedly the Dutch aren't known for diplomacy either). They are prone to small caring gestures. One day as I was limping along the street trying to exercise my leg after an injury, an immaculately suited gentleman who spoke not a word of English offered me his arm and firmly escorted me back to my apartment. I wasn't able to explain that I was walking there on purpose, for exercise, and didn't want to appear ungracious by rejecting his friendliness.

Mongolians love the arts and many are composers, writers, poets, and painters besides their main occupation. The directors of our Agriculture Sector Development Program, whom I have depicted as provincial government officials wanting more government control over the loans, were artists as well: I found one hard at work composing a song and writing the music out; another had written a book. Ulaanbaatar's many little statues are delightful, even if they are being overwhelmed by the noise, bustle and growth around them.

The country has great economic potential. The practical, energetic Mongolian people will use their riches and shape their destiny in their very own and unique way, but I am far away and have reached the end of this narrative. So I shall pour myself a glass of vodka, toast the good times had by all, and drink it down.

ACKNOWLEDGEMENTS

It has been so much fun working with my Mongolian colleagues! They have been the greatest source of inspiration to me and were essential because they spoke English and had to interpret and explain what I heard and saw. First and foremost, I want to thank my close colleague Shombodon, who is a main personage in this book and with whom I did most of my traveling in the rural areas. There are many more: in fact, over the seven years I worked in Mongolia there have been too many to mention. They include my first team of the Credit Mongol project, colleagues of the Agriculture Sector Development Project, and my team in the IFC Mongolia Leasing Project. I'll just single out Javhlan, because she was my first project assistant and because she voluntarily spent much time with my husband in the hospital to act as an interpreter, and Tsolmon, who was a long-term director of Credit Mongol and became a good friend. I also want to thank all the people who were so graceful and hospitable when I interviewed them.

I have never seen myself as a writer and was beset by self-doubt while writing the first drafts so I am grateful for the support of Dawn Marano, Meg Kinghorn and my beloved Salt Lake City writing group: Colleen Down, Jenette Purdy, Jennifer Foresta, Mary Louise Bean, Don Halveson, and Sheri Morris. A special thank-you goes to David Vessey who joined me on my 2012 travels as a photographer and reminded me that I needed to look at Mongolia with "new eyes" if I was to describe things to people who have never visited the country. I would like to thank friends who have read and commented on different parts of this book for their encouragement: Tico Cohen, Pete Morrow, Richard Austen, Joost Storm, Fred Stultz, Harrie Oppenoorth, Ingrid Fisher, and Arnoud Boerwinkel. Sadly, Tico and Pete passed away before I was able to publish this final version. I also want to express thanks to Stephen Stratford who edited the final manuscript.

Without my husband, Terry, this book would not have been possible because I would have been spending my time and energy in remunerated employment. In 2011 he became the breadwinner and gave me the gift of time to write as well as support for the project. Thank you!

BIBLIOGRAPHY

Per chapter, in order of use.

Chapter 1:

Jagchid S. and Hyer Paul. *Mongolia's Culture and Society*. Westview Press, Boulder, Colorado, 1979.

Bawden, C.R. *The Modern History of Mongolia*. Frederick A Praeger, Publishers, 1968.

Batbayar, Bat-Erdene (or: Baabar). *Twentieth Century Mongolia*. The White Horse Press, 1999; Mongolia and Inner Asia Studies Unit, University of Cambridge, 2005.

Moses, Larry W. *The Political Role of Mongol Buddhism*. Indiana University Uralic Altaic Series Vol. 133. Asian Studies Research Institute, Indiana University, Bloomington, Indiana, 1977.

Dilowa Khutugtu. *The Diluv Khutagt of Mongolia: Political Memoirs and Autobiography of a Buddhist Reincarnation*. Polar Star Books, 2009.

Avery, Martha. *The Tea Road: China and Russia meet across the Steppe*. China Intercontinental Press, 2004.

Moses, Larry, and Halcovic, Stephen A. Jr. *Introduction to Mongolian History and Culture*. Bloomington: Research Institute for Inner Asian Studies, Indiana University, 1985.

Batsaikhan Ookhnoi. "The Mongolian National Revolution of 1911 and the Bogdo Jebtsumdamba Khutuktu, the last Monarch of Mongolia" in *Mongolians After Socialism: Politics, Economy, Religion,* ed. Bruce M. Knauft and Richard Taupier. Admon Press, 2012.

Lattimore, Owen. *Mongol Journeys.* Doubleday, Doran and Co., 1941.

Chapter 2:

Avery, Martha. *The Tea Road: China and Russia meet across the Steppe.* China Intercontinental Press, 2004.

Dilowa Khutugtu. *The Diluv Khutagt of Mongolia: Political Memoirs and Autobiography of a Buddhist Reincarnation.* Polar Star Books, 2009.

Sablov, Paula L.W. *Does Everyone Want Democracy? Insights from Mongolia.* Left Coast Press, 2013.

Batbayar, Bat-Erdene (or: Baabar). *Twentieth Century Mongolia.* The White Horse Press, 1999; Mongolia and Inner Asia Studies Unit, University of Cambridge, 2005.

Bawden, C.R. *The Modern History of Mongolia.* Frederick A Praeger, Publishers, 1968.

Moses, Larry, and Halcovic, Stephen A. Jr. *Introduction to Mongolian History and Culture.* Bloomington: Research Institute for Inner Asian Studies, Indiana University, 1985.

Lan, Mei-hua. China's "New Administration" in Mongolia, in Kotkin, Stephen and Ellerman, Bruce E. *Mongolia in the Twentieth Century: Landlocked cosmopolitan"* M.E. Sharpe, 1999.

Urgunge Onon and Derrick Pritchartt. *Asia's First Modern Revolution: Mongolia Proclaims its Independence in 1911.* Brill, 1989.

Lattimore, Owen. *The Mongols of Manchuria. Their Tribal Divisions, Geographical Distribution, Historical Relations with Manchus and Chinese and present Political Problems.* George Allen & Unwin, 1935.

Worden, Robert L. and Matles Savada, Andrea, editors. *Mongolia: A Country Study.* Washington: GPO for the Library of Congress, 1989. (The full text is available at http://bit.ly/2Dp8ucN.)

Jagchid S. and Hyer Paul. *Mongolia's Culture and Society.* Westview Press, 1979.

Batsaikhan Ookhnoi. "The Mongolian National Revolution of 1911 and the Bogdo Jebtsumdamba Khutuktu, the last Monarch of Mongolia" in *Mongolians After Socialism: Politics, Economy, Religion,* ed. Bruce M. Knauft and Richard Taupier, Admon Press, 2012.

Diener, Alexander C. "The Borderland and Existence of the Mongolian Kazakhs: Boundaries and the Construction of Territorial Belonging" in *The Ashgate Research Companion to Border Studies* ed. Wastl-Walter, Doris. Routledge, 2011.

Murphy, George S. *Soviet Mongolia. A Study of the Oldest Political Satellite.* University of California Press, 1966.

Moses, Larry W. *The Political Role of Mongol Buddhism.* Indiana University Uralic Altaic Series Vol. 133. Asian Studies Research Institute, Indiana University, 1977.

Chapter 3:

Lattimore, Owen and Urgungge Onon. *Nationalism and Revolution in Mongolia.* Oxford University Press, 1955.

Sanders, Alan J.K. *Historical Dictionary of Mongolia.* The Scarecrow Press, 2003.

Lattimore, Owen. *Mongol Journeys.* Doubleday, Doran and Co., 1941.

Rupen, Robert A. *The Mongolian People's Republic.* Hoover Institution Studies: 12, Stanford University, 1966.

Bawden, C.R. *The Modern History of Mongolia.* Frederick A Praeger, 1968.

Moses, Larry, and Halcovic, Stephen A. Jr. *Introduction to Mongolian History and Culture.* Bloomington: Research Institute for Inner Asian Studies, Indiana University, 1985.

Urgunge Onon and Pritchartt, Derrick. *Asia's First Modern Revolution: Mongolia Proclaims its Independence in 1911.* Brill, 1989.

Batbayar, Bat-Erdene (or: Baabar). *Twentieth Century Mongolia.* The White Horse Press, 1999; Mongolia and Inner Asia Studies Unit, University of Cambridge, 2005.

Palmer, James. *The Bloody White Baron: The Extraordinary Story of the Russian Nobleman Who Became the Last Khaan of Mongolia.* Basic Books, 2011.

Dilowa Khutugtu. *The Diluv Khutagt of Mongolia: Political Memoirs and Autobiography of a Buddhist Reincarnation.* Polar Star Books, 2009.

Andrews, Roy Chapman. *Across Mongolian Plains: a Naturalist's Account.* D. Appleton and Company, 1921; Fredonia Books, 2001.

Humphey, Caroline and Sneath, David. *The End of Nomadism? Society, State and the Environment in Inner Asia.* Duke University Press, 1999.

Moses, Larry W. *The Political Role of Mongol Buddhism.* Indiana University Uralic Altaic Series Vol. 133. Asian Studies Research Institute, Indiana University, 1977.

Chapter 4:

Morozovna, Irina Y. *The Comintern and Revolution in Mongolia.* White Horse Press/ Mongolia and Inner Asia Studies Unit, University of Cambridge, 2002.

Murphy, George S. *Soviet Mongolia: A Study of the Oldest Political Satellite.* University of California Press, 1966.

Batbayar, Bat-Erdene (or: Baabar). *Twentieth Century Mongolia*. The White Horse Press, 1999; Mongolia and Inner Asia Studies Unit, University of Cambridge, 2005.

Moses, Larry, and Halcovic, Stephen A. Jr. *Introduction to Mongolian History and Culture*. Bloomington: Research Institute for Inner Asian Studies, Indiana University, 1985.

Rupen, Robert A. *The Mongolian People's Republic*. Hoover Institution Studies: 12, Stanford University, 1966.

Batsaikhan Ookhnoi. "The Mongolian National Revolution of 1911 and the Bogdo Jebtsumdamba Khutuktu, the last Monarch of Mongolia" in *Mongolians After Socialism: Politics, Economy, Religion,* ed. Bruce M. Knauft and Richard Taupier, Admon Press, 2012.

Sablov, Paula L.W. *Does Everyone Want Democracy? Insights from Mongolia*. Left Coast Press, 2013.

Worden, Robert L. and Matles Savada, Andrea, editors. *Mongolia: A Country Study*. Washington: GPO for the Library of Congress, 1989.

Chapter 5:

Rupen, Robert A. *The Mongolian People's Republic*. Hoover Institution Studies: 12, Stanford University, 1966.

Batsaikhan Ookhnoi. "The Mongolian National Revolution of 1911 and the Bogdo Jebtsumdamba Khutuktu, the last Monarch of Mongolia" *in Mongolians After Socialism: Politics, Economy, Religion,* edited by Bruce M. Knauft and Richard Taupier. Admon Press, 2012.

Moses, Larry, and Halcovic, Stephen A. Jr. Introduction to Mongolian History and Culture. Bloomington: Research Institute for Inner Asian Studies, Indiana University, 1985.

Moses, Larry W. *The Political Role of Mongol Buddhism.* Indiana University Uralic Altaic Series Vol. 133. Asian Studies Research Institute, Indiana University, 1977.

Kaplonski, C. *Truth, History and Politics in Mongolia: The Memory of Heroes.* Routledge Curzon, 2004.

Batbayar, Bat-Erdene (or: Baabar). *Twentieth Century Mongolia.* The White Horse Press, 1999; Mongolia and Inner Asia Studies Unit, University of Cambridge, 2005.

Worden, Robert L. and Matles Savada, Andrea, editors. *Mongolia: A Country Study.* Washington: GPO for the Library of Congress, 1989.

Chapter 6:

Rupen, Robert A. *The Mongolian People's Republic.* Hoover Institution Studies: 12, Stanford University, 1966.

Batbayar, Bat-Erdene (or: Baabar). *Twentieth Century Mongolia.* The White Horse Press, 1999; Mongolia and Inner Asia Studies Unit, University of Cambridge, 2005.

Murphy, George S. Soviet Mongolia: *A Study of the Oldest Political Satellite.* University of California Press, 1966.

Kaplonski, Chris. "Thirty Thousand Bullets, Remembering Political Repression in Mongolia" in *Historical Injustice and Democratic Transition in Eastern Asia and Northern Europe. Ghost: at the Table of Democracy* ed. Christie, Kenneth and Cribb, Robert. Routledge Curzon, 2002.

Moses, Larry, and Stephen A. Halcovic, Jr. *Introduction to Mongolian History and Culture.* Bloomington: Research Institute for Inner Asian Studies, Indiana University, 1985.

Worden, Robert L. and Matles Savada, Andrea, editors. Mongolia: *A Country Study.* Washington: GPO for the Library of Congress, 1989.

Chandler, David, Cribb, Robert and Narangoa, Li general editors. *End of Empire: 100 days in 1945 that changed Asia and the World.* NIAS Press, 2016.

Chapter 7:

Rupen, Robert A. *The Mongolian People's Republic.* Hoover Institution Studies: 12, Stanford University, 1966.

Moses, Larry, and Stephen A. Halcovic, Jr. *Introduction to Mongolian History and Culture.* Bloomington: Research Institute for Inner Asian Studies, Indiana University, 1985.

History of the Mongolian People's Republic. Translated from the Mongolian and annotated by William A. Brown and Urunge Onon. East Asian Research Center. Harvard University, 1976.

Murphy, George S. Soviet Mongolia: *A Study of the Oldest Political Satellite.* University of California Press, 1966.

Worden, Robert L. and Matles Savada, Andrea, editors. *Mongolia: A Country Study.* Washington: GPO for the Library of Congress, 1989.

Khongorzul, D. *Three Aspects of Economic Transition: The Case of Mongolia.* PhD dissertation. Ritsumeikan Asia Pacific University, 2010.

Chapter 8:

1921-1981: *National Economy of the MPR.* National Statistical Office of Mongolia, 1981.

Weatherford, Jack. *Genghis Khan and the Making of the Modern World.* Broadway Books, 2005.

Boldbaatar, J. "The 800th Anniversary of Chinggis Khaan: The Revival and Suppression of Mongolian National Consciousness." in Kotkin, Stephen and Ellerman, Bruce E. *Mongolia in the 20th Century: Landlocked cosmopolitan.* M.E. Sharpe, 1999.

Worden, Robert L. and Matles Savada, Andrea, editors. *Mongolia: A Country Study*. Washington: GPO for the Library of Congress, 1989.

Moses, Larry, and Stephen A. Halcovic, Jr. *Introduction to Mongolian History and Culture*. Bloomington: Research Institute for Inner Asian Studies, Indiana University, 1985.

Kaplonski, Chris. "Archived Relations: Repression, Rehabilitation and the Secret Life of Documents in Mongolia" in *History and Anthropology*, Vol. 22, No 4, December 2011.

Chapter 9:

1921-1981: National Economy of the MPR. National Statistical Office of Mongolia, 1981.

Chapter 10:

Worden, Robert L. and Matles Savada, Andrea, editors. *Mongolia: A Country Study*. Washington: GPO for the Library of Congress, 1989.

Chapter 11:

Bruun, O. and Odegaard, O. "A Society and Economy in Transition" in *Mongolia in Transition: Old Patterns, New Challenges*. Nordic Institute of Asian Studies, 1996.

Sablov, Paula L.W. *Does Everyone Want Democracy? Insights from Mongolia*. Left Coast Press, 2013.

Chapter 12:

Bruun, O. and Odegaard, O. "A Society and Economy in Transition" in *Mongolia in Transition: Old Patterns, New Challenges*. Nordic Institute of Asian Studies, 1996.

Sablov, Paula L.W. *Does Everyone Want Democracy? Insights from Mongolia*. Left Coast Press, 2013.

Sanders, Alan J.K. *Historical Dictionary of Mongolia*. The Scarecrow Press, 2003.

Hoeflaken, van, Maaike. *Herder Livelihood Profiles*. Paper prepared for World Bank. Ulaanbaatar, 2007.

Other sources:

Atwood, Christopher P. *Encyclopedia of Mongolia and the Mongol Empire*. Facts on File, 2004.

Becker, Jasper. Mongolia. *Travels in the Untamed Land*. Tauris Parke Paperbacks, 2008.

Human Relations Area Files: Subcontractor's Monograph HRAF-39 Wash-1. Mongolia's People's Republic (Outer Mongolia). New Haven, Connecticut, 1956.

Lattimore, Owen. *Mongol Journeys*. Doubleday, Doran and Co., 1941.

Needham, Wesley E. "Dilowa Gegen Hutuktu (1883-1965): Eighteenth incarnation of Telopa, Indian Buddhist Saint (988-1069)" in: *Studies in Comparative Religion, Vol. 2, No. 2,* 1968.

Ossendowski, Ferdinand. *Beasts, Men and Gods. A Tale of Travel and Adventure in Mongolia during the Years 1920-21*. Polar Star Press, 2010.

Rossabi, Morris. *Modern Mongolia: From Khans to Commissars to Capitalists*. University of California Press, 2005.

Sanjdorj, M. *Manchu Chinese Colonial Rule in Northern Mongolia*. C. Hurst & Co, 1980.

Sneath, David. "Pastoralism in Mongolia: Mobility, Technology, and Decollectivisation of Pastoralism in Mongolia" in *Mongolia in the 20th Century: Landlocked cosmopolitan*. M. E. Sharpe, 1999.

Uradyn E. Bulag. "Introduction: The 13th Dalai Lama in Mongolia, or the Dawn of Inner Asian Modernity" in *The Thirteenth Dalai Lama on the Run (1904-1906): Archival Documents from Mongolia* ed. Champildondov Chuluun and Bulag, Uradyn E. Koninklijke Brill NV Leiden, 2013.

APPENDIX 1: HISTORICAL PERSONAGES

Note: in Mongolian names, the name after the comma is the patronymic (usually precedes the name in writing often as initials). Western names have the family name, comma, given name.

Alton Khaan (1507-1582) Sixteenth-century Khaan who reintroduced Tibetan Buddhism to Mongolia.

Amar, Amandine (1886-1941) Twice Prime Minister in 1928-1930 and 1936-1939. Executed in 1941 because of his opposition to increasing Soviet influence in Mongolia.

Bat-Erdene, Batbayar. Nickname: Baabar (1954-) Post-transition politician and author of Twentieth-Century Mongolia.

Bakich, Andrei Stepanovitch (1878-1922) White Russian general and ambassador to Mongolia in 1912-1913 who escaped from the Red Army and traveled to Harbin and from there to Australia, carrying Korostovets's diary.

Bakich, Olga The granddaughter of who realized the historical significance of Korostovets's diary and published it.
Bodoo, Dogsomyn (1895-1922) A lama and the first Prime Minister after the revolution of 1921. Executed in 1922 in early internal power struggles.

Brezhnev, Leonid (1906-1982) Head of the Soviet Union from 1962-1982.

Chapman Andrews, Roy (1884-1960) American naturalist and explorer who led a series of expeditions into the Gobi desert and Mongolia in the early 20th century. He published Across Mongolian Plains in 1921.

Chen Lu Chinese commissioner in the early days of independence (around 1914).

Chinggis Khaan (1162-1227) Born Temujin, he united the Mongol tribes and built the Mongol empire.

Choibalsan, Khorloogiin (1895-1952) Most important Mongolian communist leader in the period 1930-1952.

Dalai Lama Head of the dominant "Yellow Hat" Tibetan Buddhist school of thought.

Dambijansten (also: Ja Lama) (1862-1922) A warlord of unknown origin, claiming to be a lama, who fought for Mongolian independence and established his own power base from where he operated independently until the communist-leaning government executed him in 1922.

Damdinbazar, Sodnomyn. Titles: Jalkhanz Khutugtu (1874-1923) A high-ranking lama who fought for independence and served as Prime Minister twice (1921 and 1922/23), the second time after his predecessor D. Bodoo was purged.

Damdinsuren, Jamsrangiin Title: Manlaibaatar (1871-1921) Early freedom fighter and diplomat. Fought for the liberation of Khovd.

Damba, Dashyin (1908-1989) Left-leaning revolutionary who joined the Mongolian Revolutionary Youth League in 1924 and the MPRP in 1930. He served in high positions, even taking over Tsedenbal's place as first secretary of the Central Committee, but shortly thereafter was replaced by Tsedenbal. Removed from power in 1959.

Danzan, Soliin (1885-1924) An early freedom fighter and founder of what was to become the MRPP.

Dilowa Khutukhtu (or Dilowa Gegeen Khutukhtu) (1883-1965) A high-ranking lama who fled Mongolia in 1931 in advance of the purges. His autobiography The Diluv Khutagt of Mongolia, Political Memoirs and Autobiography of a Buddhist Reincarnation, first published in 1982, was republished in 2009 by Polar Star books.

Genden, Peljidiin (1892 or 1895-1937) Prominent politician serving as president and Prime Minister. He was executed for his nationalism, standing up to Stalin and resisting plans to purge Buddhism.

Genghis Khaan See Chinggis Khaan.

Gorbachev, Mikhail (1931-) The last leader of the Soviet Union. His policies of glasnost (openness) and perestroika (restructuring) aimed at reducing high-level corruption and making the socialist economy more efficient, but ultimately hastened the Soviet Union's dissolution.

Hagenbeck, Carl (1844-1913) German merchant in wild animals.

Ja Lama See Dambijantsen.

Javsandamba Khutukhtu Title: Bogd Khaan A reincarnation of the first Bogd Gegeen, Zanabazar, and the third most important Buddhist official after the Dalai Lama and the Panchen Lama. The head of Mongolian Buddhism. The eighth Bogd Khan (1869-1924) was independent Mongolia's first head of state.

Kaizerling, Alfred (1861-1939) Count Alfred Kaizerling visited Mongolia as a Russian emissary around the turn of the century and described his meetings with the Bogd Khan in his diary.

Kahn, Albert (1860-1940) A wealthy French banker who, between 1909 and 1937, financed cultural and scientific expeditions around the world to preserve images of the societies and ethnicities of the period.

Khutulun (1260-1306) A great-granddaughter of Chinggis Khaan, famous for her warrior skills.

Korostovets, Ivan Russian ambassador to Mongolia 1912-1913 who signed the first friendship agreement between (Tsarist) Russia and Mongolia.

Kublai Khaan (1215-1294) The grandson of Chinggis Khaan who, in 1271 established the Yuan dynasty ruling over what is now Mongolia, China and Korea.

Lattimore, Owen (1900-1989) American scholar of China, Central Asia and Mongolia in particular. A friend of Dilowa Khutugtu, he was instrumental in assisting him to settle in the US.

Lenin, Vladimir Ilyich (1870-1924) Communist revolutionary of the Bolshevik revolution of 1917 who became the first head of state of the Russian Soviet Federative Socialist Republic and the Soviet Union which it became in 1922. Most famous symbol of Soviet-style communism in Mongolia (and elsewhere).

Leontiev, Konstantin (1831-1891) Conservative Russian philosopher who advocated Russia's expansion to the East.

Lkhümbe, Jambyn (1902-1934) A high-level official in the MPRP who was famously purged in the "Lkhümbe affair". Soviet and Mongolian Party officials falsely accused him and hundreds of others (most of them mistrusted Buryat Mongols) of being Japanese spies and imprisoned, executed or sent them to the USSR.

Luvsandanzan A Gegeen lama of the early 18th century.

Magsarjav, Khatanbaatar (1877-1927) An early leader in the struggle for independence who, together with the Ja Lama, Damdinsüren, and others liberated Khovd from the Manchus in 1912. He received the title of People's Hero in 1924.

Marx, Karl (1818-1883) A German philosopher who, together with Friedrich Engels, laid the theoretical foundations of communism and was involved in the early communist movements in Western Europe.

Stalin, Joseph (1878-1953) Important leader of the Bolshevik revolution and from 1922 general secretary of the Central Committee. He consolidated power and became the dictator of the

Soviet Union after Lenin's death in 1924, holding power until his own death in 1953.

Sukhbaatar, Damdin (1893-1923) The most famous freedom fighter and hero of the revolution of 1921. He was a talented military leader and founder of the Mongolian People's Party. Ulaanbaatar's central square was named Sükhbaatar Square before it was named after Chinggis Khaan and his statue is still there, in front of the parliament building.

Sun Yat-Sen (1866-1926) A revolutionary fighter who was instrumental in overthrowing the Manchu dynasty in 1911, he became the first president of the Republic of China. In 1949, his government retreated to Taiwan which became a de facto separate state.

Tömor-Öchir, Daramyn. (1921-1985) A member of the Politburo who was expelled from the Party and exiled to a remote part of the country because of his involvement in organizing the 800th anniversary of Chinggis Khaan.

Tsedenbal (1916-1991) Educated in Russia (Irkutsk and Ulan-Ude) he quickly became an important politician in the MPRP and, backed by the Soviet Union, purged his opponents and became Mongolia's head of state after Choibalsan died in 1952. While visiting Moscow in 1984 he was forced to retire and stayed there until his death in 1991.

Ungern-Sternberg, Baron von (1885-1921) Anti-Bolshevik lieutenant-general turned warlord who ousted the Chinese from Mongolia and was in turn defeated by the Red Army in 1921.

Voroshilov, Kliment Yefremovich (1881-1969) Early Bolshevik military leader and a member of the Soviet Union's Central Committee from 1925 to 1961. He was particularly powerful during the Stalin era, occupying different high-level positions.

Xu Shuzen (1880-?) A general (also called a warlord) who was despatched to what the Chinese still considered their province of Outer Mongolia with the intention to abolish its autonomy and reannex it. His heavy-handed subduing of Mongolian resistance had the opposite effect of strengthening it.

Younghusband, Sir Francis Edward (1863-1962) A British Army officer and explorer who, in 1904, led the British expedition into Tibet that confronted Tibetan militias (mostly monks) and overwhelmed them, causing thousands of casualties: the expedition was later called an invasion. It caused the Dalai Lama to flee to Mongolia.

APPENDIX 2: PLACES

Alderkhaan Soum is in Zavkhan aimag, surrounding its capital Uliastai

Altai city: Capital of Gobi Altai aimag

Altai Soums are soums in Gobi Altai and Bayan Olgi

Altai mountains are the most Western mountain ranges

Altanbulag Soum is in Selenge aimag, close to Siberian border

Amur: Western Siberian region

Arkhangai Aimag is in the Khangai mountain region

Arkhust Soum is in Töv aimag, east of Ulaanbaatar

Arvaikheer: Capital of Övörkhangai aimag

Baganuur: Mining town on the border between Töv and Khentii aimags

Baruunturuun Soum is in Uvs aimag (former state farm)

Bayan-Tumen: Former name of Choibalsan, capital of Dornod aimag

Bayan-Olgi: Westernmost aimag (the only Kazakh-majority aimag)

Bayankhongor: South western aimag

Bogd Mountain overlooks Ulaanbaatar from the south

Bugat Soum is in Govi-Altai aimag, bordering China

Bulgan: Center-north aimag, bordering Siberia

Chandmani Soum is in Khovd aimag

Choibalsan: Capital of Dornod aimag

Choir: Capital of Govisümber aimag (on the north-south railroad)

Dadal Soum is in Khentii aimag, on Siberian border

Darkhan: Third-largest city, capital of Darkhan-Uul aimag

Dauria: Another name for Transbaikal, the area east of Lake Baikal

Dornod: Easternmost aimag

Dornogovi: Southern aimag, in Gobi region

Dörgön Soum is in Khovd aimag

Erdene Zuu Monastery is in Övörkhangai aimag (Kharkhorin soum)

Erdenekhairkhan Soum is in Zavkhan aimag

Erdenet: Second largest mining city, capital of Orkhon aimag

Galshar Soum is in Khentii aimag

Gobi Altai: Southwestern aimag

Harbin: City in northeastern China, on China Eastern Railway

Ikh Khüree: Name for Ulaanbaatar before 1911

Ikhkhet Soum is in Dornogovi aimag

Inner Mongolia: Chinese autonomous region, borders Mongolia on the southwest

Jargalant Soum is in Khovd aimag, surrounding Khovd city

Kalgan: Town in China to the southeast of Mongolia (Zhangjiakou)

Khairkhandulaan Soum is in Overkhangai aimag

Khalkh Gol Soum is in Dornod aimag, location of the Khalkhin Gol battle

Khank Soum is in Khövsgöl aimag at the far end of Lake Khövsgöl

Kharkhorin Soum in Overkhangai aimag, location of Erdene Zuu monastery

Khentii Aimag lies northeast of Ulaanbaatar

Khiagt: Northern border town in Altanbulag soum (Khyagta in Russian)

Khomiin Tal Nature reserve is in western Gobi Altai

Khovd: A western aimag and its capital city

Khovsgol aimag and lake Khovsgol are in northern Mongolia

Khüree: Old name for Ulaanbaatar

Khustai Nuuru: Nature reserve west of Ulaanbaatar

Kukhmorit Soum is in Gobi Altai

Lun soum Soum is in Töv aimag

Manchukuo: Japanese name for Manchuria (before World War Two)

Manchuria Region is in northeastern China

Manzshir: Destroyed monastery just south of Ulaanbaatar, on the south side of the Bogd mountain

Nalaich: Mining town southeast of Ulaanbaatar

Niislel Khüree: Old name for Ulaanbaatar

Otgontenger: Sacred mountain in Zavkhan aimag

Outer Mongolia: Name of Mongolia when it was a province of the Manchu Empire

Overkhangai: Aimag southwest of Ulaanbaatar

Oyu Tolgoi: Mega mining project in Omnogövi aimag near the Chinese border

Port Arthur: Old name for Lüshunkou District in Manchuria, China, famous for the 1904 Battle of Port Arthur between Russia and Japan

Sain Noyon Khaan: One of the four Khalkh aimags under Manchu rule

Sanguin Khot: Name for location of Manchu Fort at Uliastai

Selenge: Northern aimag

Shargaljuut hot springs are in Shagaljuut soum in Bayankhongor aimag

Shariin Gol: Coal mine in Darkhan-Uul aimag

Sinkiang: Northwestern province of China, now Xinjiang

Sükhbaatar city: Capital city of Selenge aimag, on the border with Russia in the north

Sükhbaatar Aimag is in the southeast of Mongolia

Sumber: The soum around Choir on the railroad to China in the tiny aimag of Govisümber

Terelj: A national park and tourist area about 60 kilometers east of Ulaanbaatar

Tes Soum is in Uvs aimag, formerly a state farm

Tosontsengel Soum is in Zavkhan aimag, formerly a large wood-processing plant

Töv: The central aimag that surrounds Ulaanbaatar

Transbaikal: The area east of lake Baikal. Also called Dauria

Tseel Soum is in Govi Altai aimag

Tsengel Soum is in Bayan-Olgi aimag Tsogt Soum is in Govi Altai aimag Tögrög Soum is in Govi Altai aimag

Turt Soum is in Khövgol aimag, at the northern tip of lake Khövsgol (also called Khank)

Tuul river: River that flows by Ulaanbaatar

Ulaan Ude: Capital city of Buryatia in Siberia

Ulaanbaatar: Capital of Mongolia: the contemporary name

Ulaangom: Capital of Uvs aimag

Uliastai: Capital of Zavkhan aimag

Uriankhai: A group of ethnicities in western Mongolia, also territories where they lived

Zasagt Khaan: One of the original four Khalkh aimags under Manchu rule

Zavkhan: A northwestern aimag

Zun Choir monastery: Monastery close to Choir in Govi-sumber aimag

APPENDIX 3: THE DILOWA KHUTUKHTU

The Dilowa Khutukhtu was the reincarnation of a 10th-century Buddhist saint from India by the name of Telopa. The name Dilowa is the Mongolian pronunciation of the Indian saint's name; Khutukhtu is a Mongolian title meaning saintly, used for eminent reincarnations and the highest clergy. He starts his autobiography by recounting that he was born in 1884 in the northern part of what is now Zavkhan Aimag in a poor herder household that owned only 20 sheep, four cows and two horses, having lost many cattle during a dzud. That number of animals would not have been sufficient for the survival of the household without assistance from outside. His father was an old man of 67 when Dilowa was born; his father in turn had been 86 when Dilowa's father was born. Dilowa's grandfather, then, was born in 1731, bringing the past unimaginably close! The infant was identified as the reincarnation of the previous Dilowa who had died shortly before:

"The monastery took me when I was five years old. It was in the third month of spring [about April], when the ground was still lightly covered with snow. When the monastery envoys arrived, they made their camp next to my father's, and I remember that my mother was very busy preparing their welcome. During the daytime I would play about the camp of the envoys, but at night I would cry and ask to return to my mother's tent. Sometimes I wanted to go with them, sometimes I didn't. I do not remember exactly what happened in the ceremonies of invitation that preceded my departure, except that part of it was the placing of an amulet around my neck and that one of the officials got very drunk. When I left, the whole family came along, bringing all their cattle and possessions with them, even the family dogs. Later they settled near the monastery. I made my trip in a camel cart."

The Dilowa Khutukhtu was brought up, as Owen Lattimore describes it, "deeply imbued with the ethos of Tibeto-Mongolian Buddhism, a system of ideas and beliefs that had not changed since the Middle Ages". He lived an interesting life indeed, being caught up in a rapidly changing world where the disintegration of the Manchu empire led through turmoil to Mongolian independence under its religious leader, the Bogd Khaan, to the establishment of the People's Republic of Mongolia and the persecution and elimination of Buddhism as a power structure and as a religion.

In 1931 he wisely fled the country after being charged with anti-revolutionary activity but not convicted because no witnesses were found to testify against the "living saint". Between 1931 and 1949 he traveled and lived in Buddhist monasteries in Inner Mongolia and Beijing, and made a pilgrimage to sacred Buddhist locations in India, Nepal and Tibet. He also served as an adviser to Chiang Kai-shek for Mongol-Tibetan affairs in Chungking (now Chongqing), a sinecure position, according to Lattimore's introduction to the autobiography. Early 1949, at Lattimore's instigation he moved to the US, living the last 15 years of his life in New Jersey, dying in New York in 1964. His life reflected the turbulent times of the first half of the 20th century and his autobiography is a gem.

APPENDIX 4: THE PREZEWALSKI HORSES

Mongolia is the place where the last of the earth's wild horses was seen in their natural habitat (in 1968 in Gobi Altai aimag). The wild horse was first scientifically described in 1881 by a Russian colonel of Polish descent, Nikolai Prezewalski, and named after him. Of course, the Prezewalski horse already had a name among the Mongols: takhi.

In 1900 Carl Hagenbeck, a German who dealt in wild animals for zoos and circuses, captured about 15 Prezewalski horses and they were placed in zoos over the world. In the 1870s Hagenbeck also pioneered human zoos, in which he displayed human "savages" in their "natural state" with their tents and other artifacts. He displayed Nubians, Samoans, Sami and Inuit in European capitals, next to wild animals. I imagine he might have tried to recruit Mongol displays — they certainly wouldn't have gone for that!

All Prezewalski horses alive today descend from those 15 that were captured. In the Nineties several projects started re-introducing the horses to the wild in three main areas: the Great Gobi B strictly protected area in the border areas of Khovd and Gobi-Altai aimags; the Khar Us Nuur national park further north in Khovd; and in the Khustain Nuruu national park about 100 kilometers west of Ulaanbaatar. The latter was a Dutch project that I visited several times. I felt sorry for the first generation of not-so-wild horses who were used to the lush Dutch vegetation and temperate Atlantic climate in the parks where they lived before being transported to Mongolia. How did they survive their first Mongolian winters? And what a shock it must have been when their foals were attacked by wolves! But I was told the real danger to them is the herders, who eagerly discuss among each other the possibility of interbreeding their domestic horses with the takhis and producing a tough new horse. I imagine that a century worth of careful takhi breeding, followed by the costly venture of re-introducing them to the wild, could be undone quite quickly!

ABOUT THE AUTHOR

After graduating from the Agricultural University of Wageningen, the Netherlands, Maaike van Hoeflaken spent most of her career working as an international technical adviser managing projects in Africa, Latin America and Asia for a variety of donors, among them European Union, International Finance Corporation (World Bank Group), Asian Development Bank, African Development Bank, UK's Department for International Development. She specialized in gender, social inclusion, and banking for the poor and for small businesses. From 1999 to 2006 she worked in Mongolia, in the area of improving its business environment and increasing access to financial services for small businesses. She currently lives with her husband in New Zealand.

Printed in Great Britain
by Amazon